In the Field

A Field Experience Manual for Internship and Service Learning Students

Bassim Hamadeh, CEO and Publisher
Laura Pasquale, Specialist Acquisitions Editor
Gem Rabanara, Project Editor
Alia Bales, Associate Production Editor
Jess Estrella, Senior Graphic Designer
Stephanie Kohl, Licensing Associate
Don Kesner, Interior Designer
Natalie Piccotti, Senior Marketing Manager
Kassie Graves, Vice President of Editorial
Jamie Giganti, Director of Academic Publishing

Copyright © 2019 by Cognella, Inc. All rights reserved. No part of this publication may be reprinted, reproduced, transmitted, or utilized in any form or by any electronic, mechanical, or other means, now known or hereafter invented, including photocopying, microfilming, and recording, or in any information retrieval system without the written permission of Cognella, Inc. For inquiries regarding permissions, translations, foreign rights, audio rights, and any other forms of reproduction, please contact the Cognella Licensing Department at rights@cognella.com.

Trademark Notice: Product or corporate names may be trademarks or registered trademarks, and are used only for identification and explanation without intent to infringe.

Cover image copyright © Depositphotos/AllaSerebrina.
Interior Design Images
Copyright © Source: https://pixabay.com/en/thought-idea-innovation-imagination-2123970/.
Copyright © Source: https://pixabay.com/en/business-idea-planning-business-plan-1240830/.

Printed in the United States of America.

ISBN: 978-1-5165-1501-1 (pbk) / 978-1-5165-1502-8 (br)

In the Field

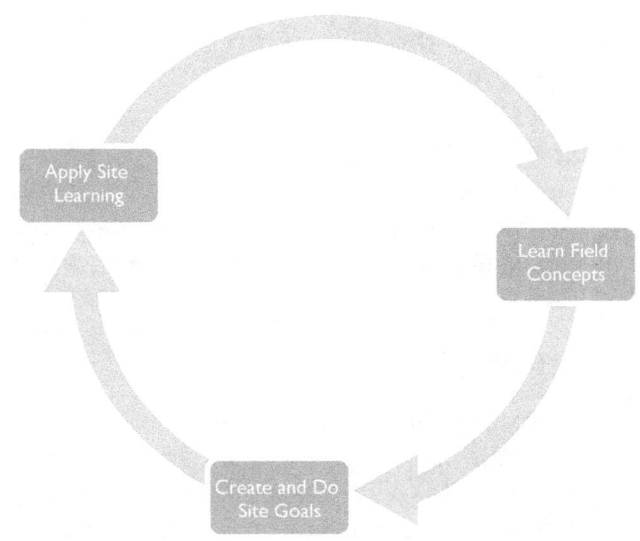

A Field Experience Manual for Internship and Service Learning Students

FIRST EDITION

Lisa Hollis-Sawyer, Ph.D.

Northeastern Illinois University (Chicago, IL)
Department of Psychology and Gerontology Program

Table of Contents

Acknowledgments vii

Preface viii

SECTION I Preparing for the Internship or Service Learning Experience 1

Chapter I Optimizing Socialization, Learning, and Professionalism in the Workplace 2

The chapter offers both informational resources and interactive exercises/activities to best prepare you to understand the concept of socialization within organizations, to contemplate social learning onsite, and to assume appropriate social roles within the organization (e.g., professionalism). Resources and guided exercises are presented for you to work through these important foundational concepts.

Chapter II Identifying the Community Site and Your "Fit" Within It 20

The chapter presents informational resources and interactive exercises/activities to help you to self-reflect upon your personal interests as they pertain to field-related training and associated community service areas ("person analysis"), to analyze the expected job requirements within your chosen field focus ("task analysis"), and to identify specific training sites, assessing the degree to which they match your field training needs and interests ("organizational analysis"). Resources and guided exercises are offered to assist you in learning these important process issues.

Chapter III Creating Site-Related Goals for the Field Experience 38

The chapter provides interactive exercises/activities and informational resources for you to brainstorm and develop "actionable" goals to prepare for your site-related activities under the guidance of both a designated site supervisor and your faculty supervisor. Informational resources and guided exercises are provided to assist you in navigating through this important planning process.

Chapter IV Creating Academic Objectives for the Field Experience 54

The chapter presents practical advice, interactive exercises/activities, and informational resources to guide you in how to research training-related theories and concepts and develop academic objectives for your field training experience. Resources and guided exercises are offered to assist you in your research-related skill development process.

Chapter V Creating a Learning Contract or "Plan of Action" 73

The chapter provides informational resources and interactive exercises/activities to guide you in the process of creating a complete draft of your learning contract, covering the integration of both the developed site-related goals and academic objectives to date. Resources and guided exercises are offered to assist you in creating a complete learning contract draft.

Chapter VI Getting Feedback about Your Learning Contract and Associated Approvals 92

The chapter presents informational resources and interactive exercises/activities to advise you in the processes of how to best solicit constructive feedback regarding your draft learning contract and how to finalize the details of this learning contract for approvals from your supervisors before you can officially begin onsite. Advice regarding how to effectively address feedback revisions from multiple sources and how to achieve an approved learning contract is presented through both guided exercises and informational resources.

SECTION II Getting Onsite and Starting the Learning Process 111

Chapter VII Contacting Your Site Supervisor and Beginning Your Site Activities 112

The chapter guides you through interactive exercises/activities and informational resources in how to effectively initiate your field training experience and how to optimize your organizational socialization onsite. Advice regarding how to create a productive mentoring relationship with your site supervisor and begin activities onsite is presented through the chapter's informational resources and guided exercises.

Chapter VIII Starting the Site-related Journaling Process: Introspection in Action 129

The chapter presents informational resources and interactive exercises/activities for you to analyze your learning through a journaling process regarding self-reflections on both your onsite and academic research learning. Guided exercises and other supplemental information are proffered to assist you in your journaling of this ongoing learning.

Chapter IX Seeking Performance Feedback: Utilize 360 Degree Feedback Opportunities 145

The chapter provides informational resources and interactive exercises/activities to help you collect, synthesize, and address constructive performance suggestions from multiple feedback sources (i.e., your site supervisor, peer interns, coworkers, and faculty supervisor), and to use this feedback to optimize your learning. Resources and guided exercises are offered to assist you in seeking and responding to performance feedback.

Chapter X Receiving and Adjusting to Performance Feedback: Be Open to the Process 162

The chapter gives informational resources and interactive exercises/activities to guide you in how to accurately interpret and effectively adapt to constructive performance feedback in response to multiple feedback sources. Resources and guided exercises are provided to assist you as you optimize the onsite feedback-revision process for your overall learning experience.

SECTION III Identifying Learning Outcomes and Concluding the Site Experience 181

Chapter XI Analyzing the Results of Your Site-Related Learning 182

The chapter offers informational resources and interactive exercises to guide you in the process of identifying learning-related "themes" from the content of your journaled self-observations. The purpose of this activity is for you to reflect upon the theoretical and/or conceptual bases of your onsite training outcomes. Resources and guided exercises are provided to assist you in this self-reflection process from your ongoing journaling.

Chapter XII Writing the Results of Your Site-Related Learning 200

The chapter presents informational resources and interactive exercises/activities to guide you in the process of writing about your culminating learning experiences in the form of a field paper. Resources and guided exercises are offered to help you put together the information from your site-related learning and academic research focus as your onsite training approaches completion.

Chapter XIII Presenting the Results of Your Site-Related Learning 220

The chapter guides you in how to prepare for an onsite presentation regarding your culminated learning over your training weeks, and how to provide constructive feedback to the site (e.g., ways to improve onsite training feedback communication). Informational resources and guided exercises are presented to assist you in developing an onsite presentation of your learning outcomes using a PowerPoint program or other presentation options.

Chapter XIV Reflection on Your Culminating Learning Experience and the Next Steps 238

The chapter guides you through interactive exercises/activities and informational resources in how to best reflect upon what you learned through the entire training experience and how to utilize these self-observations to take the next steps in your educational and career development goals. Informational resources and guided exercises are provided to assist you in this culminating step of your field training.

References 256

Glossary of Terms 267

Appendix A: List of Suggested Supplemental Book Readings by Chapter 273

Appendix B: List of Career Training Resources by Field of Study 277

Appendix C: Learning Contract Template 334

ACKNOWLEDGEMENTS

The author would like to give a heartfelt "thank you" to the people who helped and supported her throughout the manual writing process. There were many people who generously contributed to this publication, and I want to sincerely thank each one for sharing their wonderful wisdom and insights about the field training experience. Lastly, the author would like to thank Tom, Josh, and May for their wonderful support and understanding during this busy time. Without their assistance, this manual would not have been possible!

PREFACE

This manual was created for use as either a main or a supplemental text in the teaching of both undergraduate and graduate classes across many fields/disciplines related to internship/field experience placements and service learning courses.

This original manual on how you can prepare for and conduct your onsite field training is useful for emerging professionals in a variety of applied professions. The manual is unique in that it:

- Assumes placements often occur outside of a clinical, mental-health setting.
- Is written for either an undergraduate or graduate audience.
- Is designed in a workbook format, rather than as a theory-focused textbook.

Utilizing a knowledge- and skill-building structure ("scaffolding") within each chapter, you can select the chapters that best apply to your unique training needs in your field/discipline. The manual offers students pedagogical features in the content of the weekly sections related to:

- Appropriate weekly learning goals,
- The incorporation of relevant case studies regarding learning processes/outcomes,
- Informational "boxes,"
- Guiding exercises to assist in learning activities and goal planning (e.g., developing onsite learning goals, journaling activities), and
- Discussion/application questions at the end of each section.

The purpose of this manual is to guide you through the many different preplanning, planning, and onsite stages of both your career-development and academic learning involved with an internship/field experience or service learning placement.

You may not engage in every step of the process suggested in the manual, based upon your specific field's or discipline's training requirements, but this manual will help you think more critically of what you should consider at each step in the process to ensure a successful launch and completion of your field training experience. The general aim of this manual is to make you more aware of the developmental nature of your learning across stages, even before you start the first day in your training site. It is important to make sure that you utilize all available support resources (e.g., your faculty supervisor), and please contact your site supervisor as early as possible to start your learning experience successfully!

SECTION 1

Preparing for the Internship or Service Learning Experience

Fig. 1.1: Source: https://pixabay.com/er men-employees-suit-work-greet-ing-1979261/.

CHAPTER I

Optimizing Socialization, Learning, and Professionalism in the Workplace

FIELD LEARNING FACTOID

"College students continue to realize how much employers value work experience in the candidates they recruit. In fact, nearly all the employers taking part in NACE's Job Outlook 2015 survey said they prefer to hire job candidates who have work experience. Furthermore, relevant work experience is preferred by almost 75 percent of employers, and 60 percent of employers say they prefer work experience gained through an internship or co-op experience."

Source: National Association of Colleges and Employers (www.naceweb.org)

Introduction

Across your lifespan, you will be faced with the situation of entering a new workplace and the associated "new learning" involved in this process. A realistic and accurate understanding of what it means to be a professional and how to best "fit in" onsite is the rationale underlying the use of field training in an academic program across multiple fields/disciplines (Bay, 2006; Clayton & Myran, 2013; Varner, 2007; Wesley & Bickle, 2005). It is important to acknowledge that you may feel anxiety about starting your first work experience through this field training, but this is a universal experience for most interns and a natural anticipatory reaction to this important learning step in your professional development.

The degree to which you are prepared to enter your field-related training, be it a singular internship/field experience or a service learning course, is a topic that needs to be discussed regardless of your area of specialization (e.g., social work and nursing) (Abuhusain, Chotirmall, Hamid, & O'Neill, 2009; Fisher, Thompson, & Garcia, 2007; McCord, Houseworth, & Michaelsen, 2015). Field training preparation is vital to ensuring that your internship/field experience or service learning experience will be a beneficial learning and career development process for all involved (i.e., you, the intern; the educational institution; and the training site) (Miller, 1991; Stedman & Hatch, 2000; Stedman, Hatch, & Schoenfeld, 2001; Stephenson, 2005). The professional standards and performance expectations within a chosen discipline/field should be understood by you *before* beginning your training (e.g., Phelps & Swerdlik, 2011).

One major benefit from onsite training is creating learning opportunities in career professionalism for students (Loh & Nalliah, 2010; Martimianakis, Maniate, & Hodges, 2009; Roth, Zlatic, & American College of Clinical Pharmacy, 2009). There are "universal" professionalism concepts related to work conscientiousness, team commitment, task persistence, and employee trustworthiness for interns to learn onsite (Brennan, 2010; Dotson & Dotson-Blake, 2015; Garman, Evans, Krause, & Anfossi, 2006; Glazer, 2008).

Learning Goals for this Chapter

Chapter I offers both informational resources and interactive exercises/activities to prepare you to:

- → Anticipate your organization socialization process as an in-coming intern,
- → Engage in effective social learning onsite in anticipation of your onsite training, and
- → Assume an appropriate " intern role" in your training workplace (e.g., understand expected employee conduct behavior).

Look It Up!
Define and Understand Important Concepts

When preparing to start an internship/field experience or service learning placement in your chosen field, you should have a knowledge of specific learning concepts. Please consult the word glossary provided at the back of this manual and look up the following terms discussed in this chapter.

Organizational Socialization: _____
_____
_____
_____

Job Adaptation: _____
_____
_____
_____

Organizational Culture: _____
_____
_____
_____

Business Etiquette: _____
_____
_____
_____

Work Professionalism: _____
_____
_____
_____

What Do I Think About ... ?

1. What is a good informational resource(s) (e.g., books) to consult about how to plan for my upcoming training experience?
2. What personal factors should I consider in this pretraining preparation process?
3. Who is a good person(s) to ask for advice when planning my internship/field experience or service learning placement?
4. What is the biggest challenge I anticipate in preparing for my field training?
5. What is the biggest opportunity I hope to encounter through my anticipated training?
6. What do I feel will be an error to avoid in preparing for my onsite training?
7. What advice would I give a peer in my academic program regarding preparing for his/her onsite training experience?

Phase I: Steps in the Socialization Process as an Intern

Before you begin the process of selecting your field-training site, you should understand what organizational socialization means within your chosen field and how you can best prepare ahead of time to anticipate these field-related performance expectations on the job to best adapt to the job-related tasks (job adaptation) and culture of the internship site (organizational culture). What are the steps that you need to take to have an understanding of these ideas? Let us go through some general ideas of what you should do in preparing for this step in the process:

1. *Research the concept*—What does it mean to engage in a socialization process in your upcoming training site? According to the Oxford Handbook, "organizational socialization" is defined as a social learning and adjustment process that enables an individual to adapt to an organization's norms, rules, and cultural values.

2. *Ask other student interns*—Sometimes the best insights you can gain come through asking peers about their training experiences. Seek out their advice regarding how to best prepare for a student internship/field experience or service learning placement within the industry you are interested in entering as an emerging professional. Ask classmates whether your shared academic coursework training creates supportive "transfer of learning" to onsite performance or whether additional preparation is needed.

3. *Visit a career placement office*—A great resource for you in preparing for your onsite training is your on campus career development and placement office. Talk with an advisor regarding steps in your anticipatory professional development (e.g., creating an effective résumé). Ask whether you could take a career interest inventory to verify you are on the correct career path and to identify your professional strengths. Additionally, there are opportunities for professional training through career development and placement services (e.g., interviewing skills).

4. *Acquire a field-related mentor*—As you contemplate how to best prepare for your internship/field experience or service learning placement, it helps to find an industry professional who will agree to become your career mentor. Unfortunately most students may not do this step until after graduation, which may not be the best timing.

Let us check in on your perceptions of this preplanning process at this point. The following are some important questions to ask yourself when preparing for your impending internship/field experience or service learning assignment:

Before proceeding, you should review what you have learned so far. In the following, there will be a review exercise related to the information you learned through the activities suggested in Phase I.

"Let's Review!" Phase I Learning

1. What did you learn about potential sources of information regarding organizational socialization onsite within your training field? _____
   _____
   _____
   _____
   _____
   _____
   _____

2. As you engaged in the suggested learning activities, what were some important concepts related to organizational socialization that you learned? _____
   _____
   _____
   _____
   _____
   _____
   _____

3. Which informational source(s) did you find to be the most helpful in your understanding of this preplanning process? Why?_____
   _____
   _____
   _____
   _____
   _____

4. Please describe something you learned that you did not anticipate learning._____
   _____
   _____
   _____
   _____
   _____

Phase II: How to Engage in Social Learning in The Field

Before you choose a potential internship/field experience or service learning placement site, you should learn what it means to be a career professional in your area of specialization. When thinking about engaging in the proceeding activities, it is important to develop a "timeframe" to guide your activities:

> Week 1: Do your research and identify potential career fairs and/or professional development activities in your area within the current month.
>
> Week 2: Contact potential sources to interview or "shadow" in order to learn specific roles.
>
> Week 3: Collect information related to identified professional resources, ranging from community activities to professional contacts.
>
> Week 4: Synthesize the information to guide your understanding of professionalism in your field.

Let us go through some general ideas of what you should do in preparing for this step:

1. *Interview a working professional in the field*—Contact a professional working in the industry or field you will be training for as an intern. Meet and discuss topics related to onsite organizational learning and associated performance expectations. Get advice on how to best prepare for industry-wide performance expectations from the perspective of a career entrant.
2. *Attend and "network" at a field-relevant professional society meetings*—One of the best ways for you to learn about your training field is to attend associated professional society gatherings. Much information can be learned through these events, and it also offers the opportunity for you to engage in invaluable career networking. Professional networking may also produce information for you to apply for employment opportunities.
3. *"Shadow" a field-relevant professional*—Through your career networking efforts, ask a practitioner within the field if you can visit the organization and "shadow" him/her for a day, week, or longer. This observation opportunity, if possible, would help you develop your understanding of what it means to be a working professional in your field.
4. *Find and attend a job fair in your community*—There are many opportunities for you to learn about different companies in your area of specialization. For example you might research and find semi-annual job fairs in your community for both information gathering and making potential career contacts by speaking with industry representatives.

FROM A SITE SUPERVISOR'S DESK

Marie Gurnik, Executive Director at Brookdale Living Communities:

The beauty of internship programs is that students usually find out during the experience whether the job would be a good fit for them. To prepare for an internship, the student really needs to spend some time deciding what areas would be most appealing to them. They then need to do some research on those areas and see what locations offer these specific services and whether these locations would work. It is beneficial for you to take into consideration proximity to home, whether public transportation is available (if necessary), whether the locations offer internship programs, and once they have met with the site supervisor and discussed the details of the internship, whether it is a good "fit" for both the site and the student. Students also need to decide how much time they will be willing to spend each week at the site, and how this fits into the expectations of the site supervisor.

Please remember to always dress in a professional manner. An internship site is a work setting, so clothing that is acceptable for class may not be acceptable at the site. Ahead of time, please have a discussion with the faculty supervisor prior to beginning the internship and get some clear guidelines of appropriate dress. Also, after starting the internship, the intern should be proactive and discuss any work-related issues with both the site and faculty supervisors to rectify the situation as soon as possible. The goal is for both parties to get the most out of the time spent in the internship, thus creating a "win-win" for everyone!

What Should I Do?
Putting Your Learning into Action

1. Identify field-relevant professional societies on the Internet to join and associated professional meeting/networking opportunities to attend.
2. Talk to professionals in your field, both faculty members and current practitioners, about how to best prepare for your internship/field experience or service learning placement experience.
3. Arrange to visit and observe the workplace of a professional who occupies a job position reflecting your immediate career plans and aspirations.
4. Speak with an on-campus career counselor about both general advice regarding factors to consider in making field training decisions and educational support resources for your use (e.g., workshops on résumé development).
5. Journal about what you have learned to date regarding factors to consider and informational sources and resources to consult during this preplanning process.
6. Interview someone who currently works in the job and career you are interested in. Ask this person about his/her training background as a student. Finally, get some advice about choosing a field training opportunity.

Before proceeding, please review what you have learned in Phase II! In the following, there is a series of review questions related to what you learned in doing the activities and exercises. To best help you with this ongoing learning process, please be accurate in your responses to assess what areas of learning may need further review.

"Let's Review!" Phase II Learning

1. What did you learn about sources of information regarding the range of occupations in your field? _____
   _____
   _____
   _____
   _____
   _____

2. As you engaged in the suggested learning activities, what did your various sources (e.g., field-relevant practitioners) share with you about performance activities in the workplace?
   _____
   _____
   _____
   _____
   _____
   _____

3. Of the different people you spoke with, who shared information about what to think about in identifying different training opportunities in your field? Who was the most helpful? Least helpful? Why? _____
   _____
   _____
   _____
   _____
   _____
   _____

4. Please describe something you learned that you did not anticipate learning. _____
   _____
   _____
   _____
   _____
   _____
   _____

Phase III: Work "Role" Assumption in an Organization

Based upon an understanding of the concepts we have reviewed to date, let us next examine anticipated role-related issues you may enounter as an intern. In developing your ideas about assuming your intern role, you should focus upon many different areas of anticipated performance. You should be cognizant of proper ettiquette (business ettiquette) and expectations of professional behavior in the workplace (professionalism).

For example, you should think about how to improve your communication skills in anticipation of your intern role when onsite. Communication comes in many forms, from verbal to nonverbal modes of self-expression. The language used to communicate with others onsite must be well understood (e.g., workplace "jargon") to convey both your ideas and general competencies to your supervisor and those within the workplace. Diversity sensitivity is another consideration to be cognizant of when conveying and responding to workplace communications. Let us focus on one example of a communication approach, the workplace e-mail. The following is a summary of elements to consider in structuring an appropriate e-mail:

1. Opening with your contact's appropriate title and name spelling (e.g., Dear Sir/Madam/Title:)
2. Explain the purpose of the e-mail correspondence.
3. Give a brief overview of the points to be covered in the correspondence. Convey ideas in a clear and succinct manner (e.g., use succinct wording in your sentences).
4. Use appropriate work "jargon," if applicable, but avoid the use of improper grammar, unknown abbreviations, or word contractions (e.g., "you're" should be "you are").
5. Provide a closing message, with possible follow-up correspondence information, if applicable.
6. Closing with your name, affiliation, and contact information (e.g., Cordially, Your Full Name, Phone Number, E-mail Address, Fax Number).

Both the verbal and nonverbal communication you engage in onsite can potentially affect your work performance and how people perceive you within the workplace. Personal body language usage is an issue to learn more about before you step onsite as an intern.

Based on an organization's culture, the following characteristics of body language may create an impression of you as a competent intern (or not) and/or whether you "fit in" onsite. In addition to these issues, organizational communication applies to broader legal concerns of ethical workplace behaviors (e.g., perceived sexual harassment). As you prepare for your upcoming onsite experience, do your research, and possibly engage in some professional ettiquette training related to the following nonverbal behaviors:

- Eye contact (e.g., eye gaze time length)
- Posture/stance/sitting
- Duration of a behavior (e.g., duration of a handshake)
- Social space (social distance between others)
- Facial expression (e.g., smiling)
- Volume/tone of voice
- Physical contact (e.g., hugging)
- Touch (e.g., firmness of a handshake)
- Use of technology (e.g., wearing headphones onsite)
- Gestures (e.g., a "thumbs up" gesture might be considered rude in some cultures)
- Courtesy behavior (e.g., expressing gratitude)
- Personal etiquette (e.g., table manners during a business lunch)

In addition to different forms of communication, you should be aware of the general impression you make on others. "First impressions" can be relatively persistent thoughts we use when interacting with others on a daily basis. Therefore, it is important for you to make a good first impression at your future training site. A part of this process is identifying work-appropriate norms for your appearance onsite (e.g., choice of clothing) acccording to your training field.

Think About It!

Here are topics to consider as you think about "dressing for success" at your upcoming internship/field experience or service learning assignment:

1. As an intern, what impression am I making in the workplace through my clothing choices?
   _____
   _____
   _____
   _____
   _____

2. Do my clothing choices relate to the nature of my onsite work? How so? _____
   _____
   _____
   _____
   _____

3. How can I find an appropriate example of how to dress as an intern when onsite? Who should I ask for advice? _____
   _____
   _____
   _____
   _____

Apply Your Knowledge!

The following are some suggested ideas for you to consider when planning to assume your role as an intern in a workplace:

1. *Be a role model*—Exemplify the behavior that you would like others to adopt in the workplace. Model professional behavior through your onsite activities, exemplifying punctuality, dependability, and conscientiousness in your work.
2. *Be an achiever*—Always strive to give 110% in your work activities. When difficulties arise in onsite situations, identify issues and proactively problem solve in a collaborative effort to support workplace initiatives.
3. *Be open to new opportunities/ideas/people*—Diversity appreciation is a valued aspect of employee behavior. Encountering new people, ideas, and situations is a wonderful learning and growth-related opportunity for you during your onsite training.
4. *Be conscientious, dependable, and trustworthy*—Be the workplace source that others consult with to discuss ideas and plan projects. When assigned onsite tasks, fulfill (and exceed) others' expectations. Be consistent and reliable.
5. *Be respectful and courteous*—Treat others in the workplace as you would wish would be treated. Be considerate of other's perspectives, needs, goals, and feelings as you engage in team-based activities and interact with others.
6. *Be a team player*—Offer to help others when you have the time and/or resources available. Be available to lend your time and knowledge to others onsite but be careful to not neglect your own onsite assignments in the process.

Try It Out!
Role-Play Exercise

Role-Play Exercise Brief: Part of the preparation process before beginning your internship/field experience or service learning placement is to practice your anticipated role as a future intern. A role-playing exercise with other classmates or an instructor gives you the opportunity to think about what you need to prepare for in assuming this upcoming professional role in your future internship/field experience or service learning placement.

For the following role-play exercise, please assume the role of an intern at Site X. You are approached by another intern ("Pat") who is asking for your advice regarding how to do better work onsite. You have noticed that Pat the intern is always late to work and seems to avoid work assignments if possible. Also, you have observed that Pat does not answer e-mails in a timely manner and only sporadically attends intern meetings.

Your Role: Cover the following topics to practice some constructive feedback: how to access workplace policies, professionalism techniques (e.g., being on time), and effective communication. This exercise is limited to 30 minutes.

After completion of the Role-Play Exercise, ask yourself the following:

1. What did I learn about my feedback communication skills in this role play exercise?
2. What was the hardest aspect in giving feedback to Pat the intern? Easiest? Why?
3. If I did the role play exercise again, what would I do differently?
4. What do I need to work on in preparation for my field training based on this exercise?

There is much to consider in preparing for your training as a future intern, from what is expected of you to how you should develop a "plan of action" (e.g., choice of proper career attire). Let us go through some general ideas of what you should do in preparing for this step in the process:

1. *Attend professionalism development workshops for students*—On-campus academic departments (e.g., business departments) or career counseling offices often provide opportunities for your professional development as a student, ranging from business etiquette training to how you should prepare to answer questions in an internship or job interview. These on-campus support resources are especially relevant to you at this stage of your professional development.

2. *Research professional standards of conduct*—Anticipating what the focus of your career would be after you graduate, you need to understand the professional standards and expectations from relevant industry-related publications. There are various published guidelines across many disciplines related to professional expectations of conduct in interacting with multiple constituents (e.g., APA standards of professional conduct with clients). It helps you to understand these standards and professional expectations of behavior as you begin to plan for your upcoming internship/field experience or service learning assignment.

3. *Know workplace laws regarding ethical employee behavior (e.g., Title IX)*—Become familiar with national and industry-related legislation regulating appropriate workplace behavior in United States (and other countries, if applicable). It is both your right and responsibility to be familiar with legislation governing your behavioral conduct onsite. For example, as an intern, you should be aware of workplace rules pertaining to identifying and reporting possible incidences of perceived sexual harassment.

4. *Brainstorm ideas with faculty and peer interns*—You will encounter diverse social attitudes and beliefs in the workplace as an intern. Plan to have repeated discussions with multiple constituents, such as supervisors, related to workplace issues of preparing for diversity sensitivity, impression management, seeking and giving feedback, and other issues underlying effective work role engagement in preparation for and during your onsite learning.

5. *Talk to a job recruiter*—A job recruiter, or a "head hunter," has an in-depth understanding of what makes an ideal candidate for a specific job positions. He/she may offer unique insights into what can make you an ideal candidate within a large pool of intern and/or job applicants. He/she can give you insights related to the characteristics of effective employees, managers, and/or leaders within an organization. When talking with a job recruiter, ask about what you need to plan for to become that ideal intern when onsite.

6. *Visualize yourself within the work role*—Mental preparation is an important part of this preplanning process. You should try to visualize yourself as an intern in your anticipated job or workplace. Why is this important? A person's self-concept is an integral factor during the assumption of a work role. Ultimately, your motivation to do well within the short-term intern position can stem from your ability to see yourself within the intern role. Again, introspection related to this concept is significant for both your experiential learning and the setting of your personal career goals.

Search the Web!
Learn About Your Field of Study

Search the Internet for different websites regarding your chosen area of career training. Check out at least three different websites pertaining to professional career preparation within your area of study. As you review this information, please answer the following questions:

1. What were the top three pieces of advice you found regarding career preparation within your field of study:

   a. _____
   b. _____
   c. _____

2. How much of the advice related to professional ethics? Professional demeanor and appearance? Other issues?

   _____
   _____
   _____
   _____
   _____
   _____
   _____
   _____

3. How challenging was it to locate Internet information related to professional development and preparation within your chosen field of training? Of those resources found, which resource(s) was the easiest to locate through your Internet search? Please explain.

   _____
   _____
   _____
   _____
   _____
   _____
   _____
   _____

There is much to consider as you embark on this exciting step in your planning. Let us review what you have learned so far! On the next page, there is a series of review questions related to what you learned in reviewing the information and doing the exercises.

AN INTERN'S INSIGHTS

Josephine Brylak: It is never too late to discover new passions or drives in life. Not everyone can realize their true calling at an early age. Those individuals that do, however, seem to have an advantage in that they may be able to maximize their time at university by focusing all their attention and energy on achieving their true calling and reaching that single goal, instead of taking a more winding path. However, many young adults are not as confident about future career goals, and must, instead, explore meandering avenues. These individuals, like myself, take every new experience as an opportunity to narrow down interests, develop laboratory and professional skills, and create a sense of career focus.

After taking some general education courses, I soon became captivated by the field of psychology. I was encouraged to apply to my university's summer research program and could work intimately with another psychology professor studying and coding gesture speech. I presented my data from that summer at multiple conferences where I could develop my oral and written communication skills, despite never having done any prior public speaking! What is more, the professors leading my biology and psychology senior seminar course challenged me to explore new experiences and gain more priceless real-world experience. As you are exploring internships, look for opportunities that will challenge you and do not be discouraged if you do not have a defined career goal still do not know what I want to be when I "grow up." Discover your passion and learn from the experience!

"Let's Review!" Phase III Learning

1. What information was the most helpful regarding thinking about developing a professional work role? Least helpful? Please explain. _____
   _____
   _____
   _____
   _____
   _____

2. As you engaged in the suggested learning activities, what were some important concepts related to professional development that you learned? _____
   _____
   _____
   _____
   _____
   _____

3. When speaking to different people about preparing for your upcoming field training, who was the most helpful in terms of advice? Why? _____
   _____
   _____
   _____
   _____
   _____
   _____

4. Please describe something you learned that you did not anticipate learning. _____
   _____
   _____
   _____
   _____
   _____
   _____

Summary of the Chapter

This chapter examined issues of what to think about and what informational resources to consult in preparing for your upcoming field experience/internship or service learning placement. There is much to consider, ranging from a knowledge of your chosen field to how you can best "fit in" once you start your field training. This preplanning process is important to do, but it is rarely done. You will benefit from this significant "learning curve" experience throughout your entire field training process. There are multiple constituents (e.g., your faculty supervisor) to consult at every stage of your training process—do not hesitate to ask for advice and support resources along the way!

What Did I Learn?

Self-reflection is a vital part of your learning process throughout the field experience process. Without looking back in the chapter, please list what you feel were the main three points of learning that were personally relevant to you regarding focus of the chapter (please explain why each is personally relevant to your learning):

1. _____
   _____
   _____

2. _____
   _____
   _____

3. _____
   _____
   _____

Discussion Questions

1. What can academic programs do better to prepare students for this preplanning step?
2. What do you anticipate will be the benefits of the training for your long-term career goals?
3. Do you feel finding a site is a relatively straightforward process for your onsite field training? Why or why not?
4. In general, when do you think is the best time to start preparing for your onsite field training? Should it have been earlier or later in your educational training?
5. Self-reflection on your ongoing learning is vital to your professional development over time. Is this an easy or arduous process?
6. Interns bring diverse backgrounds and interests to the workplace. Is this a topic important to discuss with your faculty supervisor? Why or why not?
7. Preparing for your onsite training experience can be potentially stressful. Would it be beneficial for students to develop a peer support group related to this stage of a student's professional development? Why or why not?
8. How challenging is it to learn about an organization for decision-making purposes? Did this initial investigation influence which organization(s) you may choose? Why?
9. What did you learn most about yourself when thinking about concepts underlying professionalism in the workplace?
10. If you were to design a preplanning workshop for intern students, how would you design it? What specific factors would you consider in the design of this informational workshop? What issues do you think are important to discuss?

Additional Information Links

- Monster.com website: Discussions by former interns about the benefits of internship/field experience or service learning placements
  http://www.monster.com/career-advice/article/students-benefits-internships
- Vault.com website: A search database for internship/field experience or service learning placement opportunities
  http://www.vault.com/wps/portal/usa/companies
- thebalance.com website: Advice for students regarding using an internship/field experience or service learning placement to increase marketability
  https://www.thebalance.com/complete-internship-more-marketable-1986736
- Chron.com (Small Business) website: Ten characteristics of professionalism are presented
  http://smallbusiness.chron.com/10-characteristics-professionalism-708.html
- Naceweb.com website: A website for students promoting linkages between education and employment opportunities
- National Association of Colleges and Employers (*www.naceweb.org*)

Fig. 2.1: Source: https://pixabay.com/action-analysis-business-2277292/.

CHAPTER II

Identifying the Community Site and Your "Fit" Within It

FIELD LEARNING FACTOID

"Internship positions are available in several disciplines. They can be arranged through your school or the organization for which you will work. And they often provide either pay or academic credit—sometimes, both. Regardless of how it is coordinated, completing an internship increases your chances of getting a job that you will enjoy. Not only do you discover your job likes and dislikes, but you enter the job market with experience that is related to your career goals."

Source: U. S. Department of Labor: "Internships—Previewing a Profession" (www.bls.gov/careeroutlook/2006/summer/art02.pdf)

Introduction

Ask yourself the following: What are my long-term career goals? What is the professional training I need to attain my career goals? Onsite field training is a significant step in your career development, and it will entail you undergoing multiple stages of planning and decision making to successfully complete this experience (Rodolfa, Haynes, & Kaplan, 1995). Creating an optimal "fit" between your career training needs and the requirements of your onsite field training is necessary for you to have a productive and beneficial training experience (Jacob, 1987; Keilin, 1998).

Consider the career-related factors that are meaningful to you when evaluating potential internship/field experience or service learning placement sites (Leversha & Stuart, 2016). You should deliberate on many different inclusionary and exclusionary factors involved in making this site-related training choice (Rodolfa et al., 1999). You need to have a "voice" in the site selection process, as it can have both a short- and long-term impact upon your career and other key stakeholders in the process (McHugh, 2016).

An optimized match between you and a field training site can be a great launch for you as an emerging professional in an industry (Merluzzi, 2016; Miloro, 2016). This matching process may take a while, but it is a critical step in the professional development process (Rivero et al., 2016). There should be careful thought given to your field's job trends and how this relates to your site selection options (Spencer, Atencio, McCullough, & Hwang, 2016; Stewart & Stewart, 1996).

Decision-making assessments will be made when engaging in this preplanning process. You assess a range of organizations to judge which choice best matches your career training needs, and sites assess your qualifications to become a selected intern (e.g., perceptions of your professionalism) (Bajwa, Yudkowsky, Belli, Vu, & Park, 2016; Doran & Cimbora, 2016; Ransburg, Sage-Haywood, & Schuman, 2016). You should investigate, and anticipate, how you will be evaluated before you apply to different field training sites (e.g., Hersh & Poey, 1984)

The choice of a field-appropriate training placement site can significantly affect your later career viability (Gherardi, Gherardi, Perrotta, & Perrotta, 2016; Mitchell, 1996). Deliberate decision making on your part helps ensure that you are getting the career training you need and desire, as well as equally ensuring that you will be a qualified intern for the training site (Holsti et al., 2015; Hutchinson & Hyden, 2016; Mackenzie, Assaf, & Cusolito, 2016; Stedman, Neff, Donahoe, Kopel, & Hays 1995). The site you choose should relate to your ideas about leadership roles with your field/industry (Starineca, Zolle, & Stein, 2016).

Learning Goals for this Chapter

Chapter II offers both informational resources and interactive exercises/activities to best prepare you to:

→ Self-reflect upon your personal interests related to field-related training and associated community service areas ("person analysis"),

→ Analyze the expected job requirements within your chosen field focus ("task analysis"), and

→ Identify specific organizations and assess the degree to which their organizational characteristics (e.g., mission statement and values) correspond to your field training needs and interests ("organizational analysis").

The proceeding parts in this chapter will review "matching" factors to consider, as well as sources to consult, when you are selecting a field training site. Please refer to Appendix B for list of potentential organizations by field that might help you generate some ideas for your selected training site. Keep in mind that a training organization is also looking for a good match among its internship applicants. It behooves you to understand what sites are looking for in an ideal intern and how you can embody those same site-related expectations. This should be a mutually-beneficial match for both you and your selected field training on many different levels (e.g., match on core values and beliefs regarding customer service).

Before beginning to discuss specific issues related to your onsite field training, let us explore some foundational concepts for this chapter:

Look It Up!

Define and Understand Important Concepts

In preparation for the onsite training in your chosen field, you need to have background knowledge in specific learning concepts. Please consult the word glossary provided at the back of this manual, and look up the following terms discussed in the current chapter.

Person Analysis: _____
_____
_____
_____
_____

Task Analysis: _____
_____
_____
_____
_____

Organizational Analysis: _____
_____
_____
_____
_____

Organizational Fit: _____
_____
_____
_____
_____

Phase I: Reflection Upon Your Personal Career Interests ("Person Analysis")

Before you begin the process of finding your site, you should reflect upon your career interests and motivations. As a student, one of the main benefits of doing an internship/field experience or service learning assignment is that it is a wonderful "stepping stone" for you to launch your career. You should make your training site choice(s) after a careful consideration of both your career aspirations and your performance capabilities. What are the steps of this person analysis process? Let us go through some general ideas of what you should do in preparing for this professional self-analysis step in the process:

1. *Research the field*—Do background research on your field of training, including looking up information on the fields of teacher education, social work, or business management through books, articles, and industry "blogs."
2. *Review professional society websites*—Visit and review the websites of professional organizations related to your career training focus. Information related to professional standards, current research, educational, and/or community-related outreach activities on the local, national, and/or global level can help you better understand the general philosophy and professional expectations within the field.
3. *Talk to an existing and/or former field-relevant student intern*—If given the opportunity, talk to a former or current intern in your field. Ask him/her about decision-making strategies in choosing a field site that best fits both career interests and training needs from a peer's perspective.
4. *Discuss these concepts with faculty in your field/discipline*—In addition to discussing issues of choosing a beneficial training site with other interns, brainstorm these same ideas with faculty members in your department. For example, ask a faculty member to give you some practical advice in how to find a training site that matches well with your personal values and beliefs about protecting the environment (i.e., "green" corporations).
5. *Engage in introspection*—As you plan for your field training, there is the need to always check in with yourself regarding your personal goals, perceptions, and even concerns related to your anticipated learning experiences.
6. *Develop a draft résumé*—As you think about your professional development, you should draft a résumé detailing the following points:

    - Career goals—describe the career you wish to attain.
    - Career-related attributes—list your strengths related to technology skills, industry-related knowledge, and communication/language skills.
    - Educational background—list current and completed educational attainments with associated grade point averages and any academic awards (e.g., Dean's list).
    - List of personal references—list four to five references who can attest to your career-related potential.

7. *Learn how to prepare for and participate in an interview*—you will be interviewing many different career-related professionals in the coming weeks for your professional training experience. Here are some tips about interviewing:

- Research the background of the person and/or company that will be the focus of the interview.
- Dress to impress and think about the appropriate "uniform" for the person/company you are interviewing.
- Prepare interview questions ahead of time based upon the amount of time you will be given for the interview (e.g., five interview questions for a 20–30 minute interview).
- Have a business card to hand to the interviewee at the completion of the interview, in addition to your résumé.

As you begin this introspective process, ask yourself several questions regarding the next steps in your internship/field experience or service learning planning. With these decision factors in mind, consider the many different resources and social networking opportunities that you will need to coordinate your planning efforts around. The follow are some important questions to ask yourself when engaging in this ongoing planning process:

What Do I Think About ... ?

1. What factors should I consider in my field training site decision?
2. What am I looking for in an organization's website or corporate materials?
3. Should I visit a potential field site ahead of time? What am I looking for onsite if I visit the workplace and observe its employees?
4. Who is a good person(s) for me to ask for advice when selecting a field training site?
5. What did I learn about myself through this self-reflection process?
6. What are my immediate career goals? Long-term career goals?
7. Finally, what do I hope to achieve through my field training?

"Let's Review!" Phase I Learning

1. What did you learn about your personal career goals and field-related training expectations? _____
   _____
   _____
   _____
   _____

2. Why is conducting an "organizational analysis" important? What did you learn through this process? _____
   _____
   _____
   _____
   _____
   _____
   _____

3. As you engaged in the suggested learning activities, what did you learn through the "person analysis" process? _____
   _____
   _____
   _____
   _____

4. Which informational sources did you find to be the most helpful during this learning process? Why? _____
   _____
   _____
   _____
   _____
   _____
   _____

Phase II: Expected Job Requirements ("Task Analysis")

As you start the process of selecting a potential field training site, ask yourself what it means to be a professional in your chosen career training focus. More specifically, what are the exact job requirements ("tasks") associated with the job position (task analysis):

1. *Research the career/field experience*—In selecting a field site, do your research about the specific occupation(s) you may be entering as an intern. Read books, and review Internet resources (e.g., blogs) related to the area of work you are considering.

2. *Search online career placement websites*—In addition to searching for online job information, it may help you to peruse relevant career placement websites (e.g., monster.com) to see different job titles in employment ads and the applicant's abilities sought by employers. This will give you a better understanding of what to plan.

3. *Interview job-relevant professionals*—To identify the optimal field training choice for you, it is good to interview a sample of professionals who work in the job position related to your anticipated field training position. Beyond what you can learn through books or online resources, a practitioner can give you "real world" advice and can recommend specific training options to enhance your future career viabillity.

4. *Examine career-related professional society websites*—Lastly, identify and review a sample of professional societies (e.g., American Psychological Association) to better understand the professional practices, standards, and ethical guidelines within your career area of interest. You might find some great resources for placement opportunities and/or scholarships for students/early career professionals.

FROM A SITE SUPERVISOR'S DESK

Kristine Pierre, Northeastern Illinois University Senior Director—Academic & Community Partnerships:

- Do Your Research: Be sure to make time to research all you can about the organization you are applying to. You will be better prepared for your internship and show initiative.

- Clarify Expectations: You want to make sure you are on the "same page" as your supervisor. Talk through your expectations and listen to the expectations of your site supervisor.

- Learn the Office Culture: Observe and ask questions about the norms and values of the organization. Taking time to evaluate the "nuances" makes it much easier to fit in. This includes issues like appropriate dress, personal phone calls, and tone of voice in meetings.

- Be Prepared to Do Some Grunt Work: A part of being an intern is making the work lives of other employees easier. All jobs have menial tasks. "Pitching in" will help others see you as a team member and may help you get more challenging assignments.

- Manage Your Time: Show up to work when you are expected and avoid taking long breaks or lunch periods. You should prioritize your time in completing multiple assignments.

- Communication Skills: Always use respectful and professional language in your written and verbal communications. Be sure to carefully proofread all written work.

- Ask for Feedback and Advice: Ask your supervisor every so often what you could be doing to improve your performance. Make it easy for them to share feedback that will help you grow professionally.

What Should I Do?
Putting Your Learning into Action

1. Discuss with your faculty mentor different approaches to researching prospective field sites, and associated decision factors to consider.
2. Find and visit different community-based volunteer fairs.
3. Attend an on-campus career fair and talk to organization recruiters about your field training interests and/or your long-term career interests.
4. Register for a field-relevant professional conference and attend the social networking opportunities through these conferences to learn more about potential training or job options.
5. Develop a résumé or work on an existing one to better reflect what you have learned from your ongoing field training research. You should express your career skills and interests in a clear and concise manner in the beginning, so a human resources (HR) manager can best understand your "fit" with the site.
6. Sign up for a professional networking website (e.g., LinkedIn) to network with professionals who occupy the careers you are interested in entering as an intern and/or as a job hire.
7. Journal what you have learned to date and remember to refer to it as you go through the subsequent stages of your field training.

Before proceeding, you should review what you have learned in Phase II! It is good to assess what you have learned thus far in your review of the information in this chapter. The next section contains a series of review questions related to what you learned in doing the activities. Think about how this information will support your decision-making processes in the coming weeks.

"Let's Review!" Phase II Learning

1. Based upon the suggested sources of information and activities, what did you learn about the process of conducting a detailed "task analysis" for a job or career you are interested in? _____

2. A "person analysis" (Phase I) and a "task analysis" (Phase II) can, in combination, yield important insights for you regarding your percieved preparedness for entering a specific field training opportunity. What insights did you learn about yourself at this stage of the process? _____

3. Were you able to find a published job description about the internship/field experience or service learning placement position you are interested in? If so, what did you learn? If not, why do you think it was difficult to find? _____

4. Based upon what you have learned so far, have your attitudes toward beginning your career changed? Yes or no. Please explain. _____

Phase III: Field Sites for Matching Purposes ("Organizational Analysis")

As important as it is to understand your training interests and needs as a potential intern and the typical job requirements of the anticipated field placement position, it is equally beneficial for you to thoroughly investigate the possible training sites (organizational analysis).

Researching the organizations you would like to apply to as an intern or future job hire is a multi-step procedure. The first step is learning how to identify potential internship/field experience or service learning placement sites. Once you identify organizations you are initially interested in, you should carefully review each organization's historical background (e.g., "founder" story), "niche" within the industry, organizational culture (i.e., mission statement, goals, values/beliefs, and long-term industry goals). You might want to research specific employees, as you might be interviewed by this person and/or work with him/her later.

Resources to Learn about Organizations

The following are some helpful resources to learn more about an organization as a potential internship/field experience or service learning placement site:

- Company's website
- Professional society websites containing information regarding top-industry organizations
- Relevant industry publications (e.g., Forbes)
- Organization's social media accounts (Twitter, Facebook)
- Internet resources for industry rankings and related performance (Crain's)
- Professional networking websites to connect with chief executive officers (CEOs) or upper management personnel (e.g., LinkedIn)

Think About It!

Here are topics to consider as you engage in an analysis of different organizations that you are interested in for your upcoming onsite field training:

1. What was the most informative resource I reviewed during the organizational analysis?
   _____
   _____
   _____
   _____

2. How does the organizational analysis help me develop my short-term internship goals?
   _____
   _____
   _____
   _____

3. What are the cultural values of an organization that would be important to me? _____
   _____
   _____
   _____
   _____

4. How does the industry ranking of an organization impact my decision-making process?
   _____
   _____
   _____
   _____

5. What personal societal concerns do I hold that influence my field training site choice? _
   _____
   _____
   _____
   _____

6. What is one benefit of doing my training at a site that matches my personal values? ___
   _____
   _____
   _____
   _____

Apply Your Knowledge!

The collected information during the organizational analysis can be utilized beyond the selection of an appropriate field training site. All of your accumulated knowledge should help you develop a clearer perspective on what type of career best fits both your personal and professional goals (organizational fit). Here are some further applications of this knowledge:

- Develop an online profile reflecting your understanding of the industry you would like to enter as an intern and/or an employee.
- Tailor your cover letter and/or e–mail correspondence to each potential field training site with specific details regarding the target organization.
- Communicate your research knowledge during professional networking opportunities at community volunteer fairs, career fairs, or other social events.
- Demonstrate your site-specific knowledge when conducting a preliminary onsite meeting(s) (e.g., an interview) with site representatives.
- Revise your résumé to reflect your updated understanding of what would be a good fit between your knowledge, skills, abilities, and other characteristics (KSAOs) and industry standards regarding employee qualifications.
- Speak to a career placement office representative regarding your site placement interests, and seek advice about how to contact organizations for internship/field experience or service learning placement opportunities.
- Reflect upon your learning to engage in more refined professional development processes and preplanning steps (see Chapter I).

Try It Out!
Work Sample Exercise

Work Sample Exercise Brief: A work sample test presents a portion of the actual job you might do in the workplace. You can create a work sample based upon one of the major work behaviors from a sample job description(s) you have collected during the "task analysis" step of your onsite research. For example, a work sample could be designed to reflect daily decision-making activities and could be assessed using an "in-basket" testing approach (e.g., a series of correspondence you receive and respond to in an "in box"). You can work with your faculty mentor and/or classmates to create industry-specific hypothetical scenarios to address (e.g., scheduling issues).

Your Role: For the following work sample exercise, please assume the role of a new trainee employee at Site X. You are approached by a site manager who asks you to participate in some policy decision-making tasks for training purposes. You are in a meeting with the manager and reviewing some recent employee and customer/client issues. You are to respond to various workplace issues and incidents. You are to make written comments on hard copy materials related to Site X memos and one-page policy postings. This exercise is limited to 30 minutes.

After completion of the Work Sample Exercise, ask yourself the following:

1. What did I learn about my decision-making capabilities through the in-basket exercise? Do I think that this exercise is relevant to what I might be doing onsite as an intern?
2. Based upon my learning, what skills should I continue to work on before getting onsite?

Search the Web!
Learn More about Your Field of Study

Search the Internet for different resources regarding how to best select a field training site. Also, discuss different resource options with your faculty mentor. Understand that this decision-making process can help you prepare for your career before graduating. Check out at least three different Internet resources pertaining to this training site decision process. As you review this information, please answer the following questions:

1. What were the most beneficial resources you found regarding choosing an optimal training placement? Explain why. _____

   _____
   _____
   _____
   _____
   _____
   _____
   _____
   _____

2. What did you find out about the availability of site placements within your field, and what were the associated selection criteria that organizations use to choose interns? _____

   _____
   _____
   _____
   _____
   _____
   _____
   _____

3. If you were giving advice to another student intern regarding how soon he/she should begin research training site options, what would your advice be? Please explain. _____

   _____
   _____
   _____
   _____
   _____
   _____
   _____
   _____

AN INTERN'S INSIGHTS

Elizabeth Tabet: Having an internship is exciting. It is an opportunity to take everything learned in the classroom to a professional setting. In preparing for an internship, you should first decide what kind of job you want to pursue. Take the time to think about what you want.

A key component of preparing for an internship is not only finding an organization that fits for the student, but it involves finding an organization that the student will be a good fit for. Students should start by researching organizations and finding the answers to questions like: What does this organization specifically do? What is their mission statement or organizational goals? Then, contact different sites and ask if they have any internship opportunities available.

Before starting any work at an organization, I think it is essential to discuss and agree upon some activities that you will be a part of and some goals you want to achieve. Agreements should be made before starting any work so both sides will clearly understand what the student is going to do, what the organization expects from you and it solidifies what your boundaries are as a student intern. By coming to these mutual agreements, it reaffirms your place and appropriate fit at that organization. An internship is essentially a "trial run" for students. It gives students a chance to experience what working in their chosen field will be like, so it should be taken seriously with that in mind. Getting an internship is a process and it takes preparatory action on the student's behalf. The more prepared you are for an internship, the more enjoyable, meaningful, successful and rewarding the experience will be.

"Let's Review!" Phase III Learning

1. What did you learn about the benefits of researching organizations for choosing field training site? Please explain. _____
   _____
   _____
   _____
   _____

2. How has your understanding of your future career training and potential career opportunities changed since you started researching organizations in your field? _____
   _____
   _____
   _____
   _____

3. What was the easiest information that you could find regarding organizations you were interested in doing your internship/field experience or service learning placement with? Most difficult information to find? Please explain. _____
   _____
   _____
   _____
   _____

4. How has the "organizational analysis" process improved your preplanning process?
   _____
   _____
   _____
   _____
   _____
   _____
   _____
   _____
   _____

Summary of the Chapter

This chapter reviewed different steps to be taken by you in choosing a site for your field-related training. The chapter reviews the processes of conducting three diverse types of analyses, which should influence this decision-making process: person analysis, task analysis, and organizational analysis. Each of these information-gathering steps covered in this chapter should help you become clearer about your training needs, motivations, and options. It is not a simple decision to make, and many personal and field-related factors should be considered when determining an internship/field experience or service learning placement site choice.

What Did I Learn?

As you reflect upon what you learned about this decision-making process, think about what you know to date (and what you still need to review). Without looking back in the chapter, please list what you feel were the main three points of learning which were personally relevant to you regarding focus of the chapter (explain why each is personally relevant to your learning):

1. _____
   _____
   _____
   _____

2. _____
   _____
   _____

3. _____
   _____
   _____

Discussion Questions

1. After completing the exercises and reviewing the content of this chapter, what would you say was the biggest lesson you learned about yourself regarding your chosen field?
2. Have your career goals changed in focus after you conducted the suggested person, task, and organizational analyses? If yes, how?
3. Based upon your research to date, what are two suggestion you would make to other students regarding how to find local and/or national site placements?
4. In reflection upon what you learned in this chapter, have your learning outcomes helped you better prepare for your long-term career? If yes, how so?
5. Of the three different analysis approaches (person, task, and organizational), which one was the most useful to you in finding a good training site option? Least useful? Why?
6. In researching different organizations, was it easy or difficult to identify and understand their organizational values and beliefs? If easy, what pieces of information indicated these values and beliefs?
7. In preparing to best reach out to different sites for training opportunities, how have you updated your contact letter, résumé, or other content after completing this chapter?
8. A job description is a beneficial source of information to help you match your career-related interests to your academic training. What did you learn about a job?
9. Creating a good "fit" between you and your chosen training organization is critical for your success onsite. What concept(s) discussed in the chapter helped you in this aim?
10. If you were to develop an informational workshop for your classmates regarding how to choose a training site, what would be four to five topics you would cover?

Additional Information Links

- LinkedIn: http://www.linkedin.com
- Glassdoor: http://www.glassdoor.com
- Internships.com: http://www.internships.com
- Internmatch.com: http://www.internmatch.com
- YouTern: http://www.youtern.com
- Idealist: http://www.idealist.com
- CoolWorks: http://www.coolworks.com

Fig. 3.1: Source: https://pixabay.com/e board-business-company-creative-2445

CHAPTER III

Creating Site-Related Goals for the Field Experience

FIELD LEARNING FACTOID

"Creating Measurable Goals: ... Investigate an issue present at my internship site through research and share my findings through a reflection with my mentor and the Internship Coordinator. Present, suggest, and collaborate good solutions, changes, or alternatives to my mentor after investigating an issue. Create a strategic plan with my mentor to implement solutions and changes over a two-month period."

Source: U.S. Denver Center for International Studies website
(https://sites.google.com/site/dcisinternships/creating-goals)

Introduction

Drafting your site-related learning goals helps you to have a clear understanding of the goal expectations of your selected training site, as well as the broader training expectations of your field (Basow & Byrne, 1994; Nagel, 2014). There should be conscious planning on your part regarding ways to create learning goals onsite that will correspond to your academic goals and knowledge (Borzak & Hursch, 1977; Calico, 1985; Little & Robinson, 1997). These interrelated goals will form the basis of your overall learning outcomes from the experience and will help you develop into an emergent professional (Compton & Davis, 2010; Kaufman, Israel, & Rudd, 2009). Because of the criticality of this learning experience, you should devise field-related goals that truly prepare you for the real-world workplace (e.g., diversity in the classroom training of preservice teachers: Phillion, Miller, & Lehmen, 2005). Meeting as early as possible with your site supervisor will help in this planning process.

Internships/field experiences and service learning experiences can be highly beneficial and yield invaluable outcomes for students, organizations, and the broader community (Alpert, Heaney, & Kuhn, 2009; Green, 1997). This applied training experience, if planned in a thoughtful and detailed manner, can support your successful entry into your chosen career field (Beenen & Rousseau, 2010). The key to this step is being open to this intensive learning process and accepting both the challenges and opportunities presented in a proactive manner (e.g., O'Neill, 2010). This is a unique learning opportunity for you. Enter this experience with clear goals for both your short- and long-term career training aspirations, as well as an open mind to the many training opportunities offered.

Achieving your learning goals, both in and out of the classroom, can facilitate feelings of positive self-motivation and personal self-efficacy (Zimmerman, Bandura, & Martinez-Pons, 1992). Ongoing goal setting during your learning and task performance can enhance your ability to "anchor and adjust" your cognitive and/or physical task performance for effective self-regulatory strategies to utilize during your field training (Curtis, 2000; Oettingen, Pak, & Schnetter, 2001).

A field training opportunity can be transformative, creating a more enriched knowledge base in your early career development, as well as empowering you to be an active learner (Angelique, 2001; Taylor, 2004). Among the many training outcomes, you will learn more about yourself through the processes of self-introspective journaling (Grow, 1991; Kuiper, 2004) and external assessments (Weigand, Richardson, & Weinberg, 1999). Additionally, this is an opportunity for you to "pilot test" a career position to see if you like it (Cunningham & Sherman, 2008; Johari & Bradshaw, 2008; Ottesen, 2007).

As you review and do the activities presented in this module and all of the modules presented in this manual, please think about the many benefits you will acquire during your learning. Experiential learning, and service learning more specifically, will provide clear benefits to you (and other interns) in many ways, from building your knowledge, skills, and abilities for your increased career viability to more generalized benefits of personal development in communication effectiveness (e.g., oral presentation of ideas), self-presentation/impression management tactics to best adapt to different social situations, task organization, and other interpersonal capabilities beyond the workplace.

Learning Goals for this Chapter

Chapter III offers both informational resources and interactive exercises/activities to best prepare you to:

→ Learn about the concept of "action goals" and apply it to field learning,
→ Engage in the goal planning process with both your faculty and site supervisors, and
→ Articulate and refine challenging but doable site-related learning goals through interactions with your faculty and site supervisors.

The focus of this chapter will be to understand how to develop these types of goals for your upcoming onsite field training. Before beginning to discuss specific training issues related to your field experience, let us explore some foundational concepts for this chapter:

Look It Up!

Define and Understand Important Concepts

In preparing to start drafting your site-relate goals for your field training, it is vital to have a background knowledge in specific learning concepts. Please consult the word glossary provided at the back of this manual, and look up the following terms discussed in the current chapter.

Goal: _____
_____

Learning Goal: _____
_____

Goal Setting: _____
_____

Actionable Goal: _____
_____

Needs Analysis: _____
_____

Job Analysis: _____
_____

Job Description: _____
_____

Phase I: How To Develop and Refine "Actionable" Goals for a Site-Related Learning Experience

The goals that you develop under the guidance of your supervisors are the foundation of your experiential learning. An important part of this goal development process is the determination of the criteria to assess your learning progress (Ledoux, Thurlow, McHenry, Burns, & Pugh, 2007; Li et al., 2015). The benefits of this goal setting go beyond the training experience, helping you in your career-seeking behavior and other related decision-making tasks (Noordzi, Hooft, Mierlo, Dam, & Born, 2013; Taing, Smith, Singla, Johnson, & Chang, 2013).

Goal setting is a critical part of your site-related learning planning and process. We all engage in goal-setting behaviors on a daily basis. You will find that the process of articulating your specific short-term training goals onsite will assist in refining your long-term career goals. You will find that you engage in goal setting in an ongoing manner throughout your internship/field experience or service learning training.

Before you can step onsite to start your field training, you must plan each of your activities with a specific focus on establishing each as a learning goal. You will develop and revise these goals through the process of flexible goal setting in response to the dynamic nature of each actionable goal for the training experience.

There are many different sources of information that can help you in this process. A key aspect of this procedural step is your reflection upon personal motivations and capabilities projected onto the expectations of the upcoming field training experience, as well as areas for improvement (needs analysis).

Let us go through some ideas of what you should do in preparing for this step in the process:

1. *Review information about the industry*—It is important to know what is typically done by people who work in the industry that you will be doing your internship/field experience or service learning placement. Conduct Internet research regarding typical industry-related activities and trends that can give you a better idea of typical job duties similar to what you might be doing.

2. *Discuss the task-related needs fulfilled through your internship/field experience or service learning placement duties ("needs analysis") with your site supervisor*—Part of the process should involve consulting with the site-related supervisor(s) regarding expectations of the training experience and what will be done. His/her input will be invaluable in helping you conceptualize your onsite activities and link these onsite ideas to your academic objectives.

3. *Meet with your faculty supervisor about your initial research focus*—There are typically two parts to any field training experience, with one being experiential and the other being academic. Develop a plan of action for your internship/field experience or service learning placement under the guidance of your faculty supervisor. If the opportunity is available, discuss these preliminary planning steps with other interns in the classroom.

4. *Interview current interns for their insights*—In addition to asking for advice from site-related sources, remember to interview a few current interns in addition to collecting information at the site for the goal-setting process.

5. *Think about yourself in the goal-setting process*—What are your career goals that you would like to achieve through this internship/field experience or service learning placement experience? Your thoughts and input are a critical part of the decision-making process as you start to articulate through writing the objectives and learning outcomes you are thinking about.

6. *Embrace "serendipity"*—In creating your site-related goals and planning your professional training focus, consider that you should embrace the opportunities available to you and make the most out of available resources.

The process involved in writing your onsite goals can be an iterative experience of collecting information and comparing it to the expectations of performance standards from different feedback constituents. Think about ways to further investigate these expectations from multiple perspectives in the proceeding:

What Do I Think About ... ?

1. What do I personally want to learn through my field training?
2. How do I begin the process of writing my learning goals?
3. Are my learning expectations realistic?
4. Do my learning goals correspond with others' expectations of me?
5. What are the most common errors committed when writing learning goals?
6. Lastly, who is the best person(s) to ask for advice in how to develop my learning goals?

CHAPTER III Creating Site-Related Goals for the Field Experience | 43

"Let's Review!" Phase I Learning

1. What did you learn about conceptualizing your overall learning goals for the internship/ field experience or service learning placement? _____
   _____
   _____
   _____
   _____
   _____
   _____

2. As you engaged in the suggested learning activities, what were some important concepts you learned regarding your goal-related writing process? _____
   _____
   _____
   _____
   _____
   _____
   _____

3. Which informational sources did you find to be the most helpful to you during this learning process? Why? _____
   _____
   _____
   _____
   _____
   _____
   _____

4. Is it challenging to come up with detailed site-related performance goals? Why or why not? _____
   _____
   _____
   _____
   _____
   _____
   _____

Phase II: How to Conduct a "Job Analysis" of a Site Placement Position

As you start the process of determining what you will be doing onsite in a more detailed manner, it would be beneficial to conduct a thorough analysis of the job tasks (job analysis). A job description can be a critical part of this analysis process. Let us go through some ideas:

1. *Find online job descriptions*—Sometimes the best way to understand the requirements of an internship/field experience or service learning placement position is to evaluate the major work behaviors commonly conducted on the job. A job description offers information of both essentiual and marginal job functions, creating a realistic job preview.

2. *Interview job-relevant professionals ("job analysis" interview)*—To better understand your potential job duties as a future intern, it is a good idea to interview a sample of professionals who work in the job related to your anticipated site placement. Ask the incumbents about what they do on the job and any advice they can offer.

3. *Observe the "job" in the workplace*—With the permission of your site supervisor, visit the arranged field training site, and observe the employees conducting the duties related to what you will be doing as an intern in the coming weeks. Take notes, and discuss your observations with your faculty and site supervisors.

4. *Watch a job-related video*—As you check out online resources for possible job descriptions, see if you can find online videos (e.g., eHow or YouTube videos), which may present someone performing the tasks related to your upcoming field training experience. This is a good "second option" if you are not able to do preliminary observations of employee work behaviors at your anticipated training site.

FROM A SITE SUPERVISOR'S DESK

Dr. Hilary Ward Schnadt, Associate Dean for Academic Services & Programs, University Center of Lake County:

I am offering two bits of advice for students embarking on internships. I am offering them together, because I think the relationship between the two is powerful, and because I fear that, if each was heard individually, these ideas might be contradictory instead of complementary.

The first is "make a plan." Know what you want to get out of the internship and how you want to gain that knowledge or experience. Granted, some of the structure of your internship may be imposed by the course, through which you will earn academic credit, or by the site. However, you likely had some choice of sites, and you are responsible for the logistics of adding the internship into your academic, working, and family life. Developing a clear plan for what you want to gain from the internship will help you prioritize the many demands on your time and energy and will keep you working towards your long-term goal.

At the same time, be prepared to "embrace serendipity." An internship is an opportunity for you to learn about the details of a career and how to navigate it. Do not get so focused on following a previously-developed plan that you fail to seize unexpected opportunities that come your way. Having a conversation with a client at your site or observing interactions among the staff may lead you to an important insight that you would not have otherwise gained. Remaining mindfully "present" and using your peripheral vision is crucial!

What Should I Do?
Putting Your Learning into Action

1. Research the concept of "goal setting," and identify issues of human motivation and associated workplace performance.
2. Contact and meet with a human resources manager at a company related to your chosen field. Ask about goal setting in the workplace, and how it relates to being a highly effective employee.
3. Reach out to a job recruiter and ask about the attributes of strong candidates for job positions within your industry.
4. Go online and try to find examples of sample learning contracts or associated job duty paperwork (e.g., employee training manuals).
5. Meet with your career placement office and ask how to write learning goals related to your field training in a clear and effective manner.
6. Discuss your developing learning goals with your faculty and site supervisors to see if you are correct in your conceptualization of the process.
7. Meet with peer intern students to compare notes regarding the site-related observations and collected information. Multiple perspectives may help you further refine your thinking regarding potential site-related goal activities.

Before proceeding, please review what you have learned in Phase II! The next section contains a series of review questions related to what you learned in doing the activities and exercises. To best help you with this ongoing learning process, please be accurate in your responses. This ongoing self-assessment of learning will help you identify both what you understand to date and what information you still need to work on.

CHAPTER III Creating Site-Related Goals for the Field Experience | 47

"Let's Review!" Phase II Learning

1. Based upon the suggested sources of information and activities, what did you learn about the process of developing goals for your draft learning contract? _____
   _____
   _____
   _____
   _____
   _____
   _____
   _____

2. Learning how to conduct research on topics as they relate to specific learning outcomes is an important skill to develop. What insights did you learn about yourself during this stage in the learning process? _____
   _____
   _____
   _____
   _____
   _____
   _____
   _____

3. Matching site-related goals to academic objectives may be challenging in the beginning. What were the challenges, if any, that you encountered during this process? _____
   _____
   _____
   _____
   _____
   _____
   _____
   _____

4. Were you able to find examples of learning contracts online? If so, what did you learn about the structure and content of typical learning contracts? If you were not able to find examples within your field, why do you think examples were difficult to find? _____
   _____
   _____
   _____
   _____
   _____
   _____
   _____

Phase III: Make the Site Goals Your Own

Part of the process of creating site-related goals is to personalize the planned activities based on your unique skills and interests. Understanding what you can bring to an organization through your field training participation entails a certain amount of brainstorming about how to tailor your proposed onsite activities to both satisfy an organization's workplace needs and fulfill your career development aspirations.

Introspection is a key part of you understanding your career development goals. Most workers rarely take the time to analyze their motivations and interests before they enter the workplace. More importantly, this process of evaluating your career goals and interests should be done periodically throughout your career. The following will discuss some ways for you to apply these ideas in how to create more personally relevant and motivating goals for your upcoming field training experience.

Resources to Learn about Your Goal Related Skills and Needs

There are many online sources of information available to help guide you in this vital step in your learning. The following are some helpful resources to learn more about how to assess your work-related aptitudes and abilities regarding:

- Career goals: *mindtools.com, careeronestep.org*
- Interpersonal skills and listening skills: *skillsyouneed.com*
- Basic math and verbal skills: *jobtest.com/Wunderlich-BST-sample*
- Basic computer skills: proprofs.com/quiz-school/story.php?title=basic-computer-skills-assessment

---

Think About It!

Here are topics to consider as you engage in the process of writing your site-related goals. It is beneficial for you if these goals are a good fit with your long-term career aspirations and interests.

1. As you write the site-related goals, do you feel that they are "doable" activities for you? Why or why not? _____
   _____
   _____
   _____

2. Do you see a correspondence between your site-related goals and your broader career interests? Please explain. _____
   _____
   _____
   _____

3. Who is best suited to help you best match your skills to your planned onsite activities? Please explain. _____
   _____
   _____
   _____

Apply Your Knowledge!

Beyond choosing your declared academic major and associated academic training, you may not have given much consideration to the aptitudes and abilities you will bring to your chosen field. You might surprise yourself regarding unexplored career interests or talents. There are many resources available, both on-campus and online, for you as a student and emerging professional within your field. It is important for you to utilize these resources to assess your potential during this critical career development process.

Take the time to consider using different assessment approaches to determine your aptitude and skill levels, as well as needed areas of training. This step is an important part of your overall learning outcomes, so it is critical to consider many different factors. The timing of this assessment process in parallel with writing your site-related goals is crucial to the creation of a productive, growth-oriented experience. Here are some helpful steps to follow to begin this self-assessment process of your career-related aptitude and abilities. With the following suggestions, please discuss your assessment outcomes with your supervisors:

- Make an appointment with a career counselor on campus to discuss your career goals,
- Take an online or on-campus career interest inventory,
- Complete a physical ability test to receive feedback regarding your physical capabilities,
- Complete a general intelligence and/or intellectual reasoning test to assess your intellectual capabilities, and
- Talk with the instructors in your academic program about their feedback regarding your career-related aptitude as demonstrated through your past or current performance.

Try It Out!
Leaderless Group Discussion Exercise

Leaderless Group Discussion Exercise Brief: This exercise is an assessment of two important skills related to people's work on the job: being able to work well with others in a group and being able to assume the role of the leader within a group. This approach is commonly used in assessment centers to test job applicant candidates or promotion applicants for managerial positions. The results of this assessment have great insights for individual's performance in team or workgroup contexts.

There are many published leaderless group discussion exercises you can find online, or you can develop your exercise to possibly conduct during a class meeting with the permission of your faculty supervisor. Gather a group of four to five individuals and ask them to discuss a topical issue that needs a decision (e.g., "What do you think is the biggest issue on campus regarding student services, and what should be done?"). Observe the group as they start the task. You will take notes on the behavior of the individuals as they work through the process of assuming roles. Who is the emergent leader? If so, are there diverse types of leaders who convey different messages? Who are the followers? How are they behaving and interacting during the task? Was there a consensus decision? This exercise is limited to 30 minutes.

After completion of the Leaderless Group Discussion Exercise, ask yourself the following:

1. What did I learn about assessing job-related skills through this approach?
2. What can I learn about my leadership attributes as I observed others engaging in this type of activity? My "follower" attributes?

Search the Web!
Learn About How to Write Well Articulated and Measurable Site Goals

Search the Internet for different resources regarding how to best write a goal statement. An effective goal statement fully expresses the tasks and/or outcomes involved in the behavior. A goal statement conveys information that is measurable for assessment purposes. There is an "art" to goal writing that transfers to proficient writing in general, conveying information in a clear and concise manner.

Check out *at least* three different Internet resources pertaining to goal writing. As you review this information, please answer the following questions:

1. What were the most beneficial resources you found regarding how to write learning goal statements? Please explain why these were particularly helpful resources. _____

2. What did you learn about goal setting processes in general? _____

3. If you were giving advice to another student intern regarding how to write learning goals, what would your advice be? Please explain. _____

AN INTERN'S INSIGHTS

Tracy Hernandez: As a part-time graduate student entering my program "cold," meaning I was not already working in the field, I really needed an internship to get a tangible feel for work after graduation. I am happy to share those lessons I learned:

First, choose wisely. Find a position that you find interesting, and that also plays to your strengths. It never hurts to make suggestions for a customized role, and most sites want the relationship to be as mutually beneficial as possible. Also, avoid diving into something entirely separate from your larger body of research and experience.

Second, do your homework on your site. Have in-person conversations with your potential site supervisor and get to know their work style, expectations, and schedules. Be very thoughtful about the language in your contracts and ask yourself early and often if this is a good fit for *you*. If you have doubts, look for something new sooner rather than later.

Third, stay organized. Managing your timeline, objectives and professional goals is time consuming, in addition to daily work on your site. Budget time to frequently rework your schedule, outline everything, and keep up with your notes and journals. You will need all of this for your term papers, and (more importantly) to apply what you have learned in the real world.

Fourth and finally, power through! Wrapping up graduate courses is exhausting and often comes down to the wire. This is doubly true for internships. You have obligations not just to you and your advisor, but to your site and any populations they serve. You can do it!

"Let's Review!" Phase III Learning

1. What did you learn about writing site-related learning goals for an internship/field experience or service learning placement? Please explain. _____
   _____
   _____

2. How has your understanding of goal setting processes within a learning context changed? Please explain. _____
   _____
   _____

3. What was the easiest information to access regarding how to write effective goal statements? Most difficult to access? Please explain why you think this is true in each case.
   _____
   _____
   _____

4. Do you anticipate that your writing of clearly-articulated site goals will help you in your later onsite learning and paper writing? Why, or why not? Please explain. _____
   _____
   _____

Summary of the Chapter

This chapter presented ideas related to thinking about developing site-related "actionable" goals for your upcoming internship/field experience or related field training (e.g., service learning experience). The creation of such site-related goals entails an understanding of both the training site's requirements/needs and your personal capabilities and motivations (e.g., career training aspirations). This goal setting stage in the planning process is a critical "building block" for the subsequent steps in your further planning and experiential learning processes.

What Did I Learn?

As you reflect upon what you learned about developing site-related goals for your upcoming field training, think about what you have learned so far (and what you still need to review). Without looking back in the chapter, please list what you feel were the main three points of learning that were personally relevant to you regarding focus of the chapter (explain why each is personally relevant to your learning):

1. _____
   _____
2. _____
   _____
3. _____
   _____

Discussion Questions

1. What did you learn about the goal setting process for your approaching field-related training? Was it more challenging than you anticipated in developing these learning goals for your learning contract? Please explain.
2. How important was it to learn about the placement site and your site-related activities ahead of time in conjunction with writing your site goals? In this process of collecting information about your upcoming field training site, was it easy to acquire this information, or did it take more steps than anticipated? Please explain.
3. Who was the most informative source of information regarding writing goals? Least informative? Please explain?
4. Why do you think it is critical to have site-related goals established prior to beginning your onsite field training?
5. Is it challenging to write well-articulated onsite performance goals? Why, or why not?
6. What did you learn about yourself in this examination of your field-related capabilities and performance strengths (e.g., good problem-solving skills)?
7. Through this self-assessment process of your knowledge, skills, and abilities, what did you learn about your training needs? How will you address these training needs?
8. What did you learn about your perspectives on leadership activities in conducting the leaderless group discussion exercise?
9. Were there helpful resources for writing site-related goals on the Internet? In your library?
10. Finally, do you anticipate that your onsite learning goals will evolve in focus over the course of your field experience? Why, or why not?

Additional Information Links

- Smart Sheet website:
  https://www.smartsheet.com/blog/essential-guide-writing-smart-goals
- Look Sharp website:
  https://www.looksharp.com/blog/setting-summer-internship-goals
- Business, Entrepreneurship, and Society Program website:
  https://sites.google.com/site/besacmprogram/BES-Program/internship-syllabus/internship-learning-goals-strategies-assessments
- Our Everyday Life website:
  http://oureverydaylife.com/goals-should-during-internship-5641.html
- Psychological and Counseling Internship Goals:
  https://caps.ku.edu/internship-goals-and-objectives
- Chron website:
  http://work.chron.com/learning-objectives-goals-finance-internship-23704.html
- InternshipUSA:
  https://www.internship-usa.com/blog/2011/09/09/choosing-internship-goals/

Fig. 4.1: Source: https://pixabay.com/glasses-office-reading-books-568405

CHAPTER IV

Creating Academic Objectives for the Field Experience

FIELD LEARNING FACTOID

"Before you can decide on a focus, you need to explore your topic, to become informed about the topic, to build on your knowledge and experience. You will be locating books, articles, videos, internet and other resources about your topic and reading to learn! You are looking for an issue, an aspect, or a perspective on which to focus your research paper. This is the first step in which you will probably be checking books out of the library. Encyclopedias won't be much help here. You are looking for treatments of your topic which are either more comprehensive or more specific than an encyclopedic treatment, with various authors' summaries, analyses and opinions. But, until you've chosen a focus, you are not really on a mission of gathering information. If you gather information on the topic you will waste a lot of time doing it and have way too much to sort through when you are ready to write your paper. Resist the temptation to 'gather' until you've chosen a focus."

Source: Excerpt: "A+ Research & Writing for high school and college students" by K. L. Schwartz (http://www.ipl.org/div/aplus/step3.htm#sec1.1)

Introduction

In creating effective, actionable site goals, it is critical to construct equally accomplishable academic objectives that reflect your career education and exploration interests (Ducat, 1980; McGoey & Ross, 1999). As your site-related goals were primarily developed in working with your site supervisor, your academic objectives are developed in consultation with your faculty supervisor.

Before proceeding, the importance of information literacy as it relates to research and professional development should be acknowledged. The learning associated with this ongoing research process will assist in your knowledge base, as well as important research skills, which will generalize to your overall effectiveness as a learner and future professional in the field. The information you gain and maintain over time will help you create more sophisticated thought and problem-solving processes on the many different work-related contexts you will encounter as an intern and beyond.

As a "value added" aspect to your ongoing learning, communication is a skill that will be developed through collaborative interactions with your faculty supervisor and this will greatly benefit you beyond the field training period (Munodawafa, 2008). Field training experience is typically thought of as training in the workplace, but it is equally important to acknowledge that research skill training is an important part of this experiential learning process (Bansal, 1998; Turunen & Tuovila, 2012). The broader field training is a meaningful integration of both practical and theoretical knowledge attainment for you as an intern (Burgin & Sadler, 2016; Rogan & Anderson, 2011).

Establishment of clear academic objectives that meaningfully reflect upon your site goals helps to create supportive learning opportunities for you as both an emergent researcher and practitioner in the field (Mollica & Hyman, 2016; O'Sullivan & Tsangaridou, 1992; Scholz, Steiner, & Hansmann, 2004). This step in the development of your learning contract also has the benefit of improving your readiness to begin your internship/field experience or service learning training in the coming weeks (Stedman & Schonfeld, 2011).

You might be surprised how the process of setting clear and concise academic objectives creates a more transparent understanding of both your needs and expectations in the field training process, as well as your faculty supervisor's goals and expectations of your learning outcomes (Downey & Cobbs, 2007; Kardash, 2000). Your training will benefit you in many ways if planned well, including creating the opportunity to make a difference in your training site beyond just your daily activities (e.g., becoming an "agent of change" in the workplace) (Rogan & Anderson, 2011).

An internship/field experience or service learning situation gives you the opportunity to put your "learning into action" (e.g., Stark & Lattuca, 1997). The benefits to you as a learner cannot be understated. This approach to education emphasizes an important paradigm shift in the integration of academic and applied concepts within a career training focus (Bilimoria, 1998; Clark, 2003; Whetten & Clark, 1996). One might argue that this educational approach is an integral part of any academic training for myriad fields/disciplines (Young & Baker, 2004).

Learning "how to learn" (i.e., metacognition) is a learning theme that you will encounter at all steps in your field training (Kolb, 1984; Sims & Lindholm, 1993). The integration of both theoretical and applied aspects of your professional role is a critical step to initiate prior to beginning your onsite tasks (Whetten & Clark, 1996). Although this does not correspond to the traditional classroom model of professional instruction, it is the most innovative way of training as one of tomorrow's workforce participants within your field (Fleming, 1992; Howard, 1998; Perry, 1970; Prentice & Garcia, 2000).

There are many aspects of learning that you will encounter throughout the experiential process. One important outcome is that your ongoing learning will develop your self-reflection skills during your self-observations onsite. The associated journaling of your learning will help you integrate your academic objectives and onsite goal initiatives (Clark, 2001; Kolb, 1984; McCall, Lombardo, & Morrison, 1988). You may not have conducted such introspective processes in other classes, and that is one more reason why this training is a unique and growth-oriented learning experience for you.

Among other self-reflection skills, you may learn how to be a better critical thinker about social learning situations and how you fit within social contacts (e.g., leadership skills) (Schön, 1987; McCormick, 1993). What you learn about yourself through this field-related training will greatly assist you in your future years as a professional within the field.

Anticipate that this planning of your learning will go far beyond your internship/field experience or service learning placement (Taylor, 1988; Vaill, 1996). Your experience will be part of a larger partnership of learning involving your supervisors on your site (Inkster & Ross, 1995). As much as you will learn about yourself throughout this process, you will also learn insights regarding your mentoring relationships with supervisors and how this is a mutual learning experience for all involved. You may also gain insights regarding how to best mentor others in your later career stages.

Learning Goals for this Chapter

Chapter IV offers both informational resources and interactive exercises/activities to best prepare you to:

- → Identify relevant research topics reflecting site-related learning "themes,"
- → Use library search databases and related resources to locate and collect relevant, peer-reviewed research, and
- → Begin to draft concepts relating to your academic objectives an initial interview, reflecting current field-related concepts, and avoid plagiarism in research writing.

Look It Up!

Define and Understand Important Concepts

In preparing to start researching concepts for your upcoming field training, it is vital to have a background knowledge of specific learning concepts. Please consult the word glossary provided at the back of this manual, and look up the following terms discussed in the current chapter.

Academic Objective: _____
_____
_____
_____
_____

Theory: _____
_____
_____
_____
_____

Concept: _____
_____
_____
_____
_____

Scholarly Research: _____
_____
_____
_____
_____

Literature Review: _____
_____
_____

Writing "Flow": _____
_____
_____
_____

Plagiarism: _____
_____
_____
_____
_____

Phase I: How To Develop Ideas For Your Academic Objectives

Having a good theoretical foundation for your training experience will be useful for you in many different steps in your overall professional development process. It cannot be overstated how important it is to establish this focus early in your field training.

What should I prepare for before I begin the research process? There is a great deal to consider in preparing for this crucial step in constructing your theoretical ideas for the conceptual foundation of your learning. Writing the field paper is not the only academic goal for your field training, but it is a good means to an end related to the learning process. In addition to researching and writing your field paper, which is the primary focus of this chapter, here are some additional academic objectives or goals that you can achieve from your field-related training:

- Applying theories and concepts you learned in classes to the real-world workplace
- Refining your intellectual reasoning and decision-making skills through your onsite task assignments
- Enhancing your leadership skills through team-based projects
- Learning about diverse cultures and populations by working with diverse co-workers and/or clients/customers
- Developing your self-management and meta-cognitive ("thinking about thinking") performance capabilities
- Improving upon your critical thinking and problem-solving skills in your onsite tasks, either alone or in working with others
- Refining your social and oral communication skills in interacting with different constituents in the workplace
- Enhancing your written communication and editing capabilities through different onsite assignments for diverse purposes (e.g., creating interdepartmental memos)
- Applying your understanding of social impression management to how you present yourself as an intern to others in the workplace

As you start the process of determining what you will be doing onsite and your associated planning of each academic learning goal (academic objective), you should think about how these activities interrelate in your training plan. Let us go through some general ideas of what you should do in preparing for this step:

1. *Review your draft site-related goal ideas*—Make a list of your draft site-related goal ideas, and then write down the associations that you can make between the concepts you have learned in your classes and/or broader career ideas that you would like to link back to specific training activities.
2. *Meet with a reference librarian*—Set up an appointment with a reference librarian on your campus. When meeting with a librarian, present your goal-related ideas, and ask what research databases and other information resources would be best to utilize to find relevant academic research. The aim is to collect peer-reviewed research articles and selected books.
3. *Review your collected research*—Do a preliminary review of the research collected to develop some academic objective ideas. Using your learning contract's site-related goals as bases, create associated draft academic topics to be explored.
4. *Meet with your faculty supervisor*—Discuss your draft academic ideas and associated academic objectives with your faculty supervisor. In addition, ask about feedback regarding how well the academic ideas relate to your site-related goals to create a cohesive, integrated field paper by the end of the experience.
5. *Journal about your learning*—As with all steps in the process, you need to engage in ongoing self-reflection about your learning. Journal about what you have learned related to conducting research and developing ideas related to matching academic objective goals for your upcoming field experience.

What Do I Think About ... ?

1. How I find scholarly, peer-reviewed research resources?
2. Who is the best person to speak to regarding starting the research process?
3. Which type of information is best to begin with, articles or books?
4. How do I organize the information I have collected to formulate my ideas?
5. What is the best way to begin the research writing process (e.g., develop an outline)?
6. What is plagiarism, and how do I avoid it in my writing?
7. Finally, is there a writing center or tutor on my campus to help with my writing?

Based on the information you have collected to date, which resources best helped you in developing your academic objectives for your learning contract? As you continue to explore possibilities and research field-relevant theories/concepts, you will further enhance your understanding from a dual theoretical and applied perspectives.

"Let's Review!" Phase I Learning

1. What did you learn about conducting research to create a good "match" between your site-related goals and a theory and/or concept from your empirical research? _____
   _____
   _____
   _____
   _____
   _____
   _____
   _____

2. Why is it important to identify and collect scholarly, peer-reviewed research? What strategies did you learn to identify peer-reviewed research when conducting library article searches? _____
   _____
   _____
   _____
   _____
   _____
   _____
   _____
   _____

3. Which informational sources did you find to be the most helpful during this learning process? Why? _____
   _____
   _____
   _____
   _____
   _____
   _____
   _____

4. What did you learn about time management and search strategies in conducting this research process? _____
   _____
   _____
   _____
   _____
   _____
   _____
   _____

Phase II: How to Identify a Relevant Theory or Concept Related to Your Experience

One of the most challenging tasks for you in writing your field experience paper is finding that "perfect" theory or concept that relates to what you be doing onsite. Learning how to use research databases to find relevant research in peer-reviewed sources (scholarly research) is a key step in the process. One might argue that your research skill development is equally important to your site-related skill development during the entire field experience training process as you collect, review, and write up your research (literature review). Let us go through some ideas of what you should prepare for in this step:

1. *Meet with your faculty advisor*—Your faculty supervisor will have guidance toward potential theoretical models and/or concepts that can offer a good conceptual framework for interpreting your learning outcomes.

2. *Set up an appointment with a reference librarian*—Meet again with a reference librarian on campus. Review information related to the use of different research databases and other library research resources at your educational institution.

3. *Start your research*—Make a list of different topic ideas, and use these words or phrases as search terms in databases to see what articles you may find. Remember to record your search steps (e.g., search terms used) and download any PDF articles that are relevant to what you anticipate to be doing onsite.

4. *Be organized*—When requesting research materials through interlibrary loan, make sure you understand the time it will take to receive the materials. Use note cards to take summary notes and document the citations of chosen references.

FROM A SITE SUPERVISOR'S DESK

Alyssa Vincent, Northeastern Illinois University Reference Librarian:

Honing in on an interest for a field experience or internship research paper can feel as daunting as selecting a site or engaging in the work once you are placed. Whether you are selecting your topic or are guided in a certain direction, identifying what you care about and how that impacts your site is crucial to writing an interesting, valuable research paper.

It may be simple for some people to identify what they care about, but others might draw a blank and have only vague ideas that lack a connection to their site. There are many ways to determine where your interests could lie, and one is to critically examine what drew you to your site and how it corresponds to interests you have. Writer Zora Neale Hurston once said that "research is formalized curiosity," and our curiosity is stimulated by asking ourselves questions, not by reciting easily-searchable keywords or sorting through thousands of results from a database.

Once you have identified a curiosity that you can investigate at your field experience site, then you can start formulating keywords. Some students create "mind maps," others describe their research question to someone else and have that person help them identify main concepts, and some jump into searching in library databases or Google Scholar and identify keywords that authors of helpful articles use in their work. The key is to remain flexible and understand that your research process is always evolving, especially as you are learning new things at your site!

What Should I Do?
Putting Your Learning into Action

1. Discuss with your faculty mentor your developing theoretical ideas for your field paper.
2. Make an outline of the anticipated topics to be discussed in the introductory literature review of your field paper. In parallel, make associations with your stated academic objectives.
3. Begin your writing process and think about how your chosen theoretical concepts relate to the focus of your internship/field experience or service learning placement plans.
4. As you write, please double check that you are covering the necessary topics that relate back to your site-related goals. Please keep in mind that, at this stage in the writing process, you are simply developing draft ideas to revise in the "Academic Objectives" part of your learning contract.
5. Make an appointment with a Writing Tutor on your campus and review your writing drafts with him/her to help ensure there is a good structure and "flow" in your writing. If your campus does not provide this service, form a peer writing support group to collect and share editing feedback.
6. Find an online tutorial about how to conduct research and/or academic paper writing.
7. Journal what you have learned and refer to it as you go through the proceeding stages of your internship/field experience or service learning placement training.

Remember to utilize many different resources as you engage in this learning process. Before proceeding, please review what you have learned in Phase II! The next section contains a series of review questions related to what you learned in doing the activities and exercises. Please be accurate in your any responses to assess what areas of your learning need further attention. This review will help you identify both the content that you understand, as well as the supplemental information that you still need to find and review.

"Let's Review!" Phase II Learning

1. Based upon the suggested sources of information and activities, what did you learn about the process of finding research to support your planned site-related goals? _____
   _____
   _____
   _____
   _____
   _____
   _____
   _____

2. What is the most challenging part in the finding peer-reviewed research? What was the most helpful source for information to assist you in the process? _____
   _____
   _____
   _____
   _____
   _____
   _____
   _____

3. When matching research to your site-related goals, did you identify "gaps" in literature coverage that required more in-depth research investigation? If so, was it easy to resolve? _____
   _____
   _____
   _____
   _____
   _____
   _____

4. What writing strategies helped you most in beginning this process of formulating conceptual ideas for your academic objectives? _____
   _____
   _____
   _____
   _____
   _____
   _____

Phase III: How To Plan for the Academic Writing Process

Academic objectives relate to the theoretical examination of your learning onsite. It would be good for you to consider the different ways your writing skills will be applied at different steps in the field training experience. Your writing skills will be utilized in multiple ways for your internship/field experience or service learning placement process, from drafting your goals and objectives for your eventual learning contract to journaling your learning and writing the field paper culminating from your learning outcomes. The following will discuss different issues to consider in your writing skill development.

Resources to Use in Developing Your Writing Skills

The following are some helpful resources to learn more about how to write your thoughts and research-related concepts in a clear and expressive manner that reflects your writing style.

- Steps to creativity and how to have ideas:
  http://www.righttodone.com/7-steps-to-creativity-how-to-have-ideas
- Writing good work objectives:
  http://www.nickols.us/writing_work_objectives.htm
- Tips on how to engage in effective writing:
  http://www.dailywritingtips.com/50-tips-on-how-to-write-and-good
- Knowledge of the formatting guidelines within your field: e.g., *APAstyle.org* for psychologists for social science–related fields

Think About It!

Writing is a process that everyone should practice across their lifespans. To become a good writer entails the need to understand your unique style of writing and to engage in self-criticism about what you need to work on. Here are topics to consider as you think about ways to improve your academic writing practices in preparing to begin your field training experience.

1. What do you think is the most challenging aspect of your writing process? Why? _____
   _____
   _____
   _____
   _____

2. Beyond getting a good grade, what do you consider to be the biggest benefit you derive in completing writing assignments for your classes? Why? _____
   _____
   _____
   _____
   _____

3. As you review the chapter's suggested information regarding writing skill development, what information offered the most helpful writing tips? Least helpful? _____
   _____
   _____
   _____
   _____

4. Know your strengths and habits as a writer. How did you begin the writing process for your academic objectives? Was it effective as an approach, or could it be improved upon? __
   _____
   _____
   _____
   _____

Apply Your Knowledge!

As with any skill to refine, frequent practice using multiple approaches is important for your writing development. Practice your writing to enhance both the creativity of your ideas and the effectiveness of your communication in expressing your written thoughts (writing "flow"). The following are some helpful tips in developing your writing skills across your field training.

- Write down your thoughts immediately.
- Record ideas on a daily basis (e.g., a daily journal).
- Visit places and situations that will inspire your writing and creativity.
- Attend a writing workshop on your campus.

- Join a club on campus that relates to journalism or other writing activities (e.g., a poetry club) to help hone your writing skills while engaged in a social group.
- Make an outline of topics to help organize your thoughts.
- Brainstorm and be "open" to new concepts as you journal your thought processes.
- Audiorecord your ideas if the situation does not permit you to write them down.
- Read the published works of highly-regarded writers in your field to better understand different but equally effective writing styles.
- Get a writing style book, and review the rules of grammar and techniques for effective writing.
- Share your paper drafts with others to generate more ideas and to receive editing feedback.
- Set a schedule for your writing so that it becomes part of your daily routine.

Try It Out!
"Flow of Consciousness" Writing Exercise

"Flow of Consciousness" Writing Exercise Brief: This approach to writing is about thinking outside the box and forgetting standard rules of grammar and spelling. To paraphrase the Nike slogan, "Just Write It!" Here are the steps in the process:

1. Choose a topic—Choose a topic that interests you and that you have enough knowledge about to write for an extended period. It helps if it is a topic you are interested in to motivate the creativity of your writing.
2. Get your writing tools—Some people like to write using a laptop while others prefer the traditional pen/pencil with a writing pad. Choose the method that is the easiest for you to write. Select an option that would best allow your writing to flow easily.
3. Find an appropriate writing spot—As with your studying, you probably have a preferred location that you know you can easily concentrate on your writing.
4. Record your thoughts—Write down your thoughts as quickly as they occur. Keep writing your ideas for a full 30 minutes, and do not stop to edit your work.

This exercise is limited to 30 minutes. Review the results of your writing and associated personal insights with your faculty mentor.

After completion of the "Flow of Consciousness" Writing Exercise, ask yourself the following:

1. What did I learn about my writing approach, and possible interruptions in my thought processes, as I write?
2. What should I work on more in preparation for my upcoming field training?

Search the Web!
Learn About How to Avoid Plagiarism in Your Writing

Search the Internet for different informational resources regarding how to best avoid *plagiarism* in your writing. One tip is to read a written article or document as many times as needed to fully understand its contents, take a 3 x 5 card or other format (e.g., use of an Excel spreadsheet), and record the citation of the article or document; then, put the article or document away and out of sight. Next, write down on the back of the 3 x 5 card (or another format) what you recall about the reviewed article or document in your own words. Please do not refer to the article or other document again while writing down what you remember. Do this process every time you write a literature review. In completing these steps, your writing will hopefully improve regarding how to avoid plagiarism.

Check out at least three different Internet resources pertaining to avoiding plagiarism in academic or professional writing. As you review this information, please answer the following questions:

1. What did you learn about common mistakes writers make that may lead to inadvertently committing plagiarism? _____
   _____
   _____
   _____
   _____
   _____

2. If you were giving advice to another student intern regarding how to avoid plagiarism, what would your advice be? Please explain. _____
   _____
   _____
   _____
   _____
   _____

AN INTERN'S INSIGHTS

Leticia Hill-Medrala: My initial tip regarding the internship process is understanding your interests and career aspirations. If you are unaware of your interests and career aspirations, now will be the perfect time to brainstorm. Grab a piece of paper and make a list of your career goals and interests. Your career goals should align with your interests. It would also be beneficial to obtain a job description of your future career or a job description of a similar profession. An internship may lead to employment opportunities with the company or references for your future career.

My second tip is communication. Professors and students are useful resources in locating and securing internships. Your professors and students may have connections with internship opportunities. Make sure you keep in communication with them throughout the internship process. They can also tell you what to expect during the interview, what to wear, and rehearse common interview questions.

The last tip is utilizing modern technology. Technology is your best friend and you must use it to your advantage. Now that the Internet is accessible by computer, tablet and phone we can peruse websites from anywhere. Browse websites about companies you are interested in. For further information, you may contact the company directly by phone or email. Third-party websites are often helpful because they may contain customers' and employees' ratings and reviews about the company.

If you follow these three tips, then all other areas of the internship will fall into place!

"Let's Review!" Phase III Learning

1. What did you learn about your writing skills, and what you should work on? Please explain. _____
   _____
   _____
   _____
   _____
   _____
   _____

2. How has your understanding of what is plagiarism, and how to avoid it in your writing, expanded? _____
   _____
   _____
   _____
   _____
   _____
   _____

3. What was the easiest information to find regarding techniques for good academic writing? Most difficult to find? Please explain. _____
   _____
   _____
   _____
   _____
   _____
   _____

4. Of all the information you have reviewed in this chapter, what information do you feel you might use or suggest to a peer to use in academic writing? Please explain. _____
   _____
   _____
   _____
   _____
   _____
   _____

Summary of the Chapter

The focus of this chapter pertained to writing effective academic objectives and the broader issue of how to be a good academic researcher and writer across different tasks. This chapter's activities and exercises also guided you in ways to avoid both writers block and plagiarism during your academic and work-related writing activities. Daily writing practice is vital for you to make improvements in your academic writing, as well as any written task performance onsite.

What Did I Learn?

As you reflect upon what you learned about general writing techniques and issues in writing effective academic objectives, consider what you have learned to date (and what you still need to review). Without looking back in the chapter, please list what you feel were the main three points of learning which were personally relevant to you regarding focus of the chapter (please explain why each is personally relevant to your learning):

1. _____
   _____
   _____

2. _____
   _____
   _____

3. _____
   _____
   _____

Discussion Questions

1. Part of any learning experience entails some degree of self-reflection. Through this self-reflection, what have you learned more about yourself as a writer?
2. What did you learn about writing academic objectives, and how they relate to research related concepts or theories? Do you think writing academic objectives is more challenging than writing site-related goals? Please explain.
3. There are different suggestions throughout the chapter regarding ways to increase idea generation and creativity in your writing. Which approach do you prefer? Why?
4. What did you learn about avoiding plagiarism in your writing? What surprised you about this topic that you did not know before?
5. Practice is vital for your writing skill development. How do you rehearse your writing now based on what you learned in this chapter?
6. Which information source suggested in the chapter, or that you found in your research, was the most useful in helping you develop your academic writing? Least helpful?
7. Writing requires a "plan of attack." What steps work best for you in starting your writing?
8. What did you learn about avoiding "writer's block" in your writing? Do you think that this is a common issue with writers?
9. Have you talked about your writing style with your faculty supervisor or a writing tutor? Why, or why not??
10. What advice would you give another intern about how to effectively write academic objectives and/or research-related summaries?

Additional Information Links

- How to Create Learning Objectives:
  https://www.td.org/Publications/Newsletters/Links/2015/10/How-to-Create-Learning-Objectives
- Writing Objectives Using Bloom's Taxonomy:
  http://teaching.uncc.edu/learning-resources/articles-books/best-practice/goals-objectives/writing-objectives
- iLearn Resource Center:
  https://www2.tntech.edu/ilearn/instructor/tutorials/en/creating-instructional-goals-learning-objectives.html
- How to Write Learning Objectives:
  https://www.convergencetraining.com/blog/how-to-write-learning-objectives-the-ultimate-guide
- Writing Measurable Learning Objectives:
  http://teachonline.asu.edu/2012/07/writing-measurable-learning-objectives/
- 3 Steps for Creating Effective Learning Objectives:
  https://www.learndash.com/3-steps-for-creating-effective-learning-objectives-infographic/

Fig. 5.1: Source: https://pixabay.com/en/hands-laptop-computer-typing-2069206/.

CHAPTER V

Creating a Learning Contract or "Plan of Action"

FIELD LEARNING FACTOID

"Divide the goals into four key achievement areas: academic, skill, professional and personal. For your purposes, you will want to create a corresponding list of objectives for each goal. ... Write academic goals that will allow the student to adapt what she has learned in the classroom to a professional environment. ... Draft goals that focus on the skills the student should master during the internship."

Source: Houston Chronicle article "How to Write Internship Goals" (http://work.chron.com/write-internship-goals-16438.html)

Introduction

Why is a learning contract important? A learning contract establishes a mutually agreed upon focus to your field training experience, from start to finish. In effect, it is a map that guides your learning as you proceed step-by-step through your professional development onsite. A learning contract (plan of action) can be a great teaching tool for instruction in higher education across many different fields (Boitel & Fromm, 2014; Vitton & Butz, 2014). The purpose of developing a learning contact cannot be underestimated in your preparation to begin your field training (Friedman & Neuman, 2001; Moore, Mossop, & Simpson, 2003). Writing a learning contract (plan) creates a tailored self-focus for potentially unexplored career goals and aspirations (Boulert, 2012). In addition to better understanding yourself as a future professional in the field, your plans create opportunities for your future organizational learning and skill development (Argote & Miron-Spektor, 2011). This step offers you the opportunity to personalize your learning while meeting training requirements (Freie, 1992; Rossman, 1983).

The utility of constructing a full learning contract can be explained in many ways, ranging from assessments of your learning to creating a conducive structure to the workplace training experience (Bailey & Tuohy, 2009; Iversen, 1995). The finalized learning contract will help reinforce positive work behaviors and avoid any deficient performance tendencies (Lubitsch & Shaw, 2004; Seymour, 1988). As with any planned activity, know that the learning contract should be designed in a careful manner to ensure that it conveys doable goals and objectives, which effectively motivate you during the training process (Greenwood & McCabe, 2008; Lewis, 2004; Seymour, 1988; Wald, 1978). Finally, the process of signing your learning contract helps you "own" your field learning experience (Rahmat & Aziz, 2012).

Creating a learning contract, which integrates both detailed site-related goals and academic objectives, is a significant foundation for your experiential learning (Anderson, Boud, & Simpson, 1996). Negotiating this content is a collaborative process between you, your supervisors, and the training institutions involved (Coy, 2014; Rousseau & Parks, 1993; Stephenson & Laycock, 1993).

You will find that communication and active listening are two skills that you will further develop during this process in creating a collaborative learning contract between you and your supervisors. It is natural to assume that you are a good listener and you are accurate in your information processing. What you might learn about yourself, however, is that you need to have better perspective taking and an understanding of shared expectations.

A learning contract establishes a clear expectation of your role, as well as others' roles, for your field training (Shore & Tetrick, 1994). It also allows you to "pilot test" a career without obligating yourself to a hired position (Coco, 2000; Cutting & Hall, 2008); Kim, Kim, & Bzullak, 2012). In addition, connections between you and your community can be a "value-added" outcome through your onsite activities (e.g., volunteerism) (Tovey, 2001).

There are many decisions pertaining to the development of your learning contract, involving you and your supervisors in a collaborative process (Burke & Miller, 1999; Glennon, 2008; Miller, Hickson, & Wilson, 1996). Agreement between you and these important stakeholders is critical to finalizing this learning plan (Henry, Rehwaldt, & Vineyard, 2001; Molseed, Alsup, & Voyles, 2003; Nelken, 2009). It is important to acknowledge, however, that these learning expectations can transform over time (Robinson, Kraatz, & Rousseau, 1994).

The expected learning outcomes for you, and your reflections upon developing learning contract goals and objectives, is to be grounded in field-relevant values and empirical ideologies (e.g., Watson, 1982). The entire learning plan reflects a cooperative learning exchange between you and your training institutions/sites (Rothman, 2007; Scott, Ray, & Warberg, 1990). Your field experience will have a meaningful effect on you as a new professional in the field (Feldman, Folks, & Turnley, 1999; Taylor, 1988).

The learning contract is a guide to your learning (Rye, 2008), offering a structure to your learning and associated self-reflective activities (e.g., journaling activities) (Alm, 1996; Eyler, 2002). If you think about it, the learning contract becomes a guide to which you can refer throughout your internship hours and in the writing of your final paper. It may seem like you are devoting much of your time and effort in this preliminary step, but you will later appreciate this preplanning during your onsite training, making the experience more beneficial and, hopefully, less stressful (Beard & Morton, 1999; Callanan & Benzing, 2004; Cutting & Hall, 2008).

Learning Goals for this Chapter

Chapter V offers both informational resources and interactive exercises/activities to best prepare you to:

- → Write fully-articulated learning or "process" task goals in collaboration with your site and faculty supervisors, putting those site-related goals and academic objectives you have developed to date together in a cohesive manner,
- → Develop a learning contract (plan of action) in terms of self-reflection processes, and
- → Create an associated plan regarding the content and structure of the final field paper.

As you consult with different sources of feedback (i.e., your two supervisors, peers, and other relevant site-related stakeholders), you should be creating a clearer picture of how you will accomplish your goals both in the classroom and onsite. Appendix C presents a template for you to think about how you would organize your goal-related ideas into an integrated learning contract (plan of action). You should think about how to develop both academic objectives and onsite goals that correspond well in terms of focus and overall goalsetting intent.

Goal setting is really a two-stage process involving both the establishment of broad-based Outcomes, but also details regarding the actual process steps. The experiences of collecting detailed onsite information and engaging in effective communication will only benefit you later both in your onsite performance and in writing your final field paper.

Remember to actively journal what you have learned to date (e.g., your developing communication skills and writing style). This ongoing self-assessment of experiential learning will help you identify concepts that you understand, as well the information that you still need to better understand in your training. These self-insights will greatly assist you as you continue to build your knowledge base and in your broader professional development. As with all steps in this process, there are many concepts to learn along the way. Before beginning to discuss specific issues related to your field training, let us explore some concepts for this chapter:

Look It Up!

Define and Understand Important Concepts

In preparing to write a complete plan of action (or learning contract) for your internship/field experience or service learning placement, it behooves you to have background knowledge in specific learning concepts. Please consult the word glossary provided at the back of this manual, and look up the following terms discussed in the current chapter.

Task Statement: _____
_____
_____
_____
_____
_____

Learning Contract (Plan of Action): _____
_____
_____
_____
_____
_____

Self Reflection: _____
_____
_____
_____
_____
_____

Journaling: _____
_____
_____
_____
_____
_____

Cooperative Agreement: _____
_____
_____
_____
_____

Phase I: How to Develop Accurate Task Statements for your Goals and Objectives

Before you begin the process of learning onsite, you should understand the details of a specific task (task statement) associated with a job. Develop an integrated plan of action, or a learning contract, reflecting both your site-related goal activities and associated learning objectives. A significant part of this process is that everyone involved agrees (especially your agreement) upon the onsite tasks you will be accomplishing over the training period. As with the other steps in the planning process to date, it is important for you to consult with both your faculty and site supervisors regarding their training expectations for you. Let us go through some general ideas of what you should do at this step in the process:

1. *Meet with your site supervisor about the draft learning contract*—Up to this point, you might have been interacting with your site supervisor to primarily understand the basics of what the upcoming field training site does in a general sense. At this stage in the planning process, it is good to have a discussion with your site supervisor regarding the specific details of your training (e.g., number of hours per week onsite, location(s) of your onsite activities) and any other logistical issues that should be clearly stipulated in your developing learning contract. Your site supervisor can help you develop specific task statements under each onsite training goal, giving you important guidance and insights into "how" you will accomplish each of your planned onsite learning goals. This discussion should also reflect your career-related aspirations, and how they fit into the training process.

2. *Ask an intern or job incumbent to review your learning contract*—If possible, ask an intern or a job incumbent about how to accomplish onsite activities that correspond to what you will be doing onsite as an intern. His/her task-related insights and feedback will be invaluable to you in terms of ensuring that you have the appropriate details and that you are being realistic in goals you are setting. Ask the intern and/or job incumbent about the procedures involved in doing certain tasks to further assist you in developing the task statements underlying each of your onsite learning goals.

3. *Develop your task statements underlying each onsite goal*—Before proceeding further in the writing process, please review the information that you have collected to date, and start writing your task statements. The purpose of the task statements under each site-related learning goal is to explain the process you will follow to accomplish it. Below each onsite goal should be a list of statements that explain the procedures underlying the development and achievement of the goal (e.g., "The intern will demonstrate how to import videos and other imagery to illustrate points using the recording option within a PowerPoint presentation"). These task statements should be based on the information collected from the onsite discussions with the site supervisor and other potential sources of information.

4. *Talk to your faculty supervisor about the draft task statements*—After you have developed your draft task statements underlying each of your site-related goals and further developed ideas regarding your academic objectives, you should meet with your faculty supervisor to discuss the clarity and feasibility of the draft process steps.

As you continue, you should be finding that you are "filling in the gaps" related to the who, what, when, and where of your onsite field training. Establishing these details are key to this learning and feedback process.

What Do I Think About ... ?

1. What is the purpose of developing specific task statements for my internship/field experience or service learning placement?
2. How are the task statements similar in purpose under my site-related goals and academic objectives? How are they different?
3. How can I find samples of onsite task statements to generate my task statement ideas?
4. Why is it important to have the details of these task statement stipulated in my learning contract ahead of time?
5. Who should I seek for advice designed for interns about writing effective task statements? Which sources of information are the most helpful?
6. What is the biggest benefit I can derive from developing detailed task statements?
7. What is the most common error that interns may make in this task statement writing process?
8. Finally, what will I learn about myself through this self-reflection process involving collecting and writing detailed information for my learning contract?

Preparing a learning contract is a writing-intensive process, and you should anticipate that it will involve many repeated drafts in response to feedback from multiple sources, as well as your personal edits of your writing.

Before proceeding, it is good to review what you have learned so far! The next section contains a review exercise related to the information and/or skills you acquired through the process of reviewing the information and completing the learning activities suggested in Phase I.

"Let's Review!" Phase I Learning

1. What did you learn about developing a goal-related task statement? _____
   _____
   _____
   _____
   _____
   _____

2. As you engaged in the suggested learning activities, what were some important concepts related to writing task statements for your site-related goals that you learned? __
   _____
   _____
   _____
   _____
   _____

3. Which informational sources (e.g., advisors) did you find to be the most helpful to you during this learning process? Why? _____
   _____
   _____
   _____
   _____
   _____

4. As you begin to acquire more details related to your planned field training, did this process help you further clarify your academic objectives and the focus of your eventual field paper? _____
   _____
   _____
   _____
   _____
   _____

5. Please describe something you learned that you did not anticipate learning. _____
   _____
   _____
   _____
   _____
   _____

Phase II: The Journaling and Self-Reflection Process

A significant aspect of your field experience will be your ongoing self-reflection processes analyzing your onsite learning. This self-reflection activity will be guided through your weekly journaling and is a significant motivator for the writing of your final field paper. There are different aproaches to journaling, from periodic "check in" entries at specific times of the day about ongoing activities or journaling in response to a standardized list of questions (e.g., "What did I learn today?) to broader goal-directed focused entries related to completed and future goals (e.g., "bullet journaling," http://bulletjournal.com/get-started/). Let us go through some general ideas of what you should do in preparing for this step in the process:

1. *Find different online resources (e.g., YouTube videos) about journaling*—Learning how to engage in effective self reflection about your learning through the process of journaling is a skill to develop. Go online, and find different resources related to advice designed for students on internship-related journaling (e.g., different aproaches to both writing and graphing ideas related to learning outcomes).

2. *Review your current learning goals*—Examine what you have written to date regarding your site-related learning goals. Consider what you might journal about based on the onsite goals you have developed. The connection between the journaling of your onsite learning and your stated onsite training goals has to be clear.

3. *Meet with a writing expert*—Meet with a faculty member(s) in your department or across campus outside your major (e.g., a professor of English) to discuss how to engage in journaling to assist in your writing.

FROM A SITE SUPERVISOR'S DESK

Vincent Volpert, Field Experience Coordinator at Wilbur Wright College:

To be successful in a professional endeavor, an integration between academic knowledge and practical experience must occur. Academic knowledge is acquired throughout one's educational career, culminating with a Bachelor's, Master's, or Ph.D., in one's chosen field. You need to utilize your educational background in different applied ways when learning onsite.

A program requiring a practicum and an internship provides the student with the opportunity to gain onsite experience, improve his/her résumé and obtain some valuable networking connections. Both programs allow the student to integrate what was learned in the classroom (e.g., theories, concepts, ideas, and definitions) and apply them in a practical manner to what occurs in the workplace but to different degrees.

However, before any of these opportunities can occur, one very important element must take place—the learning contract. It can help one to realize one's strengths, and equally important, one's weaknesses. This will allow the student, together with the site supervisor and the class instructor, to tailor a document that is uniquely suited to the student.

Creating the learning contract is not a quick and effortless process, but the outcome of a well-written and well-executed one is beneficial to everyone. The goals written into the contract will act as a bridge between what was learned in the classroom and the application of this knowledge into the "real world" setting. It is, indeed, a wonderful opportunity.

What Should I Do?
Putting Your Learning into Action

1. Discuss with other interns how they perceive the internship/field experience or service learning placement process. Proactively form an intern discussion group, among either current or future interns starting a site experience soon, to share ideas, information, and social support during this learning process.

2. Get organized and set up resource materials to assist in your anticipated journaling activities (e.g., purchase and label a journal notebook designated specifically for your internship learning; consider a designated time during the week when you will record your learning observations in the dedicated journal notebook).

3. Attend a writing workshop on campus, or in your community, which may assist in both your journal writing development and self-observation skills.

4. Practice your journal writing by doing a trial run with another ongoing activity (e.g., another class or your current workplace) to practice your self-reflection writing.

5. Review your preliminary journaling practice ideas with your faculty supervisor to get his/her feedback and advice for improving the process in preparation for the task in your upcoming field training.

Remember that your overall training outcomes reflect a dynamic process of integrating your academic and onsite learning. Before proceeding, please review what you have learned in Phase II! The next section contains, there is a series of review questions related to what you learned in doing the activities and exercises. To best help you with this ongoing learning process, please be accurate in your any responses to assess what areas of learning need further attention.

"Let's Review!" Phase II Learning

1. Based upon the suggested sources of information and activities, what did you learn about the process of self-reflection and journaling? _____

2. Suggested activities relate to you reflecting upon how you learn. What insights did you learn about yourself at this stage of the process? _____

3. Were you able to find any online advice and/or support resources pertaining to effective journaling strategies? If so, what did you learn? Do you feel that these resources will be helpful to you as you journal during your field training? _____

4. Please describe something you learned that you did not anticipate learning. _____

Phase III: Putting It All Together: Goals, Objectives, and Associated Processes

At this point in the planning process, you need to understand how your site-related activities in academic objectives correspond to create a cohesive learning plan for your field training. Getting the "big picture" of how this all fits together is important before beginning your onsite learning and writing of your final field paper. Independent of this information, however, is the determination of how well your personal knowledge, skills, and abilities correspond to your planned site-related activities and broader career aspirations. Making sure all of these activities and aims align supports your personal investment of time and effort during the experience.

Resources to Use in Finalizing a Learning Contract Draft

The following are some resources to learn more about in constructing the final contract draft:

- Tutorial on learning contract development:
  http://www.sophia.org/tutorials/creating-a-personal-meaning-contract
- Sample learning contract (social work sample):
  http://www.uwosh.edu/socialwork/undergraduate-program/field-education/bsw-field/SLCsample
- Group-based learning contracts (versus individualized learning contracts):
  http://www.uwaterloo.ca/centre-for-teaching-excellence/group-work/making-group-contracts
- Role of student and faculty:
  http://www.uwaterloo.ca/centre-for-teaching-excellence/teaching-resources/teaching-tips/tips-students/self-directed-learning/self-directed learning-learning-contracts

Think About It!

At this stage in the planning process, there are many issues to consider regarding the availability of support resources and other planning details to finalize prior to beginning your on-site training. Here are topics to consider as you create a first full draft of your learning contract for your supervisors' review and feedback:

1. What do you identify as potential on-campus resources to help you in accomplishing your first learning contract draft? _____
   _____
   _____
   _____
   _____
   _____
   _____
   _____

2. At this stage in your planning process, would it be beneficial to form an intern discussion group to assist in both sharing resources and ideas? Why or why not? _____
   _____
   _____
   _____
   _____
   _____
   _____
   _____

3. Access to technology is vital for the accomplishment of your academic objectives (e.g., online library research) and writing. Do you have adequate access to technology on campus and/or at home to support your learning? If not, how can you plan to solve this?
   _____
   _____
   _____
   _____
   _____
   _____
   _____

Apply Your Knowledge!

Creating a cohesive plan for implementing effective learning goals and objectives is critical to the successful launch, continuation, and completion of your field training. The SMART goals and objectives method can be applied to the topic of developing a learning contract and is appropriate to use to assess your learning goals. Let us go through each part of the SMART method in evaluating goals and academic objectives:

- *S = specific:* Under this category of evaluation, review your site-related goals and academic objectives to judge how focused and detailed they are as written. If you feel that they are vague in wording, revise accordingly.
- *M = measurable:* With this review criteria, assess the degree to which your site-related goals and academic objectives are measurable for evaluation purposes. You might include that you need to quantify the outcomes of these goals or objectives more clearly.
- *A = achievable:* Creating "doable" goals is reflected in this same criteria. As you think about draft goals and objectives you have created, evaluate whether these aims are in fact reasonable to achieve in both effort and time.
- *R = results oriented:* Just as your goals and objectives should be measurable, they should also be evaluated in terms of the degree to which you find results from these activities.
- *T = time phased:* Finally, review your site-related goals and academic objectives in terms of the degree to which they are determinable as occurring within a certain period of evaluation.

Try It Out!
Personal Goal Plan Exercise

Personal Goal Plan Exercise Brief: It is a skill to be able to create a clear and concise goal statement. Goals apply to many various aspects of our daily lives. Let us practice developing goals for a life activity that you plan to do in the future. From the following list, please choose a life-planning topic that you consider to be relevant and that needs planning:

- Personal health
- Family activities
- Career/retirement
- Relationships
- Living situation
- Education ... among other topics you may choose.

Write four goal statements for this chosen topic. Please apply the SMART approach (i.e., specific, measurable, achievable, results-oriented, and time-phased) to evaluate each goal statement. This exercise is limited to 30 minutes.

After completion of the Personal Goal Plan Exercise, ask yourself the following:

1. What did I learn about writing goal statements for a general topic that is not directly related to my upcoming field training?
2. What should I work on to better prepare my SMART goals and objectives?

Search the Web!
Learn About Integrating Goals and Objectives

Search the Internet for different informational resources regarding how to best synchronize your site-related learning goals and academic objectives together to create a clear and cohesive learning contract and associated agreement between all key stakeholders (cooperative agreement). This is a critical step in your planning process, putting the two halves of your planned learning experience together to create a solid foundation and launch into your field training.

Check out at least three different Internet resources pertaining to creating a cohesive and well-integrated learning plan. As you review this information, please answer the following questions:

1. What were the most beneficial resources you found regarding how to create a cohesive learning contract? Why were they particularly helpful? _____
_____
_____
_____
_____
_____
_____
_____
_____
_____
_____

2. What did you find out about how to best articulate "themes" across goals and objectives to develop a clear focus for your learning contract? _____
_____
_____
_____
_____
_____
_____
_____
_____
_____
_____

AN INTERN'S INSIGHTS

Lupe Arceo de Carpintero: I was excited that I had the opportunity to intern at a senior center since I had little experience in this area. I learned some concepts and theories regarding senior centers during my classroom courses but having the opportunity of being part of the senior center program and experiencing how it impacts the community and older adults made it all more interesting for me.

Once I received the feedback from my program coordinator, I knew what areas I needed to shift my focus to. She helped me be more specific in certain areas of my research paper and how I can apply certain concepts to real life experiences. She reminded me of my skills that I already had and learned to build on it. I never felt that she held my hand and gave me the answers but instead she guided me by motivating me to ask myself more questions and learn to prioritize what was more important in my research. These questions helped me find what my learning goals should be and what academic objectives I needed to focus on. With her assistance I could concentrate on areas that she knew would interest me and help me in my future career.

Throughout my internship I knew that any feedback I received was not to be taken as criticism but instead it was a means of mentoring and guiding me in the direction she knew was preparing me for my future. To succeed in my internship, she was willing to listen and learn about my interests and I was willing to listen and learn from her experience and knowledge. I believe that having an open mind and consistent dialogue, with my program coordinator, was beneficial for my success.

"Let's Review!" Phase III Learning

1. What did you learn about how to integrate site-related goals and academic objectives together in a cohesive manner for your draft learning contract? Please explain. _____

2. How have your site-related goals and/or academic objectives changed through the application of the SMART method of evaluation? _____

3. What was the easiest information to find regarding writing a full learning contract? More difficult to find? Please explain. _____

4. Did the exercise related to creating a personal goal plan help you further refine your learning contract? Why, or why not? Please explain. _____

Summary of the Chapter

This chapter focused on the crucial step of constructing a cohesive and concise full learning contract draft. At each step in the process of developing your site-related goals and academic objectives, you have consulted with multiple "stakeholders" involved in your field training and have reviewed several sources of information and advice. You may have noticed that the process of finalizing the draft learning contract has, ultimately, come down to personal attitudes and motivations underlying your learning goals. This is your experience, and you need to personalize your career-related aims at this important juncture in the planning process.

What Did I Learn?

As you reflect upon what you learned in this chapter about creating a full draft of your learning contract, it is good for you to assess what you learned (and what you still need to review). Without looking back in the chapter, please list what you feel were the main three points of learning that were personally relevant to you regarding the focus of the chapter (please explain why each is personally relevant to your learning):

1. _____
_____
_____

2. _____
_____
_____

3. _____
_____
_____

Discussion Questions

1. What do you understand about writing a learning contract better than when you started this planning process?
2. As you examine your site-related goals in reflection upon your academic objectives (or vice versa), determine if you edited these goals and/or objectives to create a better conceptual correspondence between the two parts of the learning contract. Why or why not?
3. In addition to content editing, did you determine that some of your goals or objectives need to be reprioritized based upon the determination of personal effort or time investment?
4. Knowing what you know now, would you approach the writing of your onsite goals or academic objectives differently? Please explain.
5. Did you find some online samples to help you construct a draft full learning contract?
6. Has the application of the SMART method of evaluating goals and objectives helped you create a more concise and assessable learning plan?
7. Learning can generalize across life tasks and situations. Has the learning associated with developing a learning contract positively affected your planning activities associated with other academic work? Other activities?
8. Metacognition is a cognitive concept related to humans engaging in the process of "thinking about thinking." Do you feel that you have developed better metacognitive skills through the journaling and learning contract development process? Why, or why not? Please explain.
9. Have your general writing skills improved through the learning contract drafting process?
10. Through the self-reflection process of determining your overall field training focus in this chapter, what have you learned about yourself and/or your career goals?

Additional Information Links

- Learning Contract:
  http://www.uts.edu.au/research-and-teaching/teaching-and-learning/assessment/types-assessment/learning-contracts
- Learning Contract #2:
  https://iris.peabody.vanderbilt.edu/module/di/cresource/q2/p05/di_05_link_contracts/
- Individual Learning Contract:
  https://evergreen.edu/individualstudy/individuallearningcontracts
- Self-Directed Learning through Learning Contracts:
  https://uwaterloo.ca/centre-for-teaching-excellence/teaching-resources/teaching-tips/tips-students/self-directed-learning/self-directed-learning-learning-contracts
- Learning Contract Template #1:
  http://www.learnhigher.ac.uk/learning-at-university/independent-learning/learning-contract/
- Learning Contract Template #2:
  https://www.uky.edu/UGE/EXP-contract

Fig. 6.1: Source: https://pixabay.com/en/women-teamwork-team-business-1209678

CHAPTER VI

Getting Feedback about Your Learning Contract and Associated Approvals

FIELD LEARNING FACTOID

"If you want to turn your internship into a full-time job with the company, you need to make that fact known. More important, you need find out what you need to do to make that happen. Those I have seen successfully turn their internships into jobs did so by taking charge. They didn't wait to be recognized—and they did more than simply apply for open positions. The most impressive examples are the people who made a plan to find out how the work and performance were viewed, made personal improvements—and proactively went after the jobs they wanted."

Source: The Savvy Intern
(http://www.youtern.com/thesavvyintern/index.php/2012/02/24/-feedback-can-turn-your-internship-into-a-job/)

Introduction

Feedback seeking is a valuable strategic behavior to engage in as you finalize your learning contract, and it should help you to better engage in feedback-seeking behavior onsite, which is invaluable as an intern (Ashford & Blatt, 2003). Feedback, as a concept, can take many forms and purposes, from the conveyance of constructive advice in response to performance or coaching/mentoring to help guide future performance to seeking praise and appreciation. The processes underlying your field training experience will entail all these feedback forms at different stages of your onsite learning. An internship/field experience or service learning placement is a wonderful opportunity for you to engage in feedback-seeking behavior to optimize your personal learning and your contributions to the training site (Bok et al., 2013).

A learning contract offers a "framework" to guide your feedback seeking through conversations with your two supervisors and other relevant training contacts (e.g., onsite coworkers) (Morrison & Weldon, 1990; Park, Schmidt, Scheu, & DeShon, 2007). As a work-related behavior, among other social contexts, feedback seeking facilitates your onsite training processes and performance goal accomplishments (Crommelinck & Anseel, 2013). In a broader sense, learning how to effectively engage in feedback-seeking behavior can enhance communication both within and across managerial levels in your training site (Krasman, 2011).

Equally important to engaging in feedback seeking is understanding the motivations underlying your behavior, ranging from concerns about performance assessment to self-protection strategies (Abraham, Burnett, & John, 2006; Hays & Williams, 2011). Your feedback seeking is affected by many factors that you should consider and reflect upon during your ongoing site learning. For example, your perceptions of the social context and how others may judge you could influence your willingness to seek clarification feedback in a classroom or a training context (e.g., perceived stereotype threat) (Roberson, Deitch, Brief, & Block, 2013). Your feedback-seeking behavior, in turn, can affect how others behave and perceive you in a specific social context (VandeWalle, Ganesan, Challagalla, & Brown, 2000).

Actively seeking feedback to clarify role expectations and associated duties helps you become an effective intern (Major & Kozlowski, 1997). Only through asking questions and seeking feedback is it possible for you to best prepare for your field training in a deliberate and efficient manner (Abuhusain, Chotirmall, Hamid, & O'Neill, 2009).

This strategic behavior should be engaged in throughout your entire site-related learning process, benefitting both you and your training organization (Brooks, Cornelius, Greenfield, & Joseph, 1995). Information seeking generalizes to a broader preparation of you becoming an inquisitive researcher and practitioner in your career, actively questioning issues and developing solutions to field-related topics (Babbie, 2015; Ren, Sun, Zhang, Chen, & Liu, 2015).

These "give-and-take" situations inherent in feedback seeking exchanges prepare you well for active listening and communication skills to be engaged in onsite (Basow & Byrne, 1992). As you engage in acquiring constructive feedback, expect that you will receive feedback from multiple sources that may reflect incongruent perspectives (Badger, 2012; Bourland-Davis, Graham, & Fulmer, 1997; Harris & Zhao, 2004).

Ultimately, you will internalize the constructive feedback received, and this learning process will meaningfully shape you into the professional you are striving to become (Embo, Driessen, Valcke, & Van der Vleuten, 2010; Rothman, 2007; Subramony, 2000). You will learn a lot about yourself and others from which you seek feedback as you engage in the reiterative processes of feedback seeking and adaptation to feedback. Lastly, your feedback seeking can have a positive impact upon your relationship with your supervisors, creating both a mutual understanding of performance expectations and "open communication" opportunities between all involved (Williams & Johnson, 2000).

Feedback seeking is an opportunity for you to engage in positive self-management and to create long-lasting positive working relationships with both your faculty and site supervisors. The sharing of feedback can create a positive "bond" potential that can develop into a productive mentoring relationship for you in your career. The field training relationships that you will develop onsite and with your mentors will be important future resources for your long-term career planning, from the skills you develop to the recommendations that they can offer.

Learning Goals for this Chapter

Chapter VI offers both informational resources and interactive exercises/activities to best prepare you to:

→ Revise learning "process" goals and objectives based on feedback received from both the site and faculty supervisors,
→ Optimize the feedback-revision process through ongoing skill enhancement, and
→ Create a finalized version of the learning contract through good editing strategies and fully addressing the final feedback from both supervisors for approval purposes.

To effectively seek and accurately address feedback from involved "others" is an important skill to develop. Ahead of time, you should identify the individuals to be included in this process. We may not always correctly "hear" the social feedback we receive on a daily basis for many different reasons. You may be distracted with other issues of learning, not understand the perspective of your feedback provider(s), and/or need to work on being more attentive to social cues conveying the feedback, whether verbal or nonverbal in form. Learning how to effectively acquire and apply social feedback will greatly enhance learning throughout your training experience, and you will learn how to best interact with others in a workplace.

The process of repeating and verifying the feedback you receive will help you become a better active listener, and it may prompt the feedback source to generate even more expansive feedback ideas over time in response to revisiting their ideas. Always assume that the feedback process is an ongoing process that has many levels to investigate in the coming weeks.

Before beginning to discuss very specific training issues related to your field experience, let us explore some foundational concepts for this chapter:

CHAPTER VI Getting Feedback about Your Learning Contract and Associated Approvals | 95

Look It Up!

Define and Understand Important Concepts

In preparing for the process of engaging in seeking and responding to multiple sources' constructive feedback information, it is good for you to have background knowledge in specific learning concepts. Please consult the word glossary provided at the back of this manual, and look up the following terms discussed in the current chapter.

Feedback: _____
_____
_____
_____
_____
_____

Revision (Editing) Process: _____
_____
_____
_____
_____
_____

Active Listening: _____
_____
_____
_____
_____
_____

Feedback Responsivity: _____
_____
_____
_____
_____
_____

Integration: _____
_____
_____
_____
_____
_____

Learning Outcomes: _____
_____
_____
_____
_____
_____

Phase I: How To Seek and Effectively Address Learning Goal Revision Feedback

Before you can finalize your learning contract, there are many edits and revisions to be done. Expect that there will be more than one iteration of feedback from both supervisors, and you should always seek out constructive feedback from more than one available expert source. Remember to be "open" to the feedback process, and appreciate the revision (editing) process as a personal skill development experience. Be cognizant of your feedback-related skill needs (e.g., the need to develop better active listening skills) as you undergo this critical step in the process and journal what you are learning. It is important to effectively respond to feedback (feedback responsivity). Let us go through some ideas of what you should do in this step:

1. *Review collected feedback and edit*—Based on the feedback received from the site supervisor's review of your draft learning goals and associated task statements, you should carefully edit your learning goals to reflect any suggested revisions. Please make sure that your writing reflects proper grammar and sentence structure. Always conduct both a spelling and grammar check *before* submitting a draft document to your reviewers.

2. *Discuss your goals with your peer interns*—Peer feedback can be an important part of this feedback revision process. In or outside the classroom, check in with your academic peers to solicit their feedback regarding how your learning contract reflects their views as interns.

3. *Review your revised goals with your site and faculty supervisors*—Although it may seem like you have consulted with your site supervisor and/or faculty supervisor more than you expected, it is a beneficial process, because they might identify areas for improvement at each draft stage thay you may not see. Your aim, however, is to receive final approvals. You will be asking for final approval of your site-related and academic goals from both supervisors after all previous feedback has been addressed by you.

4. *Finalize your goals and acquire final approvals*—Finally, this is the step you been waiting for! You are to finalize your site-related and academic goals. You and your supervisors will sign the learning contract as an agreement on your activities for the entirety of the training experience. This signing process may seem like a formality, but in actuality, it is protection for you, the intern, in terms of what is expected and required of you during your training. You will be evaluated on the same exact criteria by your supervisors, so your agreement to these expectations is critical.

What Do I Think About ... ?

1. What is the biggest challenge for me in the editing process?
2. Is there an optimal singular source of feedback, or are multiple feedback sources best?
3. How do I ask for final feedback from sources in an effective and efficient manner?
4. Am I a good "active listener?" What do I need to improve upon when I seek out final revision feedback?
5. Is it important to request feedback more than once from a single feedback source?
6. What is the most common editing mistake I made in doing this revision process?
7. How many drafts should I complete before I can finalize my goals and objectives?

CHAPTER VI Getting Feedback about Your Learning Contract and Associated Approvals | 97

"Let's Review!" Phase I Learning

1. What did you learn about the process of addressing editing feedback and finalizing your site-related learning goals? Academic objectives? _____

    _____
    _____
    _____
    _____
    _____
    _____
    _____

2. Who was the most helpful source of information throughout the editing process? Why?

    _____
    _____
    _____
    _____
    _____
    _____
    _____

3. What was the most challenging aspect to the editing process? Why was it challenging, and how did you work through it (e.g., writing strategies)? _____

    _____
    _____
    _____
    _____
    _____
    _____
    _____

4. What did you learn about yourself as being an "active listener" during the feedback-seeking process? What can you do to improve upon this behavior for future feedback situations? _____

    _____
    _____
    _____
    _____
    _____
    _____
    _____

Phase II: Getting the "Bigger Picture" of Your Planned Learning Activities

Now that the details of your learning contract have been documented and your final learning contract has been approved by your supervisors, you should have a clearer idea of how your academic and onsite ideas will combine (integration) into a final field experience with associated learning outcomes. Let us go through some general ideas of what you should do in preparing for this step in the process:

1. *Research more "themes"*—Re-review your site-related learning goals to identify broader themes or concepts to research beyond your initial ideas for your academic objectives (e.g., theme of "impression management behavior"). It is helpful to anticipate what concepts you can research for your final field paper as you navigate your learning trajectory on the site.

2. *Identify conceptual factors for your journaling*—In addition to preliminary ideas for writing your final field paper, identify specific learning-related concepts that may guide your journaling prior to beginning your field experience in the coming weeks.

3. *Develop a realistic schedule*—Take the time to make a realistic, feasible plan for scheduling your onsite training hours into your daily activities (e.g., work obligations). Get a calendar and block out time from when you will need to be onsite for your internship/field experience or service learning placement. Mistakes are made when time-related logistics planning is not done ahead of time and time conflicts arise.

FROM A SITE SUPERVISOR'S DESK

Thomas Applegate, Executive Director at North River Commission:

The better prepared you are in selecting and then pursuing an internship, the more it will contribute to your career development. First, research companies, people, associations, and trends that make up your field. Second, develop compelling communications through practice and revision. Start by exploring the variety of large and small companies or organizations in your field. A terrific way to connect to people working in your area is to search on LinkedIn for alumni from your school and major. There is a good chance that they will spend 15 minutes on the phone to talk about themselves, their work, and give you quick guidance on where to look next. When I get a request from a student at my alma mater, I am always happy to help.

A key to compelling communication is practice. Use your friends, professors, career office, and anyone willing to help you practice interviewing and review your cover letters and résumés. With my team, we always set aside time for mock interviews with interns. Start with a company that you are pursuing and write a cover letter and résumé as if applying for a position there. Have one or two people roleplay as interviewers for that position. For the full effect, you and they must stay in character. Afterwards, insist that they share criticism and insight to improve your content and delivery. With feedback, revision, and practice, your written and verbal communication will be more confident and effective. Combining knowledge of your field and effective communications skills is likely to garner respect and build your career.

What Should I Do?
Putting Your Learning into Action

1. Discuss with your faculty supervisor your long-term career plans as they relate to your impending training experience. Review different career-related ideas and ask about the careers of alumni from the program.

2. Visit the library and see if you can schedule a weekly study room to create your designated workspace.

3. Schedule an appointment with the on-campus career development office and see if they can offer you any advice about how to develop an effective internship schedule. Be realistic about all your daily obligations in creating this schedule.

4. Meet with your site supervisor and discuss scheduling options for the internship/field experience or service learning placement.

5. Meet with a reference librarian to expand upon your research ideas from a review of your finalized goals and objectives.

6. Research the professional networks within your community and see if you can identify a potential career mentor who can advise you in the successful execution of a training experience. You should utilize this mentor at more than one stage of your career development.

7. Journal what you have learned and refer to it as you go through the proceeding stages of your internship/field experience or service learning placement training. This information will be helpful as you plan each step in your professional development.

CHAPTER VI Getting Feedback about Your Learning Contract and Associated Approvals | 101

"Let's Review!" Phase II Learning

1. Was it easy to identify anticipatory learning "themes" from your approaching site-related activities? Please explain. _____
   _____
   _____
   _____
   _____
   _____
   _____

2. Activities in this chapter, among other aims, relate to you expanding your professional networking beyond the confines of the classroom. Were you successful in speaking with a career mentor(s) who offered helpful advice in planning your upcoming field training?
   _____
   _____
   _____
   _____
   _____
   _____
   _____

3. Were you able to create your personal workspace and designate a specific schedule for your internship/field experience or service learning placement learning? If not, what were some difficulties you encountered in this planning? _____
   _____
   _____
   _____
   _____
   _____
   _____
   _____

4. How has the ongoing journaling process helped you become more strategic in your multi-focused skill development learning to date? _____
   _____
   _____
   _____
   _____
   _____
   _____
   _____

Phase III: Getting Final Approval for Your Learning Contract

You did it! You are finalizing your learning contract and getting final approvals from your site supervisor and faculty supervisor. This sounds like a simple step in the process, but it is the culmination of your previous efforts and outcomes to date. In fact, the criticality of this step cannot be understated. You have entered into an agreement with both your site and faculty supervisors regarding your work-related duties and outcomes for the entirety of your field training experience. Like any agreement, it behooves you to fully understand the expectations to which are agreeing for the coming months. Conversely, this learning contract is a protection for you, because you cannot be asked to do other goals or objectives beyond those statements that were agreed upon between you and your supervisors.

Resources to Do the Final Editing of a Document

The following are some helpful points for proofreading and editing the document, as they relate to the proofreading and editing skills you are developing at this stage of your learning contract process:

- Do not fully rely upon your "spell check/grammar check" options in your document program; instead, do the work manually as a double check.
- Read the statements in your document out loud—ask yourself if the content sounds grammatically correct and expresses your ideas clearly.
- Circle any possible errors on a hard copy of your document, and look up the spelling errors or other editing concerns in a systematic and methodical manner.
- Edit the content of any written work on several levels of analysis (i.e., word level, sentence level, paragraph level, and paper structure level).

Think About It!

Here are topics to consider as you engage in the final editing process of your learning contract for approval purposes:

1. Do both my supervisors have shared expectations toward my expected onsite performance? Why, or why not? Please explain. _____
   _____
   _____
   _____
   _____

2. How have my expectations toward the field training changed over time as the learning contract has developed? _____
   _____
   _____
   _____
   _____

3. Will my stated onsite learning goals anticipate all issues that I will encounter onsite? Why, or why not? Please explain. _____
   _____
   _____
   _____
   _____

4. What did I learn that I did not anticipate? _____
   _____
   _____
   _____
   _____

Apply Your Knowledge!

In signing a learning contract, you have acquired specific rights and responsibilities in the stated agreement. Beyond the explicit task statements of your onsite goals and academic objectives, you will need to fully understand your rights as an intern. Conversely, you need to be equally aware of your inherent responsibilities as an intern at the training site.

Here are some points regarding an intern's rights and responsibilities:

- Right: expect to receive responses to questions, as needed and appropriate to your learning processes and outcomes.
- Right: expect to receive constructive feedback in a detailed and timely manner from supervisors and/or relevant feedback sources.

- Responsibility: adhere to the evaluation criteria for the accomplishment of your site-related goals and academic objectives.
- Responsibility: be prepared to focus on your work and be punctual in your time obligations both onsite and in the classroom.

Here are some points regarding a supervisor's rights and responsibilities:

- Right: expect to receive the intern's work in a timely and complete manner.
- Right: expect that the intern will receive constructive feedback from you in responsive manner and ask for clarifications, if needed.
- Responsibility: adhere to agreed-upon evaluation criteria and avoid any bias or subjectivity in conducting an evaluation of the intern's performance.
- Responsibility: take the initiative in clarifying expectations and duties with the intern and/or other supervisor(s), as appropriate.

Try It Out!
Proofreading Skills Test Exercise

Proofreading Skills Test Exercise Brief: Please proofread and make editing comments on the following work schedule. Use a red pen and making your editing comments on the page. Take the time to review the document to identify all the errors.

NAME	DAYS	SHIFT DETIES	SHIFT (no more than one12-hour shift)
Adrian Henle	Th,F,S,Sun T	Wash dishes, Due stock werk	6PM–2AM 10PM–9PM
Todd Yen	Th,F,S,Sun W	Help develope scheduler; Supervise?	8PM–2PM 10AM–3PM
Sam Pratt	F,S, S, Sun, T,W,Th	Write out menue. Create weekend skedule	PM–2AM 11AM–10AM
Laura Sedillo	F,S,Sun Th	Straighn stock, due processing of orderss	8PM–2AM 1AM–2AM
Dolores Darrock	W,Th,F,S,S Sun	Clean floors, sweap up stockroom	8PM–2AM 10PM–3PM
Richard Jimenez	M,T,Sun Th,F	Create new stuck orders	8PM–2AM 10AM–10AM

This exercise is limited to 10 minutes. Go over the results of your proofreading with your faculty mentor and discuss the proofreading skills you may need to work on.

After completion of the Proofreading Skills Test, ask yourself the following:

1. What did I learn about my personal proofreading skills?
2. How do effective proofreading and editing skills relate to my future onsite work? Career?

Search the Web!
Learn About Receiving and Responding to Editing Feedback

Search the Internet for different resources regarding how to best optimize your proofreading and editing performance in response to the feedback from your supervisors and other editing feedback sources (e.g., on-campus writing tutor) to finalize your learning contract.

Check out at least three different Internet resources pertaining to effectively responding to editing feedback. As you review this information, please answer the following questions:

1. What were the most beneficial resources you found regarding addressing editing feedback in an efficient and effective manner? Explain why. _____
_____
_____
_____
_____
_____
_____
_____
_____

2. What do you think are common errors people commit in proofreading their own work?
_____
_____
_____
_____
_____
_____
_____
_____

3. If you were giving advice to another student intern regarding the process of finalizing a learning contract, what would your advice be? Please explain. _____
_____
_____
_____
_____
_____
_____
_____
_____

"Let's Review!" Phase III Learning

1. What did you learn about issues to consider regarding the shared rights and responsibilities of an intern and a supervisor during the field training process? Please explain. ____
   _____
   _____
   _____
   _____
   _____
   _____
   _____

2. How has your understanding of an intern's responsibilities changed? ____
   _____
   _____
   _____
   _____
   _____
   _____
   _____
   _____

3. What was the easiest information to access regarding the rights of interns after signing a learning contract? Most difficult to access? Please explain. ____
   _____
   _____
   _____
   _____
   _____
   _____
   _____

4. What did you learn about your proofreading skills as you did the exercise or reviewed resources on proofing and editing processes? Please explain. ____
   _____
   _____
   _____
   _____
   _____
   _____
   _____

AN INTERN'S INSIGHTS

Marina Ruiz: As a former student intern, I found that when preparing for an internship, an efficient and smooth communication process was crucial. Being able to communicate your thoughts in a clear precise manner is essential for interns. To "survive" an internship, you should communicate with your fellow interns and site supervisor to clarify each person's responsibilities.

As interns, you should prepare for all potential challenges you may encounter but it is critical to realize that nothing ever goes as planned. The best thing you can do is to be very organized, but also allow yourself to be flexible and adaptive to the circumstances which may arise. The first step is to establish clear communication lines between interns which includes getting familiar with each other and exchange contact information. This is how you establish effective communication and alleviate any stress with fellow interns.

Think about several ways to keep in contact with your group that is permitted by a field site. One very useful tool to consider is using Google docs. You can share a document in real time and make contributions as a group to one document. This is a very useful tool to have when wrapping up your final project at the end of the semester. Again, communication and sharing of information is the key to success!

Always ask questions. Students should not be concerned about sounding foolish, but rather should seek information that would have helped them achieve their internship goals.

Summary of the Chapter

This chapter covered issues in how to finalize your learning contract, as well as providing information regarding the underlying rights and responsibilities of all involved in the field training. Each person signing a learning contract has certain role-related expectations, which should be shared and accepted by all prior to finalizing a learning contract agreement. Once there is an agreement among all signees of both their explicit and implied role expectations, there can be a well-informed and successful launch to your field training experience.

What Did I Learn?

As you reflect upon what you have learned about finalizing a learning contract, it is critical to realize what you know (and what you still need to review). Without looking back in the chapter, please list what you feel were the main three points of learning that were personally relevant to you regarding focus of the chapter (please explain why each is personally relevant to your learning):

1. _____
   _____
   _____

2. _____
   _____
   _____

3. _____
   _____
   _____

Discussion Questions

1. What was the best resource you found to help you finalize your learning contract?
2. Which part of the learning contract required more final editing, your site-related goals or your academic objectives? Why?
3. Reflecting upon the prior stages of developing your learning contract up to this point, what have you learned about writing a learning contract?
4. Proofreading is an intricate skill that many writers work on their entire career. What did you learn about needed areas of improvement in your proofreading skill?
5. There are many resources that you can use to help improve your performance outcomes during your training, but some resources are better choices than others. Why are word-processing programs limited in the editing of your written work?
6. Why is it sometimes difficult for you to edit your written work? Please explain, and then offer a strategy you might use to make yourself a better "self-editor."

7. What will you practice more in your writing as you progress to the journaling and paper-writing phases of your field training?
8. What do you do if you receive conflicting editing feedback from your two supervisors or other feedback sources? Think about how you would resolve this situation to best address the overall feedback.
9. Has your feedback editing experience changed how you would convey feedback to someone else regarding his/her writing? If yes, how?
10. Finally, what advice would you give to another intern about how to finalize a learning contract? Be specific about the details you would convey.

Additional Information Links

- Getting Feedback about Writing:
  http://writingcenter.unc.edu/handouts/getting-feedback/
- 4 Steps for Getting Feedback:
  https://www.themuse.com/advice/4-steps-for-asking-for-and-getting-truly-honest-feedback
- How to Get (and Give) Feedback:
  https://open.buffer.com/how-to-give-receive-feedback-work/
- 5 Feedback Questions to Ask:
  https://www.levo.com/posts/5-questions-to-ask-when-you-re-looking-for-feedback
- How and Why to Ask for Criticism:
  http://www.yourofficecoach.com/topics/career_success/self_help_strategies/how_and_why_to_ask_for_criticism.aspx
- Examples of How to Ask for Feedback:
  http://managerbydesign.com/2010/09/specific-phrases-and-examples-of-how-to-ask-for-feedback-from-your-employees/

SECTION 2

Getting Onsite and Starting the Learning Process

Fig. 7.1: Source: https://pixabay.com/en/women-teamwork-team-business-1209678

CHAPTER VII

Contacting Your Site Supervisor and Beginning Your Site Activities

FIELD LEARNING FACTOID

"It's a simple step to starting the internship on a good note. Fifteen minutes before work starts is probably enough time to get situated. Plus, you will make a strong impression on your manager. Do all the research you can before you even arrive at your internship. Find out about the company, employees, and anything else you think is relevant. Retain what you can. It's also important to anticipate paperwork. The first day at any job will be filled with it. Bring your driver's license, social security card, and anything else you might need to help you fill things out. Bring a pad of paper and get ready to write everything down. The first day of your internship will be full of information, so write it all down to help you remember it all."

Source: 8 Tips for Starting Your Internship Off Right
(https://www.levo.com/posts/8-tips-for-starting-your-internship-off-right)

Introduction

Pretraining guidance from your supervisors can help assess your readiness to initiate your internship/field experience or service learning placement experience (Steadman & Schonfeld, 2011; Welsh, Stanley, & Wilmot, 2003). Rely upon the expertise of both of your supervisors to help you successfully begin your training and remember that the learning contract you developed for several weeks is now a "road map" for you to follow onsite. The goals presented in your learning contract empower your onsite learning (Kapoor, Tekian, & Mennin, 2010; Nutefall, 2012). The development of a mentoring relationship with your site supervisor is a distinct opportunity for professional development, and students should be prepared to develop that relationship with this goal in mind, if it is a possibility.

As was mentioned in previous chapters, communication of all forms is a critical part of successfully starting your field training on the first day and beyond. The training experience entails an ongoing social exchange between you and your supervisors (Allen, Mims, Roberts, Kim, & Ryu, 2004). The communication of ideas is also reflected through your journaling and associated underlying self-observations regarding your learning (Tsang, 2003). Anticipate that your communication skills will become more refined and situational in focus. During your onsite training, you will learn to be more conscious of your communication style as it shapes your working relationships with others.

You are embarking on an experience that will truly be transformative for your early career development (Baker, Romero, Geannette, & Paul, 2009; Bay, 2006; Diambra, Cole-Zakrzewski, & Booher, 2004). With that in mind, be cognizant of your role as an intern and the associated motivational issues inherent in your training (Johari & Bradshaw, 2008). Internships/field experiences and service learning experiences are wonderful opportunities to learn much about yourself and your capabilities. This learning experience can create opportunities for "value-added" learning, from you developing a stronger sense of self to enhancing your cultural competency through onsite exposure to diverse coworkers and social situations (Cannon & Frank, 2009; Welsh, Stanley, & Wilmoth, 2003).

This field training experience will engage you on many levels, will test your personal boundaries, and may culminate into transformational learning affecting your long-term career and broader life goals (Zanchetta, Schwind, Aksenchuk, Gorospe, & Santiago, 2013). Through this learning process, important insights about your capabilities, your attitudes, and your social aptitude in working with others may be acquired. Always remember to journal your experiences, so you can later review your notes and reflect upon your ongoing learning outcomes.

The importance of making a good impression on your first day of your field training cannot be understated. Your site experience can prepare you well for your career upon graduation and has implications towards your initial professional reputation in the industry (Baker & Cotugna, 2013; Dilts & Fowler, 1999). This is a valuable time for your professional development, entailing a meaningful integration of different knowledge and skill bases to enhance your career viability in the field (Gerken, Rienties, Giesbers, & Könings, 2012).

As exciting as this step is in your education, be prepared for the potential challenges and stressors in this stage of your professional training (Gordon, Hubbell, Wyle, & Charter, 1986). There will always be the unanticipated that goes beyond what you plan for in your learning contract, but realize that your site supervisor, faculty supervisor, and other support resources will be available to assist you in overcoming these challenges and fulfilling your goals and objectives as an intern.

Learning Goals for this Chapter

Chapter VII offers both informational resources and interactive exercises/activities to best prepare you to:

→ Successfully initiate your onsite training and associated accomplishment of onsite goals,
→ Become an effective onsite learner to optimize your onsite performance and, in turn, the-supervisor mentoring processes, and
→ Engage in effective strategies to successfully socialize into the organizational culture.

This is an exciting new phase to your field training. As with all the previous chapters, this chapter will reiterate the need for you to be an active participant in this dynamic learning process:

- Trust yourself that you are able to accomplish your established, approved goals through your learning contract.
- Be open to seeking mentoring and assistance from the many social resources you have and will encounter in the coming weeks of your internship/field experience or service learning placement.
- Understand that there will be unexpected challenges and many opportunities for success—journal your learning and actively consider how this relates to broader concepts within your academic field.

This integration of onsite and academic learning will be a "cyclical" process during your entire internship/field experience or service learning placement. In a broader sense, you will learn a lot about yourself and how you fit within your field. Across the chapters to date, you should have develped a sense that your learning will be multi-focused and multidimensional in nature. Critically analyze your ongoing learning as you finally apply your learning contract plans to the workplace.

As you can see from the previous phase in the chapter, you may have more questions than in previous planning stages as you enter this exciting onsite training stage of your professional career development. Your learning contract is a planning guide but not comprehensive in its content. You will engage in many opportunities for new learning.

Look It Up!

Define and Understand Important Concepts

In preparing the process of beginning your internship/field experience or service learning placement, you need to have knowledge of specific concepts. Please consult the word glossary provided at the back of this manual, and look up the following terms discussed in this chapter.

Expectations: _____
_____
_____
_____

Work Role: _____
_____
_____
_____

Organizational Norms: _____
_____
_____
_____

Organizational Values: _____
_____
_____
_____

Impression Management: _____
_____
_____
_____

Teamwork: _____
_____
_____
_____

Indoctrination: _____
_____
_____

Phase I: Initiation of the Site-Related Field Experience

Before starting your onsite training, you need to prepare for a successful first day onsite. If you do not have clear expectations of how to begin your role as an intern, you may make common mistakes, which can be avoided easily. It is important to understand your intended site's expectations of you (e.g., work role) in light of organizational norms and organizational values. Who should you seek advice from regarding this preparation? What are the best sources of information to research to prepare? Let us go through some general ideas of what you should do in preparing for this step in the process:

1. *Consult with your faculty supervisor for career advice*—Talk to your faculty supervisor about any advice regarding how to begin the internship/field experience or service learning placement. Your faculty supervisor can give you insights in terms of professionalism and impression management, which are critical issues to address as you form important relationships in the workplace.
2. *Check online for professionalism tips*—In addition to the advice from your faculty supervisor, it would be beneficial for you to search the Internet for any advice regarding role-related expectations and specific professional practices in the industry in which you will beginning your field training.
3. *Meet with your career placement office*—A great resource for you at any stage of your field training is your career planning and placement office on campus. Arrange an appointment with a career planning and placement advisor to discuss professional guidelines for how to start and suceed in a new job position. They should be able to offer you resources and information to support you in this important role transition from "student" to "career professional."
4. *Meet with your site's human resources manager*—You should arrange to meet with the human resources manager at your training site to review the organization's employee rules and regulations. Please make sure that you ask many questions related to the expectations of both employees and interns, so you are adequately prepared to meet those expectations prior to starting your hours.

What Do I Think About ... ?

1. How do I feel about beginning my field experience?
2. What are common reactions of interns to this stage in the process?
3. What is a common misconception I may hold about starting my field training?
4. How do I learn about the organizational culture of my upcoming training site?
5. What can I do to fit in well with employees and/or other interns onsite?
6. What should I do if I find that I have a value conflict with my training site?
7. What did I anticipate in planning for my field training? Not anticipate?
8. If I am faced with an unfamiliar onsite training task, will I be resilient and adapt well?
9. Who should I ask for advice regarding effective impression management techniques?
10. Would it help me to interview existing employees or current interns onsite?

CHAPTER VII Contacting Your Site Supervisor and Beginning Your Site Activities | 117

Through this immersive learning experience, you will learn as much about yourself as you will learn about your field of training. Before proceeding, please review what you have learned so far from completing the learning activities suggested in Phase I.

"Let's Review!" Phase I Learning

1. What was the biggest challenge in mentally preparing yourself to initiate your onsite training experience? Explain why you think this happened. _____
   _____
   _____
   _____
   _____
   _____
   _____
   _____
   _____
   _____
   _____

2. The organizational socialization process is vital for your successful integration and social acceptance within the workplace. What is social information in the workplace indicating whether you "fit in?" _____
   _____
   _____
   _____
   _____
   _____
   _____
   _____
   _____
   _____
   _____
   _____

3. Which informational sources helped you in preparing for the onset of your field training? Why? _____
   _____
   _____
   _____
   _____
   _____
   _____
   _____
   _____
   _____
   _____

Phase II: How to Engage in Impression Management Onsite

As you initiate your site-related activities, you should anticipate that there will be many people you are meeting and who are developing impressions of you. First impressions can be long lasting in nature, so it behooves you to make the best first impression possible to ensure a smooth transition and indoctrination into the workplace. Let us review some general ideas of what you should do in preparing for this step:

1. *Do your homework*—Depending upon the organization, you should be able to find information regarding your training site's dress code, behavioral code of conduct, details of their organizational culture (e.g., community events they sponsor), and other cultural factors that should give you some clues in terms of your expected appearance and behavior. This background research will help you in your socialization.

2. *Ask your site supervisor*—Your site supervisor may give you guidance regarding your behavioral expectations, ranging from informal advice to an actual employee handbook. Your site supervisor may certainly appreciate your conscientiousness regarding your motivation to fit in as well as possible, but keep in mind that they may assess you on your ability to accurately judge the social situation and adapt accordingly.

3. *Attend a professional development workshop*—Through your on-campus career development office and/or your nearby off-campus community, research if there are any professional development workshops offered free to students to help them in all aspects of professionalism and business etiquette. Business schools may offer students workshops in business dinner ettiquette, for example.

FROM A SITE SUPERVISOR'S DESK

Kate Roche, Director of Volunteer Services at Norwood Life Society/Norevolution:

Our most successful student volunteers were highly motivated, reliable, exercised good judgment, had a great deal of interpersonal flexibility, and they demonstrated that their volunteering was an important part of their educational process. There are several ways students can come to their volunteering prepared for success. Most important is to treat your interview like a job interview and when you get the internship—to treat it like a job.

Here are a few tips gained from my experience with student interns and volunteers. Prior to your interview, research the industry and come prepared with questions for your interviewer. Be ready with thoughtful answers to questions about why you are interested in the volunteer/internship assignment. Read industry job descriptions to understand expectations of various roles. Dress professionally and be on-time for your interview. Pay close attention to expectations and get clarification if you are unsure. Interviewers welcome questions!

From the first day of your internship/volunteering, be open to suggestions and constructive criticism—use this time to work on building professional skills such as communication, both written and verbal. Ask for feedback. Get to know individuals you work with as they may become references. Building and maintaining a strong professional network is one of the most important things one can do for one's career.

What Should I Do?
Putting Your Learning into Action

1. Review any online information about your field training site, ranging from its historical "founding story" to its current role and reputation within its industry.
2. Interview a recent intern or a current employee of the internship/field experience or service learning placement site to gain a better understanding of the organizational culture and manager-employee dynamics.
3. Look up the organization's stock profile to gain a better understanding of its market viability, especially since you might be asked about your organizational knowledge at some point in your training.
4. Investigate if the company has won any awards or industry-related recognition for sales performance and/or community engagement.
5. Ask your faculty supervisor if he/she can share any information regarding what you should know about your training site before you begin.
6. Finally, if applicable, assume the role of a customer/client and purchase your training site's product or service to gain a better understanding of what the organization does.

As with any step in the process of your learning throughout this field training, it is good to reflect upon what you have learned to date. Before proceeding, please review what you have learned in Phase II! The next section contains a series of review questions related to what you learned in doing the activities and exercises.

"Let's Review!" Phase II Learning

1. Among the different resource suggestions you have encountered, which one yielded the most helpful information related to you better understanding expected employee's appearance at your internship/field experience or service learning placement site? Expected employee's behavior? _____

2. What information did you learn from your site supervisor to better prepare for your intern role? _____

3. Did you develop a "schema" (idea) about your anticipated training experience? Is it possible to have a completely developed intern role schema for your training site experience? _____

4. How has your understanding of the concept of "professionalism" changed as you have contemplated the different ways you should prepare for your first day onsite? _____

Phase III: "Walking the Walk" of Your Approved Learning Contract

Now you are initiating your approved learning goals and objectives onsite and in the classroom. Acquiring approval of your learning activities was an important step in your training experience; this is where you see if what you planned is realistic and doable ("actionable").

Anticipate that what you plan may not go exactly as expected—this is certainly true with field experiences! This fact does not negate the necessity of establishing a detailed learning plan through your learning contract, but it does necessitate that you learn to expect the unexpected and learn to adapt to changing learning conditions. Personal resiliency is a key attribute of successful interns and people in everyday life. One might argue that it is a trait that only certain people have. There is also research suggest that you can learn to be more adaptive and resilient through conscious effort in both social and task-related situations.

Resources To Learn How To Be A Resilient Intern

The following are some helpful resources to learn more about resilience in the workplace:

- 10 behavioral tips to be more healthy and resilient:
  http://www.webmd.com/mental-health/features/overcome-obstacles-resilience#1
- Tips on how to become a more resilient worker:
  http://www.hrzone.com/perform/people/how-to-be-more-resilient-at-work
- Career resiliency:
  http://www.mindtools.com/pages/article/resilience.htm
- How to manage stress using resiliency:
  http://www.verywell.com/cope-with-stress-and-become-more-resilient-3144889

Think About It!

Here are topics to consider as you develop your time management and related organizational skills as an intern:

1. In some industries, a workplace can be a constantly changing environment. What do I anticipate as being a change in the field that I may encounter as an intern? _____
   _____
   _____

2. How does the concept of time management apply to me as a student? Do I think the concept applies differently to me in my upcoming role as an intern? The same? _____
   _____
   _____

3. What are my strategies for balancing the time and task commitments of being both an intern and a student during the duration of my onsite training? _____
   _____
   _____

4. What did I learn that I did not anticipate? _____
   _____
   _____

Apply Your Knowledge!

As an intern, you will need to carefully manage your time between your onsite, academic, and other life roles. The "balancing act" entailed in people juggling multiple life roles on a daily basis is a concern for most, but it is rarely planned for in a strategic manner. It is important to think about how your life will increase in complexity based upon the addition of your onsite training activities. Even if the goals and objectives that you detailed in your learning contract account for most of your daily activities, time conflicts, role overload, and inter-role adjustments may emerge during your onsite field training. Here are some further points regarding this issue to consider as you begin your internship/field experience or service learning placement:

- Identify a useful approach to scheduling tasks (e.g., using the calendar app on your iPhone) to keep track of your time obligations as both a student and an intern.
- Program your device and/or set up your scheduling system for immediate use (e.g., enter dates with specific tasks and deadlines) to help you anticipate most of the activities you need to accomplish both onsite and at school.
- Do a "test run" of your system with an upcoming event, and see how useful it is for you in meeting deadlines and completing activities. You may need to revise the process to help you better keep track of activities in general.
- Discuss other time scheduling approaches with your supervisors to get their input regarding their expectations of you as an intern and any associated scheduling concerns that are commonly encountered by students and/or employees. During these conversations with your supervisors, it would be a good idea to ask them about their own time management approaches and suggestions.

Try It Out!
Learning to Multitask: Dichotic Listening Exercise

Dichotic Listening Exercise Brief: If you can find an existing dichotic listening task program, that would be the easiest way to conduct this exercise. If not, simply have two peers record two separate messages regarding instructions for a card-sort task. The audio recordings should be no longer than five minutes each. Consult with your faculty supervisor regarding lab equipment that will permit you to listen the two audio recordings simultaneously.

To set up the card-sort exercise, create a pile of playing cards, put on the headphones, and listen to the competing messages regarding the card-sorting task, which are playing at the same time. The task for you is to listen to the competing audio messages simultaneously and to try to follow the instructions given. The difficulty of this task symbolically relates to how you might encounter situations in which you are receiving simultaneous instructions.

Ask yourself the following after doing this exercise: Did you experience any stress in attempting to do the listening and performance task? How did you adapt to the situation? If given the opportunity to do it again, would you apply a strategy to adapt to the task situation?

This exercise is limited to five minutes.

After completion of the Dichotic Listening Exercise, ask yourself the following:

1. What did I learn about my ability to simultaneously listen to multiple sources of task instructions?
2. How does this task relate to my ability to balance multiple roles in my daily activities?

Search the Web!
Learn About Impression Management in the Workplace

Search the Internet for different informational sources regarding how you can learn to apply impression management techniques and effective teamwork behavior in both the classroom and onsite. Professionalism is an important behavior associated with being a successful intern in an organization, from being punctual in response to your task-related deadlines and completing assignments in a manner that meets or exceeds your supervisor's expectations.

Check out at least three different Internet resources pertaining to impression management and teamwork onsite. As you review this information, please answer the following questions:

1. What were the most beneficial resources you found regarding professionalism in the workplace? Explain why. _____
   _____
   _____
   _____
   _____
   _____
   _____
   _____
   _____

2. What did you find out about how to avoid stress while working on a team and when encountering multiple, and potentially competing, social messages necessitating a response? _____
   _____
   _____
   _____
   _____
   _____
   _____
   _____
   _____

3. What did you learn that you did not anticipate or that surprised you? Explain why. _____
   _____
   _____
   _____
   _____
   _____
   _____
   _____
   _____

AN INTERN'S INSIGHTS

Aroma Blomquist: As I began to prepare for the internship portion of the requirement for my program, it became clear that this was not just another "elective" class I needed to take. The internship part of the program, in my opinion, is a very important determinant of what exactly it is that you want from this program, outside of this program. As you begin your search for the internship, please keep in mind your career passion and aspirations.

When determining where to conduct your internship, you should try to have a clear understanding of where you stand in terms of your role when it comes to providing for the elderly population. What are the services you feel most passionate about? For example, are you interested in improving housing for elderly or is your passion more with providing care for the elderly? Asking these questions may help you make the last step of choosing the appropriate place where you wish to conduct your internship. You may also find it helpful to seek guidance from your program coordinator who has dedicated much of his/her time to the field.

Your internship portion of this program is a fantastic opportunity to observe and partake in various steps taken in real time to help the elderly population. The internship is also very beneficial as it provides guidance from groups of individuals that specialize in that specific area (depending on the area you choose).

Guidance from these personnel is not only going to make this experience stand out but their guidance will also help you mold in to the profession you hope to attain after the completion of the program!

"Let's Review!" Phase III Learning

1. What did you learn about successfully launching your onsite training? Please explain. _____
   _____
   _____
   _____
   _____
   _____

2. Has your perspective regarding the concept of "resiliency" changed as you applied the concept to beginning your field training? Why, or why not? _____
   _____
   _____
   _____
   _____
   _____
   _____
   _____

3. What was the easiest source of information to find regarding professionalism in the workplace? Most difficult to find? Please explain. _____
   _____
   _____
   _____
   _____

4. What has surprised you about the concept of maintaining a work-life balance as you begin your onsite training? Please explain. _____
   _____
   _____
   _____
   _____
   _____
   _____

Summary of the Chapter

The focus of the present chapter was to examine the "learning curve" you may undergo as you begin your new role as an intern. Self-reflection processes in your journaling of this adaptive experience are a significant part of the analysis of your ongoing learning on many levels of analysis. Strategies in how to best engage in effective self-management, as both an intern and an emerging career professional are important developmental learning foci for you in addition to accomplishing your other learning goals. Remember that first impressions are hard to change, so make your best effort to integrate well into the social environment of the site.

What Did I Learn?

As you reflect upon what you learned about successfully beginning your field training, it is beneficial to realize what you know (and what you still need to review). Without looking back in the chapter, please list what you feel were the main three points of learning that were personally relevant to you regarding the focus of the chapter (explain why each is personally relevant to your learning):

1. _____
   _____
   _____

2. _____
   _____
   _____

3. _____
   _____
   _____

Discussion Questions

1. Much of what was presented in this chapter related to you learning how to adapt to your new role as an intern. What is one issue of onsite adaptation that you anticipate may be challenging to you during this initial phase of onsite learning?
2. Through your review of the resources presented in this chapter, what insights did you again about your resiliency capabilities as an intern? In what ways are you more resilient than other ways in response to situational demands?
3. What are specific aspects of time management planning that you have adopted based upon what was discussed in this chapter?
4. Do you feel it is challenging for most people to balance multiple life roles, such as being a full-time student and an employee? Why, or why not?
5. What personal organizational strategies have you planned to better multitask as an intern?
6. What did you learn about your listening and attentional capacities during the dichotic listening task? How does it relate to any multitasking situation?
7. What does "professionalism" mean to you, in general? Has this concept changed as you begin your onsite training?
8. Do you think it is difficult for most people to engage in impression management behavior over time in the workplace? Why, or why not?
9. Did the initial experiences of your field training match your initial expectations?
10. Based upon what you have learned to date, what advice would you give another student beginning the planning process for a training placement? What advice do you wish you had been given before you started the planning process?

Additional Information Links

- Characteristics of Effective Learning Experiences:
  http://serc.carleton.edu/introgeo/service/effective_experience.html
- Benefits of Service Learning:
  http://www.generationon.org/educators/lessons-resources/why-service-learning
- Tips for the First Day of the Internship/Field Experience or Service Learning Placement:
  http://www.internships.com/student/resources/workplace/the-first-few-days/tips-for-the-first-day
- Preparing to Start an Internship/Field Experience or Service Learning Placement:
  https://www.thebalance.com/how-to-prepare-yourself-before-your-internship-starts-1986751
- Preparing to Start an Internship/Field Experience or Service Learning Placement #2:
  http://medicalschoolhq.net/ten-tips-for-successfully-starting-your-internship/
- Making a Lasting Impression on the First Day:
  http://www.foxbusiness.com/features/2013/05/24/intern-guide-how-to-make-lasting-impression-first-day.html

Fig. 8.1: Source: https://pixabay.com/en/female-diary-write-beautiful-865110/.

CHAPTER VIII

Starting the Site-Related Journaling Process: Introspection in Action

FIELD LEARNING FACTOID

"The first step is redefining what 'journaling' is. Many people have this notion that to journal effectively you must sit down and write pages and pages of poetic language about your feelings. But really, journaling just means setting aside a little quiet, undistracted time to sit down and think about your life. It can be just by writing down a record of what you did that day; by venting about one thing that you can't get off your mind; by noting something that inspired you. Some days it may be pages and pages, and some it may only be a few words. Just as long as you're actually taking a moment to stop and think about how things are going."

Source: The Muse (http://www.themuse.com/advice/8-ways-to-stop-thinking-about-journaling-and-actually-start-journaling)

Introduction

Effective learning is based upon the need to be self-reflective upon your accomplishments and what you still need to learn or improve upon (Harris, 2008; Rhoads & Howard, 1998). As a field trainee, it may not be a conscious process daily, but it is beneficial for you to periodically review your approved learning goals from the established learning contract with your supervisors (Coleman & Flood, 2016; Kirby & Lawson, 2012). Journaling is a key aspect to this goal review process. The benefits of ongoing journaling can extend to creating meaning in your life across different daily tasks and contexts (Creede, Fisher-Yoshida, & Gallegos, 2012) and can help you become a more effective practitioner in the field (Ferrari & Chapman, 1999; Johns & Burnie, 2013).

It is important for you to create a conducive writing environment for your journaling process to ensure its success (e.g., Collay, 1998). You should make a conscious plan regarding this writing process. Before you begin each day of your field training, you should review your onsite learning goals to remind yourself about your learning goals and to reinforce your expected learning outcomes (Mezirow & Taylor, 2009; Peery, 2005). This daily practice will help keep you on track, when it is easy sometimes to lose focus during you training onsite (Stevens & Cooper, 2009). As you start this crucial step in your training, remember to use different writing tools that you know work for you to assist in your self-reflection process (e.g., a blogging writing exercise) (Bouldin, Holmes, & Fortenberry, 2006). Additionally, you should use your supervisors' feedback as a "prompt" for your journaling, because receiving and processing this feedback can potentially be an emotional experience to go through.

A review of your onsite learning goals will also help you in the general planning of your career goals as an emerging practitioner in the field (Preis & Stauder, 2014; Tsang, 2003). Here are some questions to ask yourself as you engage in a periodic review of your learning goals through the journaling process:

- What are my typical onsite learning activities, and how well do they correspond to my approved onsite learning goals?
- What should I do if my onsite activities do not correspond to my approved learning goals? If my onsite learning does correspond to my expected onsite goals, is the depth of my learning proceeding as planned? What do I need to do to create a more in-depth learning experience?
- Are there any learning goals that I have not had an opportunity work on yet? Is there a way to explain this lack of progress as "learning" in my journaling?
- When should I journal my thoughts about my ongoing onsite activities and associated learning outcomes? Is it appropriate to journal my thoughts whilst onsite, or should I wait until I leave the site after my hours are completed for the day?
- Is there an effective approach to keeping track of my learning onsite?
- Can I make an audio recording or take notes on my smartphone? Who should I ask about this?
- Is there a specific way for me to structure my journaling note taking?
- How can I find good examples of my journaling to optimize learning in my training?

This chapter will address information responding to these questions, and more, as you begin this important step in your training. Pay attention to your reactions about your learning

CHAPTER VIII Starting the Site-Related Journaling Process: Introspection in Action | 131

experiences, because you will learn much about yourself in the process (e.g., preferred learning style in response to training materials).

Learning Goals for this Chapter

Chapter VII offers both informational resources and exercises/activities to prepare you to:

→ Develop effective writing strategies for how to best document your ongoing site learning through the journaling process,

→ Establish a routine (i.e., time and location) for engaging in introspection during the writing of your journal entries, and

→ Analyze your learning goals in comparison to actual onsite activities on a continual basis.

Before beginning to discuss very specific training issues related to your field experience, let us explore some foundational concepts for this chapter:

Look It Up!

Define and Understand Important Concepts

In conducting an internship/field experience or service learning placement in your chosen field, you should have a knowledge of specific learning concepts. Please consult the word glossary provided at the back of this manual, and look up the following terms discussed in the chapter.

Self Analysis: _____
_____

Self-Directed Learning: _____
_____

Goal Relevance: _____
_____

Self-Regulatory Process: _____
_____

Time Management: _____
_____

Perspective Taking: _____
_____

Phase I: Self-Reflection During Onsite Training Experience

Before you begin to journal, you should have a good understanding of how to best approach this ongoing self analysis and how it relates to your general self-learning strategies (i.e., self-directed learning). Among other insights, you may find that your journaling reveals a deeper understanding about your personal attitudes toward working with others and the meaning of work.

Let us go through some general ideas of how to prepare for this step in the process:

1. *Research different self-reflection strategies*—Research books or online resources regarding approaches to analyzing your intern experiences during learning. It may be common sense, but it does take practice to engage in critical self analyses of your feelings and cognitive activities.

2. *Ask an expert*—Professional writers commonly engage in an analysis of their personal feelings and/or attitudes to inspire their writing. If possible, interview someone in your field who is a professional writer (e.g., a newspaper columnist), and ask about his/her strategies in writing introspective thoughts and feelings in response to different topics.

3. *Read sample journals*—Ask your faculty supervisor if he/she may have any samples of past interns' journals to see what could be field-relevant documentation of onsite learning and training outcomes.

4. *Talk it out*—Before you start writing, practice the process of "living in the here and now" while consciously reflecting upon your feelings and attitudes in the onsite training. When possible, after the experience, record your thoughts about how you felt in that situation and judge the quality of your self-observations from that learning process.

5. *Practice, practice, practice*—Practice writing a journal about your daily activities, which may not pertain to your onsite training experiences. The more opportunities you have to engage in introspection, the better will be your journal writing and overall learning insights will be regarding your ongoing skill development and learning.

Let us check in about your perceptions of the learning process at this point. The follow are some important questions to ask yourself as you initiate your onsite training and begin the journaling process:

What Do I Think About ... ?

1. How do I best manage my time to optimize my onsite learning and journaling processes?
2. Is journal writing similar to or different than other types of writing techniques for me?
3. What are common obstacles to most individuals' self-introspection experiences?
4. Will my enhanced onsite self-observations assist me in other offsite areas of learning and performance (e.g., in the classroom)? Why, or why not?
5. What are the best steps for me to follow in my journal writing? Should I take notes first and then write them out, or is there another approach better for my writing style?
6. Will journaling help improve my general writing skills? Why or why not?
7. Would it help to create a discussion group among my peers who are also doing internships to brainstorm journaling ideas?

CHAPTER VIII Starting the Site-Related Journaling Process: Introspection in Action | 133

Before proceeding, you should review what you have learned so far! In the following, there will be a review exercise related to the information you learned through the activities suggested in Phase I.

"Let's Review!" Phase I Learning

1. What is involved in self-reflecting upon my experiential learning? What are factors to consider during the self-reflection process? _____
   _____
   _____
   _____
   _____
   _____
   _____
   _____
   _____

2. How does the process of writing a journal help facilitate my introspection? _____
   _____
   _____
   _____
   _____
   _____
   _____
   _____
   _____

3. What were useful resources to consult in formulating my journal writing strategies? ___
   _____
   _____
   _____
   _____
   _____
   _____
   _____
   _____

4. What was the most challenging aspect of beginning to write a journal? The easiest? ___
   _____
   _____
   _____
   _____
   _____
   _____
   _____
   _____

Phase II: Routine Establishment for Your Journaling

Before you proceed much further into your journaling experience, you should learn how to establish a specific "routine" (i.e., time and location) to effectively engage in your focused journal reflections and writing.

Let us go through some general ideas of what you should do in preparing for this step:

1. *Meet with an on-campus career counselor*—Set up an appointment with a counselor in your on-campus career development office. Ask about advice regarding how to get organized in journaling a field training experience.

2. *Search online for life strategies/planning resources*—Conduct online searches for advice on how to engage in effective time management and/or other planning strategies while balancing an internship with other life role demands.

3. *Develop a schedule/planner*—Create a daily schedule, which, among other details, stipulates the time you will spend in writing your journal reflections. Expect to spend about 15 to 20 minutes journaling for every hour spent onsite.

4. *Reserve or create a journaling "space"*—Just as it is important to schedule a time for your journal writing, it is equally important to designate a physical space at school or at home, or even at the training site, if permitted, to create a conducive mindset for conducting your journal writing.

5. *Meet with your supervisors about memory strategies*—Ask for advice from your supervisors regarding ways to best recall training outcomes in a complete and accurate manner. Create effective memory strategies to help you recall your learning-related details when you sit down to write your journal entries.

FROM A SITE SUPERVISOR'S DESK

Michael Matos, Albany Park Community Center
Director of Adult Education Programs and Data:

A supervisor's performance feedback is always challenging. Feedback of this nature is always extremely valuable for the participants' professional development and success. This feedback is always part of a larger learning experience and provided to help motivate and understand. Whether feedback is provided to professionals, volunteers, and/or interns, we are trying to develop the skills necessary for them to function effectively.

No supervision experience is the same. Obviously, addressing performance for an intern or entry level employee is very different than for a senior level staff person, but staying mission-focused and setting priorities are very important. Providing effective feedback on performance occurs when both the member of staff and manager work together to ensure that results are achieved. Individualized quality feedback helps employees, volunteers and interns.

When addressing feedback, clearly communicate expectations. Make sure to provide employees with the tools, training, and information they need to succeed. Collaboration is always strategic when combined with communication and a climate of mutual respect. Listen and be available and transparent while taking responsibility and always giving credit where it is due. Worthy performance feedback does not just help the person reviewed; it can make the reviewer's job a lot easier and help build a productive team and successful agency mission.

You have reviewed several sources of information related to your journal writing. As with all learning, delving into the task and seeing what works is the best way to identify the best approach for you and your learning needs. Here are some suggestions for applying your learning at this step in the planning process:

What Should I Do?
Putting Your Learning into Action

1. Format a journal page or a worksheet that lists each of your learning contract's onsite goals. Designate several lines under each goal for you to take notes and write statements about your learning. Format the pages to best suit your journaling needs.
2. "Pilot" a journal writing session after a day of training onsite. Think about what you remember, and record your thoughts using a "flow of consciousness" approach in your writing (e.g., do not concern yourself with punctuation or other grammatical rules).
3. Analyze your chosen writing space for your journal entries. Is it a conducive location for contemplation of ongoing onsite learning, or do you need to reevaluate your choice to concentrate better?
4. Discuss your initial journal writing with your faculty supervisor. Ask him/her to review your journal writing and discuss with you any advice regarding how to improve the breadth, depth, and/or specificity of insights for later learning outcomes analyses.

Before proceeding, please review what you have learned in Phase II! The next section contains a series of review questions related to what you learned in doing the activities and exercises. To best help you with this ongoing learning process, please be accurate in your responses to assess what areas of learning may need further review.

CHAPTER VIII Starting the Site-Related Journaling Process: Introspection in Action | 137

"Let's Review!" Phase II Learning

1. What logistical details have you planned for in setting up your journal writing activities? Were some planning steps more involved than you anticipated? Why, or why not? ____
   _____
   _____
   _____
   _____
   _____
   _____
   _____

2. Based upon what you have done so far in response to the suggested activities, what did you find to be the easiest part of the journal writing process? Hardest? Please explain.
   _____
   _____
   _____
   _____
   _____
   _____
   _____

3. Deciding upon a conducive "time and place" to do your journal writing helps you develop a mindset to focus on your self-reflections about onsite learning. Were you able achieve this optimal writing arrangement? Why, or why not? _____
   _____
   _____
   _____
   _____
   _____
   _____
   _____

4. Engaging in introspection is a learning process in itself. What have you learned about yourself to date that you did not anticipate? _____
   _____
   _____
   _____
   _____
   _____
   _____
   _____

Phase III: Keeping Yourself "On Track" and Focused Through Your Journaling

Your ongoing journaling has many different potential opportunities for self-learning and personal growth as an emerging professional in your field. An additional, and very pragmatic, outcome from your daily journaling is an analysis of how your onsite activities correspond to your approved site-related goals from the learning contract (i.e., goal relevance). You should also analyze your personal learning processes as they relate to adapting to feedback (i.e., self-regulatory processes), time management skills, and ability to understand others' perspectives (i.e., perspective taking) during the training experience. This is a realistic concern, because it is easy to become distracted from your intended onsite activities in response to the demands the onsite training workplace.

Here are some strategies to remain "on track" in completing your approved site goals when onsite:

- Each day before going onsite, review your onsite learning goals carefully and thoroughly. This helps you create a clear expectation of what to prepare for and how to focus onsite during each training session.
- Periodically meet with your site supervisor, or another site-related manager, to discuss your learning aims as an intern based upon your approved learning contract. This helps you again focus on your learning goals but also has the added bonus of reiterating this same focus to your site-related supervisors.
- Journal immediately after you complete a training session to best recall how well your onsite activities reflect your intended learning goals. The recency of the writing process will help you remember more details of your onsite learning.

Think About It!

Here are topics to consider as you think about maintaining progress in your onsite learning as examined through your journal writing:

1. Which onsite goals have been more challenging to focus on when in the workplace? Why? _____
   _____
   _____

2. How can onsite activities be better structured to reflect intended learning goals? _____
   _____
   _____

3. Has this process of "personal accountability" in journaling onsite activities helped in the development of better critical thinking skills? Why, or why not? _____
   _____
   _____

4. How can technology be used to enhance my onsite learning and recall of site-related activities? Should permission be asked before recording my onsite activities? _____
   _____
   _____

Apply Your Knowledge!

The following are some suggested ideas for you to consider when engaging in this ongoing process of learning goal evaluation:

1. *Create a checklist*—When evaluating your ongoing learning goals, it might help to create a checklist of what you should be doing at each step in the learning process and possibly adjust the checklist as you transition in your work across different phases of training activities.
2. *Label onsite tasks according to approved learning goal(s)*—Part of your evaluation strategy could be to explicitly link your daily onsite tasks with specific, overarching learning goals for your learning contract. The labeling process will then assist you in focusing on what you are accomplishing regarding your learning goals to date and what still needs to be accomplished over time.
3. *Do a frequency analysis of onsite activities by learning goal*—A different approach could be examining the amount of time, or the frequency of behaviors, that you engage in when onsite related to each learning goal. This can assist you in better understanding the percentage of time that you devote to accomplishing each of your learning goals and the degree to which the goal-related activities overlap, as well as other issues of "efficiency," which you may be able to strategically adjust (e.g., time management).
4. *Map out your goals along a completion timeline*—Finally, a different approach might be creating a chronological timeline of your learning goals, and plotting them along a series of weeks or months (with some expected overlap).

Try It Out!
Preferred Writing Environment Mapping Exercise

Preferred Writing Environment Mapping Exercise Brief: To effectively engage in your ongoing learning analysis of your site-related goals, you need to plan your optimal writing environment in your apartment, dorm room, or other location. Just as you have a preferred study environment, it is equally important to understand preferred writing environmental factors to help you engage in your reflective journal writing. In the box below, please draw the details (e.g., furniture, entertainment equipment, "social space") that would be most conducive for your journal writing:

This exercise is limited to 15 minutes.

After completion of the Preferred Writing Environment Mapping Exercise, ask yourself the following:

1. What factors did you feel were conducive to your journal writing process? Why?
2. Conversely, which factors did you *not* include in your environmental plan and why?
3. Finally, does your preferred writing environment match your preferred study environment?

CHAPTER VIII Starting the Site-Related Journaling Process: Introspection in Action | 141

Search the Web!
Learn about Journaling for Onsite Training Evaluation

Search the Internet for different websites regarding using journals for an evaluation of personal learning. Check out at least three different websites pertaining to self-reflective journaling within your area of study. As you review this information, please answer the following questions:

1. What were the three emergent topics related to using journaling for field-related learning assessments?

   a. _____

   b. _____

   c. _____

2. Which source(s) of information were helpful in developing your ideas about journaling?

   _____
   _____
   _____
   _____
   _____
   _____
   _____
   _____

3. Is journaling commonly used for training assessments in your field of study? Why, or why not? _____

   _____
   _____
   _____
   _____
   _____
   _____
   _____
   _____
   _____

AN INTERN'S INSIGHTS

Chrisann Fahy: The number one piece of advice I can give in writing a field paper is to select a topic that you are passionate about. This will be a crucial factor in the motivational department. This type of paper may take months to develop but it is to your advantage to be driven to explore and research. The more journals and/or research that you acquire will make it easier to write your paper by expanding the thought process regarding the field topic.

When conducting your research, allow a few designated days with an adequate amount of time to sit down and gather as much information regarding your topic all at once. This will also help with limiting the time you spend repeating searches or reading abstracts. It is important to develop a timeline of completion, however. I found giving myself goals every day and every week kept me motivated and on track. Pushing yourself to complete specific tasks per week will accumulate your writing output by setting a realistic goal within your schedule, (e.g., this week I will write five pages even though my week is busy, but next week I can write ten pages).

These small goals will accumulate and result in a fully developed research paper. Writing a field paper takes dedication and hardwork, don't be afraid to ask a professor or a fellow peer for assistance. Feedback will make your life easier and don't take it personal; feedback brings you one step closer to completion. I wish you luck in the process!

CHAPTER VIII Starting the Site-Related Journaling Process: Introspection in Action | 143

"Let's Review!" Phase III Learning

1. How has your perception of journal writing changed after reviewing the information suggested in this chapter? _____
_____
_____

2. For the assessment of learning to be effective and accurate, what would you suggest is the best approach to journaling based upon your ongoing experiences as an intern? ___
_____
_____

3. How have insights about your personal memory capabilities through the suggested exercises influenced how you have tailored your journaling approach? _____
_____
_____

4. If you were approached by another intern about journaling advice, what advice would you offer? _____
_____
_____

Summary of the Chapter

This chapter reviewed information related to the process of journal writing. This process of reflective writing will assist in an effective valuation of your "on task" goal accomplishments. Learning how to engage in these self-reflective activities will greatly enhance your potential as a lifelong learner in many different contexts, especially applied toward your career development over time. Many different skills are enhanced by ongoing journaling, from a critical analysis of your personal learning to broader organizational issues of matching your onsite activities to the external criteria of learning expectations and associated performance behaviors.

What Did I Learn?

Self-reflection is a vital part of your learning process throughout the field experience process. Without looking back in the chapter, please list what you feel were the main three points of learning that were personally relevant to you regarding the focus of the chapter (please explain why each is personally relevant to your learning):

1. _____
_____

2. _____
_____
_____

3. _____
_____

Discussion Questions

1. What were the most important concepts you learned by journaling?
2. What do you feel is the least understood (but is a needed) aspect underlying effective journal writing?
3. Who was the best guide for you in developing your journaling plan/schedule? Why?
4. Based on your unique field training situation, what is the optimal memory strategy for recalling onsite activities for your later journaling?
5. How has your journaling helped you become more conscious of your onsite learning? Please explain from a self-awareness perspective.
6. Time management is always a consideration when engaging in field-related training activities. How much time is typically involved in your journaling? Do you think you could be better at time management regarding this writing process? Why or why not?
7. Creating a daily checklist to keep track of your learning goal accomplishments onsite has been suggested as a possible strategy to use. Do you use it? If yes, how do you incorporate it into your daily field training activities?
8. Establishing a designated space helps create an appropriate mindset for your journaling. What was your choice for this designated space, and why?
9. Metacognition is "thinking about thinking." What have you learned to date about your own thought processes through your ongoing site-related journaling?
10. What do you anticipate as being the benefit(s) of ongoing journaling to prepare for the writing of your final field paper or other culminating project?

Additional Information Links

- WikiEducator website:
  http://wikieducator.org/Reflective_journals
- Penzu.com:
  https://penzu.com/how-to-write-a-reflective-journal
- Assessment Resources website:
  http://ar.cetl.hku.hk/am_rj.htm
- PsychCentral:
  https://psychcentral.com/blog/archives/2014/09/27/30-journaling-prompts-for-self-reflection-and-self-discovery/
- Field-specific example—Nursing.advanceweb.com:
  http://nursing.advanceweb.com/regional-articles/features/reflective-journaling.aspx
- Field-specific example—Nicholls.edu website:
  https://www.nicholls.edu/student-teaching/student-teacher-responsibilities/reflective-journal/
- University of Texas, Arlington's Service Learning website:
  https://www.uta.edu/ccsl/for-students/reflection-journals.php
- Student Nurse Journey website:
  http://snjourney.com/ClinicalInfo/WrAndReport/ReflectiveWr.htm

Fig. 9.1: Source: https://pixabay.com/en/workplace-team-business-meeting-1245776/.

CHAPTER IX

Seeking Performance Feedback: Utilize 360 Degree Feedback Opportunities

FIELD LEARNING FACTOID

"Asking for feedback is beneficial to your personal development. Actively reaching out for advice, you learn faster and smarter. Ask yourself what you want that feedback can help you with, so you can prepare the specific questions that lead to such information. Then you need to seek out the people who might have knowledge, within your circle of connections. Finally, conduct productive feedback conversations with gratitude, clarification and commitment."

Source: Impraise Blog (http://blog.impraise.com/360-feedback/want-feedback-heres-how-to-ask-for-it-360-review)

Introduction

Performance feedback is a critical part of your daily interactions in any social and task-related environment (e.g., the workplace) (Holmboe & Hawkins, 2008). You will be engaged in learning at all stages of your professional development, and your ability to best utilize performance feedback will only help you master each of the stages in your career. Performance feedback needs to be addressed early on during your field training process to avoid potential feelings of frustration and failure. This idea of utilizing performance feedback is also relevant to the "real world" of work when you will receive and need to address performance feedback from multiple sources (e.g., customers) in an ongoing manner.

You will learn much about yourself, and learn much about others you work with, through this cyclical exchange of social feedback (e.g., expected social rules of workplace professionalism) (Kirkland, Manoogian, & Center for Creative Leadership 1998).

Being a trainee in the workplace is a great learning opportunity for you, but it is imperative that you assume an active role in the feedback-seeking and learning adaptation process. Seeking 360° feedback is a beneficial strategy for ongoing professional skill development by better understanding performance standards from multiple key stakeholders in the organizational context (Bracken & Center for Creative Leadership, 1997; Edwards & Ewen, 1996). Regardless of the feedback source, it is important for you to be receptive to the constructive feedback that you receive and to make a concerted effort to respond to the details of this information provided (Hickok, 1995). One key to engaging in effective learning experiences is to avoid thinking that feedback suggests a negative evaluation of you. Performance feedback, if conveyed properly, should not only guide you in what needs to be improved upon, but also how to do it (Fleenor & Prince, 1997; Langdon, Whiteside, & McKenna, 1999).

As you learn from this ongoing performance feedback, you will not only learn how to be a responsive feedback recipient, but you will learn how to give feedback to others based on your perceptions of the feedback recipient experience (Lepsinger, Lucia, & Lepsinger, 2009). Perspective taking can be an outcome of engaging in 360° feedback over time. Be open to this great learning opportunity regarding what works and does not work over the course of your field-related training experience (London, 2014).

As beneficial as it is, feedback from multiple sources can be overwhelming if you do not create a plan for how to document and systematically process the incoming information (Smith, 2012). Here are some suggestions regarding how to best utilize the feedback from many different and relevant performance feedback sources to optimize your learning outcomes:

- Write down information by feedback source in a systematic manner,
- Follow-up with each feedback source to clarify points, if needed,
- Compare the information received in a matrix table to note the correspondence between the feedback sources, and
- Create goals (and subgoals) related to addressing performance feedback during your field training.

CHAPTER IX Seeking Performance Feedback: Utilize 360 Degree Feedback Opportunities | 147

Learning Goals for this Chapter

Chapter IX offers both informational resources and exercises/activities to prepare you to:

→ Solicit performance feedback from multiple stakeholders for the purpose of optimizing your onsite training experience,

→ Effectively document performance feedback from multiple sources in an accurate and timely manner, and

→ Respond to performance feedback in an efficient and accurate manner to improve both your communication skills (e.g., active listening) and your general onsite performance outcomes.

You (the intern) are applying this concept to your field training site, so be open to this potentially transformative learning experience, and recognize that this is an opportunity to shape you into the professional you strive to become within your field/career focus. There will also be numerous opportunities to network with professionals in your field/discipline, which can benefit you in later steps of your career.

Look It Up!

Define and Understand Important Concepts

In conducting an internship/field experience or service learning placement in your chosen field, you should have a knowledge of specific learning concepts. Please consult the word glossary provided at the back of this manual, and look up the following terms discussed in the current chapter.

Feedback Informant: _____
_____

Feedback Recipient: _____
_____

360° Feedback: _____
_____

Self-Regulatory Learning: _____
_____

Anchoring and Adjusting: _____
_____

Adaptive Learning: _____
_____
_____

Phase I: Feedback Solicitation From Multiple Site-Related Sources

Before you ask for performance feedback onsite, you should understand how to choose appropriate targets for feedback information (e.g., a person who sees you perform on a daily basis in the training site; i.e., feedback informant) and how to approach these chosen feedback sources in a professional, proactive, and strategic manner to optimize your role as a feedback recipient. As with other work-related behaviors, impression management is important to be cognizant of when engaging in performance consultation with supervisors and other relevant feedback informants across levels in the workplace (i.e., 360° feedback).

Let us go through some general ideas of what you should do in preparing for this step in the process:

1. *Research the topic of "feedback"*—Find different sources of information regarding characteristics of effective feedback strategies conveyed in learning environments. Understand that there are different forms of feedback, as well as different purposes, to why and how that feedback is being communicated.
2. *Get advice regarding proper feedback-seeking behavior*—Ask your faculty supervisor for advice about how to best request performance feedback from others onsite in a clear, professional, and concise manner. Social communication has been discussed in more than one way across the chapters of this book, and the need to understand the nuances of effective workplace communication is meaningful in conducting this activity.
3. *Self-reflect upon your communication style*—Part of preparing to ask for performance feedback is to personally assess how you communicate your feedback needs to others. Create a clear communication approach to optimize the feedback received.
4. *Practitice your interviewing skills*—You might assume that you know how to ask someone for performance feedback, but it is a skill that you might want to practice with another person (e.g. a peer and/or your faculty supervisor).
5. *Prepare ahead of time*—It helps to anticipate what might be areas for improvement in your onsite performance before you ask for feedback. Anticipating these topics can help you create a more effective and targeted exchange of ideas between you (i.e., feedback recipient) and the person providing the feedback (i.e., feedback informant).

What Do I Think About ... ?

1. Who is the best source(s) of performance feedback for me to ask onsite? Who should I ask first?
2. Although I think I am prepared to receive critical feedback, will I have an emotional reaction if I receive critical feedback about my onsite performance?
3. Is it possible to get too much performance feedback? Can I become cognitively overloaded?
4. How should I prioritize the performance feedback, especially if there is contradictory information, from my multiple feedback informants?
5. What should I do if I need to clarify the performance feedback received? How should I approach requesting follow-up feedback?

CHAPTER IX Seeking Performance Feedback: Utilize 360 Degree Feedback Opportunities | 149

Before proceeding, you should review what you have learned so far! In the following, there will be a review exercise related to the information you learned through the activities suggested in Phase I.

"Let's Review!" Phase I Learning

1. What have you learned about the different characteristics of performance feedback? How can this knowledge help you in interpreting the feedback you receive? _____
   _____

2. What is "360° feedback," and how does this concept specifically apply to your potential feedback sources onsite? _____
   _____

3. Based upon the suggested activities, what do you better understand about how to ask for feedback as an intern? _____
   _____

4. What is your specific plan for soliciting performance feedback onsite (e.g., the first person that you will ask for feedback)? _____
   _____

Phase II: Feedback Documentation and Information Synthesis (Content Analysis)

Before you begin to proactively collect performance feedback onsite, you should determine how you will best document the incoming performance feedback information. A documentation plan will help you accurately account for all feedback details, for both immediate performance improvement and for later performance follow-ups.

Let us go through some general ideas of what you should do in preparing for this step in the process:

1. Search online for tips in how to record performance feedback.
2. Meet with your site supervisor about the best opportunities to collect feedback onsite.
3. Practice recording details of a conversation to better understand your accuracy in recalling and writing down information. "Real world" practice feedback conversations would be the best preparation for your later feedback encounters onsite.
4. Take a listening recall test to assess your active listening skills. To be an effective active listener is a skill that many people would benefit from both in and outside the workplace.
5. Develop a plan for how to respond to your performance feedback once it is recorded. If you have a response plan in place, you may be better prepared to objectively respond to the feedback you receive. You will have a guide to follow in response to the performance feedback provided based upon possible anticipated feedback scenarios.
6. In addition to establishing a response plan, you should have a detailed plan regarding how to best utilize your performance feedback in both the short- and long-term for your professional development. This will help you process the feedback in a more meaningful, career-focused manner.

FROM A SITE SUPERVISOR'S DESK

Carrie Hewitt, Elmhurst College Master's in Industrial/Organizational Psychology Coordinator:

The only way we grow as human beings is to seek out feedback from others and respond to that feedback. Bill Gates has said, "We all need people who will give us feedback, that's how we will improve." Students are in a unique situation when completing an internship or applied experience. Just like in school or classes, that environment is constructed as a learning environment. Typically, the feedback given in this type of environment is structured as such. I encourage you, as students, to listen with "open ears and open minds" to those providing you feedback in an internship experience.

The challenge for the site supervisors and program directors is to constantly provide that feedback in a nurturing, engaging and frequent way. The challenge for you is to be constantly listening for that feedback. In many situations, I encourage students to actively seek out feedback. Asking questions and obtaining developmental feedback is critical. Using what you have heard, to better yourselves and better your skill sets, is essential. The challenge is to decipher what is beneficial and what is not. Part of what is helpful to interns is that the person giving you the feedback is not usually familiar with you. Receiving feedback from someone who one does not know you can be beneficial. They want to see you succeed. They want you to do better and know how to improve. So, what do you do with this feedback once you receive it? Act on it. Make yourself greater. Strive for excellence.

What Should I Do?
Putting Your Learning into Action

1. Create a feedback journal to track the information you received from different feedback sources onsite. Review the contents before each training session.
2. Conduct a content analysis of the performance feedback you are collecting and identify potential areas for performance improvement that you can work on in subsequent training sessions.
3. Once you identify potential areas of performance improvement, meet with your faculty supervisor to verify the accuracy of how you are analyzing and/or synthesizing the collected feedback.
4. Develop a timeline for feedback follow-up questions, if needed, with your site supervisor and/or onsite constituents (e.g., co-workers, supervisors, and/or subordinates).
5. Create a goal-based feedback schedule with multiple stakeholders in the coming weeks/months of your field training experience. It is important to check in with your different feedback informants over time to verify if you are meeting their expectations for your performance improvement.
6. Talk with a career counselor on campus about how you can utilize this learning experience to further enhance your résumé and/or professional training for your future employment.

Before proceeding, please review what you have learned in Phase II! The next section contains a series of review questions related to what you learned in doing the activities and exercises. To best help you with this ongoing learning process, please be accurate in your responses to assess what areas of learning may need further review.

CHAPTER IX Seeking Performance Feedback: Utilize 360 Degree Feedback Opportunities | 153

"Let's Review!" Phase II Learning

1. What did you learn about the concept of collecting 360° feedback? Do you think it is best to collect performance feedback from multiple feedback informants? Why, or why not?

   _____
   _____
   _____
   _____
   _____
   _____
   _____

2. What did you learn about soliciting performance feedback? Is this a challenging task to accomplish onsite? Why, or why not? _____

   _____
   _____
   _____
   _____
   _____
   _____
   _____

3. Based upon your learning onsite to date, what are your ideas regarding how to most effectively document your daily onsite performance? What strategies do you use? ____

   _____
   _____
   _____
   _____
   _____
   _____
   _____

4. Are you learning how to be a more effective feedback informant based upon your experiences as a feedback recipient? How so? _____

   _____
   _____
   _____
   _____
   _____
   _____
   _____

Phase III: Feedback Responses and Self-Regulatory Processes

The process of collecting and documenting performance feedback is a moot issue if you do not accurately synthesize the information provided and proactively adjust your onsite performance accordingly. Performance improvement is adaptive and reflects true self-learning as it evolves over time.

Self-regulatory learning entails the process of internalizing the feedback received and developing a standardized "anchor" performance baseline to evaluate and adjust as needed. Think about any new knowledge or skills you have learned over the years that was moderately to highly complex in nature—you need to engage in multiple trials/practice with corrective feedback before you can proceduralize the task performance and/or the learning of a concept.

Practice is vital to this process of self-regulation and learning. The following are some YouTube videos about new learning tasks—try one or two as a way to better understand your process of anchoring and adjusting your performance under new knowledge circumstances:

- Learn a magic coin trick:
  https://youtu.be/TX-RZhYmkyl
- Learn how to draw a human face:
  https://youtu.be/7kKJW8ZLcew
- Learn how to play a piano:
  https://youtu.be/3unOs7Oekjo

When thinking about self-regulatory learning in a new onsite learning situation, it is critical to acknowledge that you are learning many new pieces of incoming information (e.g., names of co-workers) and skills (e.g., completion of workplace paperwork) as an intern. You are experiencing the need to engage in adaptive learning on a frequent basis. Here is some advice regarding how to handle this new learning:

- Focus on the "here and now" in your onsite learning to best collect and synthesize your newly-acquired information.
- Be inquisitive, and ask questions. It is a consideration to not ask "too many questions," but it does create a good impression of your work-related consciousness with your onsite supervisors and/or co-workers if it is not done appropriately.
- Identify your predominant learning style (e.g., a visual learning style), and structure your learning process as best as possible to this learning style—it may not always be possible, but research strategies to optimize your learning style within the workplace.

In addition to being the recipient of new learning and feedback, you should be proactively seeking opportunities for new learning and feedback through your workplace communications and/or work-related interactions.

The following are a few suggestions for how to optimize your messages to others onsite:

- *Clear communication*—Speak clearly, and fully articulate your ideas to minimize any possible confusion or "barriers" in your workplace communication. The social exchange of information is a critical part of the feedback cycle, and you should not underestimate its impact on the outcomes of your field training.

- *Diversity sensitivity*—Realize that you are interacting with supervisors, coworkers, and other training-related individuals (e.g., customers) from diverse backgrounds with different approaches to thinking and/or communicating ideas.
- *Perspective taking*—As you interact with multiple groups or individuals onsite, remember to be open to their perspectives. As much as it is important for you to be cognizant of your learning goals, it is equally important to understand that other individuals have achievement-related goals to be accomplished.

Think About It!

Here are topics to consider as you think about the self-regulatory learning in response to performance feedback at your internship/field experience or service learning assignment:

1. What is a good strategy for responding to others' feedback? _____

2. What have I learned about my ability to respond to others' feedback in an effective manner? What should I still work on? _____

3. Am I good at understanding others' perspectives when discussing feedback? Why? ___

4. Is it easy to be in the "here and now" when engaged in a feedback session? _____

5. What did I learn about my self-regulation skills in adapting to performance feedback? __

Apply Your Knowledge!

The following are some suggested ideas for you to consider when researching concepts of feedback-related learning and performance adaptation:

1. *Talk to your professors*—Ask faculty that you are currently taking (or have previously taken) classes with to offer insights regarding their observations of your learning style and/or how well you respond to task-pecific feedback.
2. *Watch a training video*—Find and review either onsite or online training videos related to effective feedback response behavior in the workplace (e.g., how to conduct follow-up feedback situations to clarify performance-related information received).
3. *Review your journaling*—Your observations related to daily onsite learning should also give you personal insights about how you typically respond to feedback on an emotional, attitudinal, cognitive, and/or physical level.
4. *Record your onsite performance*—Sometimes it is hard to understand others' perspectives on what changes are needed to be made to improve your onsite performance. To better understand others' observations and to make the process more objective, try recording and/or videotaping your onsite task performance to review it later.
5. *Read work-related reference materials on performance feedback*—Take the time to read a book and/or some research articles related to performance feedback strategies. Reviewing such resource materials may help you better understand ways to improve your onsite activities in response to feedback. There are many documented approaches to acquiring and using others' input to optimize workplace performance.

Try It Out!
Adaptive Reasoning Exercise

Adaptive Reasoning Exercise Brief: This exercise involves your ability to engage an adaptive reasoning, which is predictive of both successful job performance and work-related resiliency, which are important as an intern in the workplace and as a professional across your career. For example, your role as an intern requires you to be faced with new situations and/or pass a daily basis. Your ability to engage in adaptive reasoning, based upon either information presented to you or information you sought, relates directly to your ability to do well in your field training experience. One way to assess this ability is through adaptive logic testing. Here is a link for an adaptive reasoning test to take:

https://www.assessmentday.co.uk/logic/free/logicalreasoningtest1

After taking the logical reasoning test, think about your ability to adapt to the details of the testing task and how this information reflects your ability to adapt to new information in more applied situations while training onsite and in other task-related contexts.

This exercise is limited to 15 minutes.

After completion of the Performance Memory Task Exercise, ask yourself the following:

1. What did you learn about your adaptive reasoning ability during the logical reasoning test?
2. Did you get better at the test as you proceeded from item to item? Why, or why not?
3. How can you generalize your performance on the adaptive reasoning test to your performance onsite as an intern?

CHAPTER IX Seeking Performance Feedback: Utilize 360 Degree Feedback Opportunities | 157

Search the Web!
Learn About Adaptive Onsite Performance

Search the Internet for different websites regarding how to be resilient and flexible in your training performance as an intern. Check out at least three different websites pertaining to adaptive workplace performance. As you review this information, please answer the following questions:

1. What are three areas of advice from online sources regarding how to be resilient in the workplace?
   a. _____
   b. _____
   c. _____

2. Is a person trainable in situational resiliency, or is it more of a personality characteristic?
   _____
   _____
   _____
   _____
   _____
   _____
   _____
   _____
   _____

3. If it possible to be "too adaptive" to a changing workplace? Why, or why not? _____
   _____
   _____
   _____
   _____
   _____
   _____
   _____
   _____
   _____
   _____

AN INTERN'S INSIGHTS

Laura Price: Internships are used to catapult individuals to higher levels of expertise. Internships are informative and used to captivate and assimilate the intentions of students. It is important to acknowledge and grasp the internship field experiences to enhance professionalism. It is also important to set goals of an internship according to the atmosphere. For instance, I completed an internship in a geriatric psychiatric unit. A goal of mine was to become familiar with the treatment plan team. I could become acquainted by shadowing social workers, doctors, psychiatrists, nursing staff and personal care technicians working in the unit.

What I learned from the experience is that each of the mentioned professionals are pertinent to the patient's treatment plan. The cohesiveness of the treatment plan team provides the patient with support and services for the best possible outcome to recovery and/or discharging. The field work experience allowed me to interact, connect, and observe the patients across all perspectives of the unit. The experience allowed me to have a voice to ask the appropriate questions which addressed the problems and concerns of mine and the patients. Without the field experience, I would not be able to become familiar with undisclosed information and listening to the stories of older individuals both fact and fantasy as well as joyous and despairing. Nevertheless, set goals accordingly, acquire the knowledge from the field experience and be conscientious in what is to come.

CHAPTER IX Seeking Performance Feedback: Utilize 360 Degree Feedback Opportunities | 159

"Let's Review!" Phase III Learning

1. What have you learned about your ability to adapt to situational feedback based upon the suggested activities in the chapter? _____
   _____
   _____
   _____
   _____
   _____

2. Do you think it may be challenging for some people to engage in "here and now" experiences within the workplace? Why, or why not? _____
   _____
   _____
   _____
   _____
   _____

3. As you have participated in an ongoing self-introspection of your onsite performance learning and behavior, what have you learned about your personal self-awareness in the workplace? Are you more insightful about your training performance needs? Yes, or no, and why. _____
   _____
   _____
   _____
   _____
   _____

4. Is it easy to respond to onsite performance feedback, or are there limitations to how well this can be done initially before you practice it? _____
   _____
   _____
   _____
   _____
   _____
   _____

Summary of the Chapter

This chapter examined the importance of engaging in an effective feedback "cycle" of receiving and responding to constructive information for improved onsite performance as an intern. Self-understanding of how you respond to performance feedback is critical to enhancing this adaptive learning process. Engaging in a responsive "anchoring and adjusting" technique is a skill to practice in many different learning situations, and it relates well to the broader aim of your ongoing professional development as an emerging professional in your field of study.

What Did I Learn?

Self-reflection is a vital part of your learning process throughout field training. Without looking back in the chapter, please list what you feel were the main three points of learning that were personally relevant to you regarding the focus of the chapter (please explain why each is personally relevant to your learning):

1. _____

2. _____

3. _____

Discussion Questions

1. Of the informational resources you reviewed on the topic of 360° feedback, which source was the most applicable to your circumstance as an intern onsite?
2. Self-learning is important to engage in at various stages in your internship training. What have you learned about yourself to date regarding your level of feedback responsiveness?
3. Why is it sometimes challenging to receive critical feedback?
4. In thinking about how you respond to onsite feedback, have you changed how you convey constructive performance feedback to others onsite?
5. When you solicited advice about how to respond to onsite performance feedback, who was the best source of guidance? Why?
6. You should be learning more about your job attitudes and work motivations through your ongoing journaling. What have you learned about your work-related attitudes towards performance feedback from different onsite sources?
7. Communication is critical to your learning progress in the workplace. How have you engaged in enhanced communication through the suggested activities in this chapter?
8. How do you avoid becoming potentially overwhelmed by the multi-source performance feedback you receive daily as an intern? What is a good strategy to employ?
9. How have you learned to become more adept at perspective-taking with others onsite? Why is this such a critical skill in many different social feedback contexts?
10. Through the activities and exercises presented in this chapter, you hopefully better understand your potential for resiliency in the workplace. What have you learned about yourself regarding this issue?

Additional Information Links

- Wikipedia website:
  https://en.wikipedia.org/wiki/360-degree_feedbacks
- thebalance website:
  https://www.thebalance.com/360-degree-feedback-information-1917537
- Forbes.com website:
  https://www.forbes.com/sites/forbeshumanresourcescouncil/2016/11/22/tips-and-tactics-for-a-successful-360-degree-feedback-program/#6246c02f3fd1
- DecisionWise website:
  https://www.decision-wise.com/10-tips-for-using-360-degree-feedback-for-performance-appraisal/
- Management Study Guide website:
  http://managementstudyguide.com/360-degree-feedback.htm
- Chron website:
  http://smallbusiness.chron.com/benefits-360-degree-feedback-1929.html
- DecisionWise website:
  https://www.decision-wise.com/benefits-of-360-degree-feedback/
- Explorance website:
  https://explorance.com/2013/07/5-employee-benefits-of-360-degree-feedback-2/

Fig. 10.1: Source: https://pixabay.com/en/brainstorming-business-colleagues-2398550

CHAPTER X

Receiving and Adjusting to Performance Feedback: Be Open to the Process

FIELD LEARNING FACTOID

"Effective and timely feedback is a critical component of a successful performance management program and should be used in conjunction with setting performance goals. If effective feedback is given to employees on their progress towards their goals, employee performance will improve. People need to know in a timely manner how they're doing, what's working, and what's not. Feedback can come from many different sources: managers and supervisors, measurement systems, peers, and customers just to name a few. However, feedback occurs, certain elements are needed to ensure its effectiveness."

Source: OPM.gov (https://www.opm.gov/policy-data-oversight/performance-management/performance-management-cycle/monitoring/feedback-is-critical-to-improving-performance/)

Introduction

In addition to being cognizant of how to best collect feedback from multiple sources it is equally critical to be "open" to the ongoing feedback-response cycle for true performance learning progress over time (Folkman, 2006; Race, 2007). Avoid perceiving constructive feedback, if given properly, as personal criticism, but perceive it rather as an opportunity for personal and professional growth (Garber, 2004; Seashore, Seashore, & Weinberg, 1997).

This is a potentially challenging process for many individuals, because most people like to think of themselves as being competent within a performance activity, especially in a chosen field of study, but feedback is vital for anyone's ongoing learning and personal development (McCallum, 2016; Seemiller, 2013).

You will always encounter activities in the workplace that you may not be familiar with (Kurtoğlu-Hooton, 2016), so it is a necessity to seek out corrective information from other people's perspectives to best achieve effective workplace performance (Bacal, 2004). With this in mind, you will encounter many different viewpoints on how a job should be accomplished. Perspective taking is critical during this process, allowing yourself to become "ego-free" during this performance evaluation process and seeing other people's viewpoints of how well you are accomplishing your onsite training-related activities (McKenzie, Burgess, & Mellis, 2017; Miles, 1958; Sutton, Douglas, & Hornsey, 2012).

When thinking about the feedback received, identify areas for self-reflection pertaining to how others in the workplace may have different standards of performance than you (Echterling, 2016). In addition to you adjusting your own motivation and performance output to others' criteria for effective workplace performance, you also need to examine your personal preconceptions about the level of effort and/or abilities you need to apply to accomplish your onsite tasks. You need to be self-aware of your internalized attitudes and how they may influence how well you receive feedback and/or accomplish workplace activities (Maurer, 1994).

Here is some advice regarding how to become more self-aware regarding this process (i.e., the six "E's" of performance awareness in your field training):

- *Engage* in "practice sessions" of focusing on one activity you are doing without being distracted—analyze how you are feeling physically, cognitively, socially, and emotionally.
- *Embrace* your intuitive and instinctual reactions to social situations, with an appropriate follow-up assessment of how these reactions affect your onsite performance proficiency.
- *Enlist* a supervisor or co-worker to describe his/her impressions of you in different areas of onsite performance—understand that you may not be as self-aware as you need to be regarding the impressions you make on others in the workplace.
- *Enroll* in a self-awareness training course to help you focus more on your emotional reactions to social situations. This training will help you not only in your career development, but also in broader social situations you encounter daily.
- *Employ* the advice from a career counselor and/or your faculty supervisor regarding strategies to improve your onsite role-related awareness.
- *Encounter* different task-related opportunities for your internship and make note of which activities you feel efficacious in (and do not).

164 | **In the Field** A Field Experience Manual for Internship and Service Learning Students

Learning Goals for this Chapter

Chapter X offers both informational resources and interactive exercises/activities to prepare you to:

→ Assess collected feedback to both acknowledge your onsite accomplishments to date and to identify areas for future improvement,

→ Develop a series of subgoals to address various aspects of performance feedback, and

→ Participate in task- and/or time-based follow-up assessments in response to feedback.

Before beginning to discuss very specific training issues related to your field experience, let us explore some foundational concepts for this chapter:

Look It Up!

Define and Understand Important Concepts

In conducting an internship/field experience or service learning placement in your chosen field, you should have a knowledge of specific learning concepts. Please consult the word glossary provided at the back of this manual, and look up the following terms discussed in the current chapter.

Goal-in-progress: _____
_____
_____
_____

Goal Attainment: _____
_____
_____
_____

Goal Plan Responsivity: _____
_____
_____
_____

Feedback Subgoal Planning: _____
_____
_____
_____

Performance Review: _____
_____
_____
_____

Goal Follow-up Assessment: _____
_____
_____
_____

Phase I: Assessment of Collected Performance Feedback

Before you accumulate many hours of onsite training, you should understand how you are learning and your performance to date for both current (i.e., goal-in-progress) and completed (i.e., goal-attainment) tasks in ongoing self-reflection (i.e., self-assessments) throughout your field training. Your journaling is an important tool for you to use in examining your training progress, but realize that there are multiple approaches to acquiring performance feedback beyond simply journaling.

Let us go through some general ideas of what you should do in preparing for this step in the process:

1. *Systematically review your journal entries*—If done properly, your self-reflective journaling can give you great insights regarding your learning progress over time, as well as potential areas for improvement. When comparing these self insights to other people's perspectives on your progress to date, you will have a better sense of both your personal self-awareness skills and also how you can further improve upon these details in your journal writing.

2. *Request a meeting to review your training performance to date with the site supervisor/manager*—Across the chapters of this book, there has been a consistent emphasis on the need for you to periodically "check in" with your onsite supervisor and/or other managerial constituents in the workplace. This checking in process is invaluable to you to make sure that you are on track with your goal accomplishments and that you are optimizing your training opportunities for career success.

3. *Meet with other interns onsite to compare performance progress to date and to discuss goals*—In addition to checking in with site-related supervisors, it is also beneficial to check in with other interns onsite, or in your academic program, to assess both shared experiences, but also to compare your accomplishments/progress to others in similar training situations.

Let us check in about your perceptions of the learning process at this point. The follow are some important questions to ask yourself when collecting performance feedback in your internship/field experience or service learning assignment:

What Do I Think About ... ?

1. Reviewing my journal entries, what personal insights will I learn about myself related to my degree of self-awareness as an intern trainee?
2. How will I alter my approach to completing my onsite work after I more objectively review my work to date?
3. Will these acquired insights about my onsite performance positively affect my academic work?
4. When soliciting 360° feedback, will my sources give generalized or task-specific feedback? Which would be more beneficial to me?
5. If I can watch a videotape of my onsite activities, how will this refine my self-perceptions of workplace learning?
6. Is it beneficial for me to identify "gaps" (i.e., missing information) in others' feedback?
7. As I collect performance feedback, what will I learn in terms of my "thinking about thinking" (metacognitive) strategies?

Before proceeding, you should review what you have learned so far! In the following, there will be a review exercise related to the information you learned through the activities suggested in Phase I.

"Let's Review!" Phase I Learning

1. After doing the suggested activities in this chapter, how has your ability to effectively collect performance-related feedback improved? _____
_____
_____
_____
_____
_____
_____

2. Regarding ongoing metacognitive skill development, how has this feedback solicitation process affected your subsequent onsite performance effort and/or performance strategies? _____
_____
_____
_____
_____
_____
_____

3. What was the easiest feedback to collect regarding your onsite performance? Most difficult? _____
_____
_____
_____
_____
_____

4. Do you think that your request for feedback has improved others' feedback approach to you? Why, or why not? _____
_____
_____
_____
_____
_____

Phase II: Performance Plan of Subgoals for Onsite Performance Improvement

Before you proceed further into your onsite activities, you should learn how "relevant others" perceive you in the workplace regarding your needed areas of performance improvement. It is critical to understand what you are doing well onsite and, subsequently, what you still need to improve upon in reflection upon the approved learning goals (goal plan responsivity).

Let us go through some general ideas of what you should do in preparing for this step:

1. *Review again your approved learning goals*—As emphasized in previous chapters, it is always important to refer back to your approved goals to make sure you are accomplishing what you need to accomplish.

2. *Identify discrepancies between your original learning goals and your current onsite performance outcomes*—The next step involves you identifying unfulfilled or partially accomplished learning goals, in addition to needed areas for improvement.

3. *Discuss these potential discrepancies with your faculty and site supervisors*—After you have identified these potential areas for improvement, it is recommended that you meet with your faculty and/or site supervisors.

4. *Develop performance subgoals and a timeline related to areas of needed improvement*—Draft an appropriate number of performance subgoals to address needed areas of further training or activity. Construct a timeline over the course of your field training to address the accomplishment of these performance subgoals to improve your onsite training performance.

FROM A SITE SUPERVISOR'S DESK

Dr. Shedeh Tavakoli, Counselor Education Program Coordinator, Northeastern Illinois University:

Prior to the start of your field experience/internship, identify your goals and expectations and communicate them to your supervisor. Concurrently, demonstrate a genuine interest in learning about your supervisor. For example, ask about their supervision style and expectations. A seasoned supervisor will provide a clear framework that depicts responsibly and expectations for both people. It is important to know your own style and articulate your expectations and uncertainties. To impress, supervisees avoid discussing their limitations, mistakes, and apprehensions. Masking your true emotions will hinder the supervisory working alliance as well as the therapeutic relationship with clients. Be aware of how you may be triggered by the feedback style of your supervisor and how your emotional response may affect the relationship. Take responsibility, own your emotions, and be open to examining the origin of your reactions.

A strong and healthy working alliance between the supervisor and supervisee is critical in finding a way to disentangle the triangulated dynamics between the supervisee, client, and supervisor. Maintain full self-awareness, listen to the feedback without feeling a need to defend yourself, and process the information before responding. Openness to feedback regarding potential countertransference that prevent therapeutic progress is critical to your professional development, and ultimately, the quality of the therapeutic relationship. Last, always remember to Q-TIP (Quit Taking It Personally), and MIC (Maintain Interpersonal Connection).

The creation of a performance subgoal plan allows you to focus on the process of your learning, in addition to the outcomes. This strategy is beneficial to you in your broader career development, because you are learning how to better accomplish goals applied to the many stages of your professional development over time. Here are some suggestions for applying your learning at this step in the planning process:

What Should I Do?
Putting Your Learning into Action

1. Research different work-related performance improvement plan approaches online.
2. Read books and/or articles on effective self-management techniques that you might be able to apply to your field-related training.
3. Seek advice from your faculty mentor and/or other supervisors related to your training plan.
4. Integrate the collected information from different research resources and others' advice into a draft personalized performance improvement plan.
5. Meet with a representative from your on-campus career development office and discuss your plan ideas.
6. Finalize the plan that best matches the goals and activities of your onsite training and do a one-week pilot test. Assess the effectiveness of the plan in helping you improve your performance.

Before proceeding, please review what you have learned in Phase II! The next section contains a series of review questions related to what you learned in doing the activities and exercises. To best help you with this ongoing learning process, please be accurate in your responses to assess what areas of learning may need further review.

"Let's Review!" Phase II Learning

1. What have you learned about constructing a personalized performance improvement plan that you did not know before you began your onsite hours? _____
   _____
   _____
   _____
   _____
   _____
   _____

2. Do you think an effective performance improvement plan can be developed by an intern prior to starting his/her onsite training? Why, or why not? _____
   _____
   _____
   _____
   _____
   _____
   _____

3. Is it possible to create a "cookie-cutter" performance improvement plan which would apply to multiple field training sites, or are they site-specific by nature? Explain your answer.
   _____
   _____
   _____
   _____
   _____
   _____

4. When giving advice to another intern about developing a performance improvement plan, what points would you convey? _____
   _____
   _____
   _____
   _____
   _____
   _____

Phase III: Periodic Follow-up Evaluations of Onsite Activities

As critical as initial performance feedback can be for you as an intern, it is equally important to solicit ongoing onsite evaluations. Receiving responsive performance feedback, or feedback in response to your performance changes over time, is a vital process to ensure that your onsite goal-related behavior is showing expected progress (e.g., feedback subgoal planning). The responsibility of engaging in ongoing and responsive feedback is both on the onsite supervisor and you, the intern. Be proactive, and seek feedback from your site supervisor, in addition to other feedback sources (e.g., co-workers, fellow interns), to ensure that your ongoing performance goals are being addressed (i.e., goal follow-up assessment).

Here are some points to consider when seeking out follow-up feedback for your onsite performance and broader professional development:

- *Be careful what you ask for*—If requesting ongoing performance feedback, especially in response to performance changes, do not argue against it, but rather accept the constructive feedback messages in an open and flexible manner.
- *Be a good listener*—It is easy to solicit feedback but then "tune out" the feedback when it is conveyed. Listen thoughtfully about what information is being said to you, and actively take notes, so you can later recall what was said.
- *Be a good assessor*—In addition to conscientiously recording the feedback provided by others, you need to make sure that you fully understand the information suggested to improve your onsite performance. You cannot accurately improve your onsite attitudes and/or behaviors unless you understand what is being asked of you.
- *Be specific in feedback clarifications*—Make sure that you are asking accurate questions to gain needed clarity in the details to be addressed for your performance improvement.

As you seek and acquire follow-up performance feedback onsite, you should be seeking a broader audience of potential feedback informants in the workplace. Here are some issues to consider when selecting amongst multiple sources of performance feedback information:

1. What is the area of expertise of this feedback informant, and how should this guide my interpretation of their feedback?
2. Should I consider the workplace motivation of the feedback informant? Why?
3. Is it good to be selective of which feedback to pay attention to? If so, how do I decide among different choices of feedback information?
4. What is the "timing" to ask for feedback? Should I ask for performance feedback based on a specific stage in the training process, or should it be time-based (e.g., every two weeks)?
5. Should I rotate my list of feedback informants to maintain their willingness to help give me ongoing feedback across the course of my field training?

In addition to seeking repeated feedback onsite, it is helpful to engage in ongoing online research to seek feedback from field-relevant expert sources (e.g., field-relevant professional society "chat" rooms). Here are some general online sources regarding professionalism advice that would be valuable to you as an intern:

- 10 tips for work professionalism:
  https://www.live-career.com/career-tips/career-advice/professionalism
- Work professionalism from a career search site:
  https://www.monster.ca/career advice/article/10-ways-to-be-professional-at-work-Canada
- Habits to be an emerging professional in the workplace:
  https://career services.Princeton.edu/undergraduate-students/launch-your-career/professional-development-tips

Think About It!

Here are topics to consider as you think about seeking ongoing feedback to enhance your onsite performance during your training at your field site assignment:

1. Is there a way to prioritize your incoming performance feedback to maximize its benefits and avoid any potential conflicting information? _____
_____
_____
_____
_____
_____

2. Should you seek general or task-specific performance feedback at various stages in your training process? How do you decide which level of feedback focus is appropriate for your career development needs? _____
_____
_____
_____
_____
_____

3. Feedback is a mutual social exchange of ideas. Is it important to give feedback to your feedback informants at any point in the communication process? Explain your answer.
_____
_____
_____
_____
_____

Apply Your Knowledge!

The following are some suggested ideas for you to consider when seeking ongoing task performance feedback as an intern-in-training. Be organized in approaching the feedback experience. Here are some ideas regarding how to best optimize your ongoing workplace performance feedback process:

1. Develop a set of task-specific questions ahead of time to "stay on task" for both you and your feedback informant.
2. Categorize performance feedback by specific learning goals or onsite tasks.
3. Create a "strengths" and "areas for improvement" table matrix in response to incoming feedback about your onsite performance to date.
4. Within the "areas for improvement" feedback section, record your personal insights about the steps to be undertaken in improving your performance in the workplace.
5. Develop a realistic timeline for follow-up feedback to occur after you feel you can make noticeable progress in your areas for improvement.
6. At the regularly-scheduled midterm (i.e., mid-point of the training hours) and final evaluation (i.e., at the end of your training hours) time periods, "frame" the feedback discussions based on your ongoing informal feedback meetings and associated subgoal accomplishments leading up to each of the formalized assessments.
7. Put the onsite performance feedback in context, linking it back to your broader career goals and what you see as being industry trends in employer preferences for new hires. The performance feedback that you receive as an intern should give you a good foundation to enhance your career preparation in your field/discipline.

Try It Out!
Openness to Experience Assessment Exercise

Openness to Experience Assessment Exercise Brief: In addition to the many qualities associated with being a productive and successful field trainee, it is helpful for you to have an "open mind" during your onsite learning process, as well as the combined academic-applied instructional experience. To better understand your degree of flexibility and openness to experiences, it would be appropriate to assess a personality trait from the "big five" personality characteristics that correspond to this attitudinal/behavioral attribute—the personality trait of "openness to experience" (OE trait). Here is a link to a short quiz related to this personality trait, in addition to the other four trait characteristics in the "big five" assessment:

https://www.123test.com/personality-test/

After you complete the personality test and see your test scores, especially your OE trait score, please reflect upon the degree to which you agree with the score and how relates to your performance as an intern and within other task-related performance situations. This exercise is limited to 15 minutes.

After completion of the Adaptive Learning Decision Exercise, ask yourself the following:

1. What did you learn about yourself through this assessment process?
2. Do you feel your resultant score is an accurate assessment of your onsite performance as an intern? Why, or why not?
3. If you were to develop your own "openness to experience" test related to interns' training behavior, what would you develop as part of the trait-related assessment?

When you think about receiving (and giving) onsite performance feedback, it is important to realize that there are multiple domains of performance that you should actively pursue for feedback purposes as they apply to your broader professional development outcomes in your career field.

Let us go through some general ideas of what you should consider (if applicable) related to your performance feedback areas of concentration:

1. *Interpersonal skills*—To be an effective professional, it is necessary to be able to "connect" with others in the workplace and outside the workplace for business purposes (e.g., finding new clients).
2. *Managerial decision-making capabilities*—Even though you may begin at an entry-level position, there is always the need to understand the core characteristics of what an effective managerial style is and how it relates to equally effective organizational decision making.
3. *Teamwork and cooperation*—Regardless of the size the company, you will always be engaged, to some degree, in teamwork and cooperative activities. Being a supportive team player in a work-related project is a key attribute for many job positions.
4. *Learning plasticity*—Many workplaces are constantly changing and introducing new knowledge to be learned. It behooves you to develop a flexible learning schema to absorb the many informational transitions and alterations you will encounter across your career trajectory.
5. *Communication skills*—To communicate well in the workplace is a necessary skill across different occupations and industries. Communication, both nonverbal and verbal, should focus on clear and effective exchanges of ideas and information that will benefit many different people onsite.
6. *Creativity and problem-solving*—Increasingly, employers are looking for employees who can effectively think outside the box and apply creativity and problem-solving capabilities to many different issues related to industry competitiveness and corporate innovation.
7. *Diversity sensitivity*—Regardless of your chosen occupation, you may be working in an increasingly diverse workplace (e.g., training/teaching students in a classroom). Understanding diverse cultures goes beyond acknowledging differences and entails an in-depth understanding of diverse groups and their associated cultural perspectives.
8. *Organizational skills*—Your need to be organized in the workplace cannot be understated. This is a skill to develop within your industry and your occupation to optimize your time- and task-related effort allocations.
9. *Technological innovation*—Last, but certainly not least, is the need for you to engage in the utilization of technology in whatever occupation and industry you are working in. Almost all industries and occupations are impacted by technological innovations and will continue to be for decades to come.

Search the Web!
Learn About Performance Feedback Utilization

Search the Internet for different websites regarding how to best utilize performance feedback to enhance your professional development. Check out at least three different websites pertaining to workplace training and associated feedback within your area of study. As you review this information, please answer the following questions:

1. What free online resources were most helpful for you regarding how to best utilize onsite performance feedback?

   a. _____
   b. _____
   c. _____

2. Do you feel that most performance feedback is generalizable across fields, or are there field-specific areas of advice that you have encountered through your research? _____
   _____
   _____
   _____
   _____
   _____
   _____
   _____

3. Based on what you have learned for your online research, what advice would you give another intern about how to best prepare for adapting to ongoing performance feedback?
   _____
   _____
   _____
   _____
   _____
   _____
   _____

AN INTERN'S INSIGHTS

Danka Lazarevic: The best way to learn and grow through the training process requires from interns to have and improve or develop some characteristics, such as attentiveness, trustworthiness, flexibility, organization, responsibility, persistence, and confidence.

Attention is the key for successful communication by which interns can have more targeted questions and responses. Trustworthiness is also one of the fundamental characteristics that permeates all process from all possible angles; therefore, being trustworthy opens and gives many opportunities. Being flexible improves cooperation among colleagues. Thus, interns can receive others' suggestions and opinions and adjust themselves based on supervisors or employees' opinions. As a result, the intern becomes more adequate and more desirable in many different situations. Basically, the interns are more accepted if they show higher level of flexibility. Being a flexible intern also enhances flexibility from supervisors' and employees' sides and, therefore, cooperation becomes more stable and performance becomes more creative.

Being responsible and persistent intern enhances productivity. Thus, having a certain goal, the intern should undertake responsibility and be persistent to accomplish the certain goal. Also, all work should be organized and accomplished in a clear manner. As a result, throughout the training process, organization significantly helps to accomplish the goals on easier way.

Overall, each characteristic complements each other and functions together. Good luck!

Let us review what you have learned so far from Phase III! On the next page, there is a series of review questions related to what you learned in reviewing the information and doing the exercises. To best help you with this ongoing learning process, please be accurate in your responses to assess what areas of learning still need a further review.

"Let's Review!" Phase III Learning

1. What are various sources of ongoing work performance feedback that you can plan for ahead of time? Why is this anticipatory planning approach important? _____
_____
_____
_____
_____
_____

2. We tend to think of performance feedback as being a strictly observable, behavioral phenomenon. Is this completely true? Why, or why not? _____
_____
_____
_____
_____
_____

3. Which feedback performance domains do you think would be the most applicable to your career training specialization? Why? _____
_____
_____
_____
_____
_____

4. What are three factors to consider in selecting someone to provide you with ongoing performance feedback? _____
_____
_____
_____
_____
_____

Summary of the Chapter

This chapter reflected upon many different issues underlying the need to engage in ongoing performance feedback during your field training experience. Not only how to proactively respond to onsite feedback, but how to do it in a systematic and effective manner, is emphasized throughout the chapter. The OE trait is key to develop throughout your professional training and has implications towards your receptivity to constructive criticism from others in the workplace. The broader generalizable lesson is how you can be a lifelong learner in many different learning and performance contexts.

What Did I Learn?

Self-reflection is a vital part of your learning process throughout the field experience process. Without looking back in the chapter, please list what you feel were the main three points of learning that were personally relevant to you regarding the focus of the chapter (please explain why each is personally relevant to your learning):

1. _____
   _____
   _____

2. _____
   _____
   _____

3. _____
   _____
   _____

Discussion Questions

1. What is the main benefit of learning how to ask for workplace feedback? Is it easy to do?
2. What are some social role factors (e.g., gender) that you feel may impact the process of feedback-seeking behavior? Why?
3. How has technology usage impacted workers' strategies in seeking performance feedback?
4. Effective communication is an important factor underlying the process of sharing performance feedback between individuals in the workplace. What communication approach do you feel is best when sharing performance-related feedback in the workplace?
5. Is nonverbal communication equally or more important than verbal communication when sharing performance feedback? Why, or why not?
6. What did you learn about ways to avoid being overwhelmed by multiple sources of feedback during your field training?
7. Feedback is a two-way street. What does this mean according to what you have learned about approaching a feedback situation in the workplace?
8. How has your approach to soliciting performance feedback in the workplace become more effective over time? Conversely, what do you still need to work on?
9. Some performance feedback may be judged to be less of a priority than other feedback received at the same time. How do you prioritize your multiple sources of feedback?
10. As you gain experience in receiving feedback from multiple sources, you may have noted which approaches to feedback communication work better than others. What do you feel is the best feedback approach to help an intern in their learning outcomes when onsite? Please explain your answer.

Additional Information Links

- themuse website:
  https://www.themuse.com/advice/taking-constructive-criticism-like-a-champ
- Psychology Today website:
  https://www.psychologytoday.com/blog/happiness-in-world/201002/how-give-and-receive-feedback
- Buffer website:
  https://open.buffer.com/how-to-give-receive-feedback-work/
- BusinessPerformance website:
  http://www.businessperform.com/workplace-communication/constructive_feedback.html
- Psychology Today website:
  https://www.psychologytoday.com/articles/201103/how-take-feedback
- WikiHow website (video):
  http://www.wikihow.com/Accept-Criticism-While-at-Work
- Everyday Health website:
  http://www.everydayhealth.com/emotional-health/value-of-constructive-criticism.aspx
- WikiHow website:
  http://www.wikihow.com/Accept-Feedback-or-Corrective-Action-at-Work

SECTION 3

Identifying Learning Outcomes and Concluding the Site Experience

Fig. 11.1: Source: https://pixabay.com/chalkboard-classroom-teacher-female-1280967/.

CHAPTER XI

Analyzing the Results of Your Site-Related Learning

FIELD LEARNING FACTOID

"Working in an office environment (or any kind of professional setting) can be difficult to get used to—and the best (perhaps only) way to learn how to navigate the working world is through real life, hands-on experience. After your internship, you should have a better idea of the appropriate way to behave as a professional and a sense of how to play the game of office politics. 'For many students, an internship is their first exposure to a professional work setting,' says Strausser. 'Often students comment about how much they appreciated the opportunity observe workplace culture and see how professionals interact with one another and conduct themselves.'"

Source: Business Insider (http://www.businessinsider.com/what-you-can-learn-from-your-summer-internship-2015-8)

Introduction

To understand how much you have learned over time in your field-related training, it is important to revisit the original learning goals you set forth in your approved learning plan (Hatcher, Bringle, & Hahn, 2016; Newman, 2013a, 2013b). Analyzing what you have accomplished through your training is key to assessing both your effectiveness as a learner and the site's effectiveness in accomplishing its training initiatives on your behalf (Newman, 2013; Payne, 2000; Russell-Chapin & Ivey, 2004). You will attain both "hard" (i.e., specific knowledge and skills) and "soft" (i.e., the ability to effectively work with people in the organization at all levels—"people skills") skills during your training. This training perspective relates to a "micro-level" analysis of performance effectiveness within the specific site environment (e.g., collaborative team performance). It is equally important to acknowledge that your learning has implications toward the "macro-level" analysis of organizations regarding how to create a more well-trained workforce within your specific field.

Advice has been given in previous chapters related to keeping on track, but it is still a necessary meta-cognitive process to compare your original aims to your culminating field training outcomes at the end of the training time to best reflect upon your personal learning skills and areas for improvement in an ongoing manner (Azevedo & Aleven, 2013; Martin, Wright, & Danzig, 2013). The experience will also help you create instructional strategies you may use as a practitioner in your own field (Heider, 2017; Nadel, Majewski, & Sullivan-Cosetti, 2007).

Reiterative learning assessments are pervasive in many aspects of your daily activities but are particularly relevant to the workplace, as incentives are typically tied to such goal-oriented behaviors (Eyler & Giles, 1999; Gordon, 2001). Being mindful of your field training aims daily during your onsite hours is critical in maintaining continuity between the beginning and completion of your field activities, optimizing your effectiveness in community-based service (Bringle, Reeb, Brown, & Ruiz, 2016; Ferrari & Chapman, 1999).

Learning Goals for this Chapter

Chapter XI offers both informational resources and exercises/activities to prepare you to:

→ Systematically review the original learning goals you and your supervisors agreed upon and reflect upon them at the end of your experience (e.g., did you complete all your goals),

→ Analyze the content of your many hours of journaling to identify learning "themes," and

→ Compare your original goals for intended onsite learning to your journaled learning outcomes to assess the correspondence to the two foci with the intention of making a plan to explain why there might be discrepancies from a learning goal-oriented perspective.

Look It Up!

Define and Understand Important Concepts

In conducting an internship/field experience or service learning placement in your chosen field, you should have a knowledge of specific learning concepts. Please consult the word glossary provided at the back of this manual, and look up the following terms discussed in the chapter.

Learning Analysis: _____
_____
_____
_____
_____
_____

Goal Review: _____
_____
_____
_____
_____
_____

Learning Achievement: _____
_____
_____
_____
_____
_____

Goal-to-Outcome Discrepancy: _____
_____
_____
_____
_____
_____

Goal-Oriented Perspective: _____
_____
_____
_____
_____

Lift Goal: _____
_____
_____
_____
_____
_____

Phase I: Reflection Upon Original Learning Goals

Before you complete your field training, you should understand how well you have succeeded in addressing original, approved learning goals to your onsite activities (learning analysis). Here are some suggestions in how to be more mindful of your intended learning goals as you engage in onsite activities as an intern:

- If possible, focus on one task at a time.
- Be methodical and self-aware in conducting each onsite activity.
- Engage in active listening when interacting with others in the workplace.
- Pay attention to the reactions of others and be receptive to their social feedback.
- Be conscientious in your communications with different people onsite.
- Understand that intended goals and performance outcomes may not correspond for several reasons, either due to personal and/or site-related factors that may dynamically interact together.
- Proactively, conduct an ongoing goal review of intended learning outcomes and associated learning achievement.

Let us go through some general ideas of what you should do in preparing for this step:

1. Revisit your originally approved learning goals for both your onsite and academic training.
2. Review the original theoretical research that was the basis for your learning contract.
3. Research concepts related to performance goals and the assessment of your learning outcomes.
4. Meet with your faculty supervisor to discuss anticipated and unanticipated outcomes from your proposed academic goals.
5. Meet with your onsite supervisor to also discuss anticipated and unanticipated outcomes from your onsite activities and associated proposed learning aims.

The following are some important questions to ask yourself when preparing to analyze your results and learning outcomes from your onsite training:

What Do I Think About ... ?

1. Will I find that some of my intended learning outcomes changed over time as I trained in the workplace?
2. Should I consider ways to fulfill unaddressed learning goals or explain why some goals were ultimately not achievable?
3. In what ways did I learn more, and possibly more significant, workplace performance attitudes and performance lessons than I originally planned?
4. Which area of my learning goals was the most directly addressed during my onsite training? Least addressed?
5. In reflection, was there a better way for me to keep track of my goal accomplishments from the beginning of my field training?
6. In thinking about my learning processes over time, who should I have consulted with more about my learning goals?
7. If I could go back in time, would I have approached my onsite training experience differently? Why, or why not?
8. How could I use technology to keep better track of my ongoing learning?

"Let's Review!" Phase I Learning

1. What did you learn, in general, about your time management skills in accomplishing your onsite learning goals? _____
_____
_____
_____

2. Based on your review of learning to date, what change in goalsetting behavior might you adopt in future goal-related activities? Why? _____
_____
_____
_____

3. Were you realistic about the breadth and depth of your learning that you were able to accomplish onsite? Explain. _____
_____
_____
_____

4. Self-reflections on learning can help you become a more effective learner. What did you learn about yourself as a learner through this self-reflection process? _____
_____
_____
_____
_____

Phase II: Identification of Final Learning Outcomes

Before you begin to write up your final learning outcomes, you should learn how to summarize the outcomes from this ongoing review of your many documented hours onsite.

Let us go through some general ideas of what you should do in preparing for this step:

1. *Review the content of your onsite journaling*—You have been reviewing the content of your journaling for a number of weeks for the purpose of understanding what you have accomplished and what you still need to accomplish. You should begin to examine your overall learning trends related to your self-observations.

2. *Gather additional learning documentation*—In reflection upon what you see as your learning outcomes through journal writing, it might be beneficial for you to cross-reference your ideas with other documentation of your learning progress over time (e.g., mid-term evaluation from your site supervisor).

3. *Ask for feedback from coworkers/peers onsite to gain further perspectives on your learning outcomes and accomplishments in the workplace*—As with any phase in this training experience, it behooves you to check in with your coworkers and/or intern peers about their oobservations of your performance.

4. *Meet with your faculty supervisor to discuss how to synthesize multiple sources' feedback about your learning outcomes*—In gathering all of the different performance-related information, talk to your faculty supervisor about how to synthesize this multi-source feedback into a cohesive "picture" of your ongoing learning outcomes.

FROM A SITE SUPERVISOR'S DESK

Dr. Tim Andriano, Social Service Program Coordinator at Wilbur Wright College:

I am sure you are looking forward to finding a job and starting your professional career. This is a good time to reflect on your internship and to think strategically about the kind of job you would like and the type of setting in which you would like to work. Thinking strategically will help you focus your job search. You may find the following questions helpful:

- What size of agency would prefer to start your career, small, medium or large?
- Is there a particular sector you are interested in (e.g., non-profit or corporate)?
- Are you interested in working in a particular administrative support area such as finance, human resources, marketing, development, community relations, facilities, IT?

You will need to market yourself to employers. You can network by joining professional associations and advocacy associations, attending job clubs, job fairs, and conferences. Networking means putting yourself forward, in an assertive but non-aggressive way, making your skills known and getting the word out that you would make a great employee.

Lastly, do not overlook the importance of soft skills. According to Job Outlook 2016, from the National Association of Colleges and Employers (NACE), 201 NACE members listed the top "soft skill" attributes they seek on a candidate's résumé. These soft skill attributes are, in order of importance: leadership, ability to work in a team, written and verbal communication skills, strong work ethic and initiative. Congratulations on completing your career training!

What Should I Do?
Putting Your Learning into Action

1. Construct a "discrepancy" goal matrix that lists each original learning goal and the associated areas of performance learning documentation (e.g., midterm evaluation feedback).

2. Beyond the original journaling of learning outcomes, extend this writing to self-reflect upon the underlying learning processes (e.g., proceduralization of skills and "scaffolding" of learning) undertaken to accomplish your onsite learning outcomes.

3. Link your self-reflections regarding the learning process to available literature on cognitive skill functioning to gain further self-insights (e.g., conducting a cognitive protocol analysis).

4. Examine how your learning onsite transitioned from new learning to more proceduralized (i.e., automatic, unconscious) knowledge and/or behavior over time as a field trainee.

5. Discuss with faculty members in your program how you can improve upon your goal-oriented learning strategies to optimize your broader professional career development.

6. Meet with the career professional to discuss your developing knowledge and skill sets as they relate to your career viability within your chosen field/discipline.

7. Examine your existing résumé, and think about ways to integrate what you are working on onsite, as the learning outcomes can be translated into statements on this important career documentation.

Before proceeding, please review what you have learned in Phase II! The next section contains a series of review questions related to what you learned in doing the activities and exercises. To best help you with this ongoing learning process, please be accurate in your responses to assess what areas of learning may need further review.

"Let's Review!" Phase II Learning

1. What did you learn about your effectiveness in completing your onsite learning goals? Academic goals? _____
   _____
   _____
   _____
   _____
   _____
   _____
   _____

2. Based upon review of your original learning goals, do you feel you are becoming more conscious of your learning engagement activities in general through this review process? _____
   _____
   _____
   _____
   _____
   _____
   _____
   _____

3. Was it easy to find documentation to support your learning outcomes? Were some learning goals harder to document than others? Why? _____
   _____
   _____
   _____
   _____
   _____
   _____

4. What learning area appeared to be the most discrepant from your original learning goals? Least discrepant? _____
   _____
   _____
   _____
   _____
   _____
   _____
   _____

Phase III: Explain Learning from a Goal-Oriented Perspective

At this stage of your learning goals outcome analysis, it is your task to assess discrepancies between the two sources of information (i.e., goal-to-outcome discrepancy). Discrepancies between what was planned to be learned and what you learned should not be a negative, but rather should be understood from a goal-oriented perspective. You should analyze how accurate or realistic your learning goals were to proactively adjust your next learning goals, as well as to better understand your personal learning needs, which may have affected the degree to which your learning goals were satisfied. Realize that your learning goals will shift in focus as you and your situation change dynamically over time. Changes within you reflect your accumulation of new knowledge, skills, and abilities (KSAs) from your training and professional development process.

Organizations within your field, as well as beyond your field, utilize goal-orientation strategies in the following ways, which apply either directly or indirectly to your onsite training experiences. On a macro level, effective organizations adopt a goal-oriented focus in their work-related tasks:

- Personnel decision-making (i.e., employee benefits, hiring, training, promotion, and/or reduction in force) to establish and/or maintain a qualified employee resource pool
- Anticipatory strategic planning (e.g., anticipated consumer trends and associated adaptive shifts in customer service/policies) to ensure industry competitiveness among other companies in the same field/discipline
- Responsive management coaching (e.g., identification of effective employee motivators) to achieve optimal employee performance
- Societal/civic engagement (e.g., community outreach with volunteer organizations) to meaningfully contribute to societal needs and to reinforce the organization's core values and policies within its mission

Through this process of internalizing the goal-oriented learning strategies, you can become a more effective professional within your field. Learning to become more strategic and goal-focused professional will help you both in your daily activities onsite but also in your broader career planning trajectory as you proceed from one stage of your career to the next.

For each of us, it is good to engage in ongoing strategies to become more goal-oriented in our daily activities. Here are some attributes of a "goal-oriented person" in the workplace (or other achievement-related context) that you can adopt:

1. Be passionate about your goals, because you must identify them with what you are doing.
2. Acknowledge that goals are learning opportunities, regardless of whether you fail to achieve the goal the first time and must adjust your approach accordingly.
3. Understand that goal commitment, and associated task-related persistence, is key to being successful in the long-term.
4. Realize that not all goals are easily resolvable and do take time.
5. Plan your task-oriented goals in a realistic manner, taking context-dependent factors into consideration as you conceptualize both the process and the associated intended outcomes.
6. Identify timeline constraints in the accomplishment of your short-and long-term goals.
7. Be willing to fail, because failures can teach you lessons in goal setting, which may translate into later long-term success in your career and beyond.

Think About It!

Here are topics to consider as you think about the potential differences between what learning goals you originally set and your resultant learning through your internship/field experience or service learning assignment:

1. Self-reflecting on your learning was an ongoing process throughout the training experience. Did this practice help you keep on track onsite? Why, or why not? _____
   _____
   _____
   _____
   _____
   _____
   _____
   _____

2. Across the many hours of training, you have acquired new knowledge, skills, attitudes, and/or values related to your industry. Which was the most meaningful change for you? ___
   _____
   _____
   _____
   _____
   _____
   _____
   _____

3. Between your initial goals and the analysis of your learning outcomes, which area of training performance exceeded your expectations? Why? _____
   _____
   _____
   _____
   _____
   _____
   _____

4. Will you approach goal-oriented strategic planning in a different manner based upon your training experience? How? _____
   _____
   _____
   _____
   _____
   _____
   _____

Apply Your Knowledge!

The following are some suggested ideas for you to consider when engaging in broader career development goal planning. What you have learned as an intern should offer you a good foundation for a successful launch into your career, but there are always ongoing personal and professional goals to plan for across your lifespan. Here is some advice regarding topics of goal planning in your ongoing career development process:

1. *Be self-aware*—Know your values, beliefs, and motivations. Having a core sense of self will assist you in navigating your professional development path and lead you to the best options for your career success.
2. *Trust yourself*—Be confident you can achieve your career goals in the face of potential obstacles or thresholds to overcome.
3. *Make contacts*—Learn from and communicate with others about your performance goals and your related mentoring/coaching needs. Utilize the social network you develop over time to assist you at every stage in your career.
4. *Anticipate change*—Be resilient and flexible in both your solo and group work, acknowledging that there will always be the unanticipated situations to respond to.
5. *"Own" the Outcomes*—Adopt the attitude that both your failures and accomplishments are due to you and your abilities. Ultimately, this perspective will help you understand the need for ongoing training and professional development over time.

Try It Out!
Cognitive Protocol Task Analysis Exercise

Cognitive Protocol Task Analysis Exercise Brief: When you are learning to do a task for the first time, you should focus on the step-by-step process. With that in mind, it is good to practice being fully self-aware of your performance in a task as you proceeded at each step. One helpful exercise is to vocalize your performance as you do the task, creating a cognitive linkage between your mental and physical performance, which relates well to how you are thinking about your onsite performance in journaling your self-observations. For this exercise, choose a small task that you do daily (e.g., preparing dinner), and describe aloud the steps as you conduct them. As you verbalize the steps, think about the reasoning behind your actions, and analyze the motivations behind the actions taken.

After completing the short task, think about what you learned about your self-awareness and the unconscious processes underlying your behaviors and attitudes while conducting the task. This exercise is limited to 15 minutes.

After completion of the Cognitive Protocol Task Analysis Exercise, ask yourself the following:

1. What did you learn about your "mindfulness" in completing daily activities?
2. Was it difficult to verbally describe each step in the task chose for the exercise? If yes, why do you think this is true?
3. Did conducting this exercise help you better think about how to journal your onsite task self-reflections? How could you utilize this cognitive strategy in your general training? Career?

One type of goal setting that is important to consider for your professional development, as well as personal development, is referred to as a lift goal. Think about ways to apply what you have learned as strategies you can use to improve your life circumstance. Applied to the workplace, a site-related lift goal could be interpreted as a strategy for you to focus on a specific knowledge, skill, and/or ability to improve your mental health, physical health, or overall well-being on the job.

1. *Avoid destractions while working*—Constantly checking e-mails and/or overwhelming multitasking behaviors can be disruptive work habits. Focus on what you need to do to improve your work-related environment.
2. *Adopt productive "life hacks"*—Find productive shortcuts to streamline your daily activities without sacrificing quality (e.g., outsource small non-work tasks).
3. *Give yourself a short- and long-term "to do" list*—Be planful, and anticipate future goals, in addition to working current goals being accomplished.
4. *Prioritize tasks*—Choose career and/or work-related activities that are meaningful and significant to you on a value-based level.
5. *Remember to schedule "self-time"*—You can only focus on your goals and performance if you feel mentally and physically healthy. Check in with yourself periodically to assess your health needs and take the time to eat, exercise, and/or socialize to optimize your health status.
6. *Enjoy what you do*—You can better experience long-term personal growth if you are happy with what you do in the workplace and in life. Your self-concept should be congruent with the values and beliefs expressed in your job activities.
7. *Visualize your goal accomplishments*—Part of the goal setting process is being able to actually see that you can accomplish what you want. Visualize, or create a mental picture of that personal goal accomplishment in action. Dedicate some time to picturing the goals you wish to accomplish and, further, create a mental picture of you completing the goal.
8. *Identify your extrinsic and intrinsic work motivators*—Understand what motivates you in your career, both from the "internal" (e.g., self-esteem) and "external" motivating factors that may guide you in your career trajectory as you progress from being an emerging professional graduating soon from your program to your future career stages.
9. *Acknowledge and accept the "unknown"*—Lastly, understand that you will not be able to control everything or know everything that is related to your career at each stage in your professional development. Be open to the unknown, and appreciate the learning experience that you engage in as you navigate your career exploration.

Search the Web!
Learn About Strategic Goal Planning

Search the Internet for different websites regarding strategic goal planning. Check out at least three different websites pertaining to planning professional development goals within your area of study. As you review this information, please answer the following questions:

1. What are three different online resources you identified that were helpful for your career goal planning?

    a. _____

    b. _____

    c. _____

2. You have reviewed a variety of suggestions regarding onsite learning goal considerations. What information was new that you encountered through the online information? _____
_____
_____
_____
_____
_____
_____
_____
_____
_____

3. With metacognitive skills, you engage in the process of "thinking about thinking." How does this concept apply to your career goal planning as an intern and as an emerging professional? _____
_____
_____
_____
_____
_____
_____
_____
_____
_____
_____

There is much to consider as you evaluate your ongoing professional development goals. As an emerging workforce participant, be aware that you and your professional goals will evolve over time. Embrace this exciting period in your training, and acknowledge that the future will offer exciting opportunities for career growth. Your culminating field trainng experience serves as a wonderful foundation for this ongoing learning that you will engage in throughout your professional life.

AN INTERN'S INSIGHTS

Juana Vallejo: One of the most important skills and advice I can give future interns is to have good time management. Being able to manage other classes while working full-time and completing two internships was not easy for me. However, due to my time management skills I could manage all my responsibilities. Having a planner to write down deadlines served as a tool in accomplishing and planning how to complete both short-term and long-term goals.

Another advice I can give interns is to apply their listening and communication skills. Being able to listen to the needs of the organization interning for as well as what professors expect from you can improve your chances of accomplishing tasks. Moreover, being able to communicate with professors and supervisors on tasks that need to be completed can help prevent miscommunication. In addition, learning about diversity and applying our knowledge of it with the people we are working with can prevent misinterpretations from occurring due to cultural differences. The people in the organization I worked for were very diverse, therefore, during my free time, I would research diverse cultures and learn simple things such as whether giving a handshake was allowed in their culture.

Lastly, as college students we are always learning, therefore, being open to feedback is essential in completing internship goals. Applying the feedback received is a learning experience that improves not only our academic knowledge but also allows interns to provide better services for the people that the organization serves.

"Let's Review!" Phase III Learning

1. What do you understand to be a "goal oriented perspective," and how does it apply to your learning in your field training experience? _____
   _____
   _____
   _____
   _____
   _____

2. How could you apply strategic goal planning to your broader academic training? Future career plans? _____
   _____
   _____
   _____
   _____
   _____
   _____

3. How is a standard goal different than a lift goal? How are they similar? _____
   _____
   _____
   _____
   _____
   _____

4. Did conducting the cognitive protocol analysis exercise make you more aware of your goal-related task performance onsite? Why, or why not? _____
   _____
   _____
   _____
   _____
   _____
   _____

Summary of the Chapter

This chapter reviewed information related to you analyzing the outcomes of your onsite learning in comparison to your original learning goals. You were guided through the process of both identifying any discrepancies between your intended and actual onsite learning. Adopting a goal-oriented perspective in your onsite activities can help you develop more effective short- and long-term plans for your career and broader personal development. This cognitive-behavioral approach to learning can be generalized to your intentions toward self-improvement across many different performance and personal domains.

What Did I Learn?

Self-reflection is a vital part of your learning process throughout the field experience. Without looking back in the chapter, please list what you feel were the main three points of learning that were personally relevant to you regarding the focus of the chapter (please explain why each is personally relevant to your learning):

1. _____
   _____
   _____

2. _____
   _____
   _____

3. _____
   _____
   _____

Discussion Questions

1. What did you learn about your onsite goal accomplishments that has implications towards your general strategic planning behavior across different contexts (e.g., academic goals)?
2. Do you have a unique perspective about evaluating your learning goals based on the chapter's information? Why, or why not?
3. Did you forget some of your original learning goals over time when onsite? If so, why do you think this happens?
4. What is a good strategy to help you stay more focused on your learning goals in different performance sites based on what you have learned in this chapter?
5. How is effective communication a key aspect of your goal accomplishments while onsite in your field training? Off-site?
6. What are some attributes that you have learned about that relate to successful goal-oriented behaviors?
7. What metacognitive skills have you learned about related to your goal-related site activities? Career goal planning?
8. Some online sources suggest that it is good "to fail" related to your learning goals. Why is this a good suggestion pertaining to your professional career training as an intern?
9. The cognitive protocol analysis task approach can help you improve your information processing awareness during the task performance. How can this assist you in your training-related goal planning? Performance assessment?
10. Do you have specific lift goals related to your emerging career in your specific field/discipline? Give two examples.

Additional Information Links

- The Glossary of Education Reform website:
  http://edglossary.org/student-outcomes/
- MindTools website:
  https://www.mindtools.com/pages/article/kirkpatrick.htm
- MacQuarie University website:
  https://staff.mq.edu.au/teaching/evaluation/resources_evaluation/developing_unit/assess_achievement
- Industry Week website:
  http://www.industryweek.com/education-training/how-improve-your-training-outcomes
- Cornell University's Center for Teaching Excellence website:
  https://www.cte.cornell.edu/teaching-ideas/assessing-student-learning/measuring-student-learning.html
- Faculty Focus website:
  https://www.facultyfocus.com/articles/educational-assessment/student-internships-an-effective-assessment-model/
- Indiana University Bloomington's School of Informatics and Computing website:
  https://www.soic.indiana.edu/career/students/capstone-learning-outcomes.html
- University of Florida's Applied Physiology and Kinesiology website:
  http://apk.hhp.ufl.edu/index.php/academic-resources/undergraduate-programs/intern-information/apk-internship-policies-and-procedures-manual/introduction-e/

Fig. 12.1: Source: https://pixabay.com/entrepreneur-startup-start-up-man-593

CHAPTER XII

Writing the Results of Your Site-Related Learning

FIELD LEARNING FACTOID

"The 'macro' question that you are answering in this paper is "SO WHAT?" So, what that you did this internship? Whom does it affect? How might it be useful? How did your experience connect to your academic work? How did you grow intellectually and/or personally? Remember that since your internship was a highly individual experience, your paper will also be unique, addressing those specific topics and questions that concerned you. This is an important means For you and your instructor to evaluate and learn from your experience. Therefore, please include (1) a brief description of what you did daily, and (2) then demonstrate your analytical ability in your reflection on your experiences. Your journal is a useful place to recover insights, connections, changes, small incidents that highlight larger issues, and common threads. Rely on your journal for a sense of perspective on the internship; the more complete a journal you kept, the easier this paper should be to write."

Source: Swarthmore College (http://www.swarthmore.edu/arts-social-change/guidelines-internship-reflection-paper)

Introduction

You are at the phase in your field training when you are beginning to write the results of your onsite learning, and this is a critical step in your professional development (Cohen, 2014). Your outcomes should be regarded as meaningful contributions to the community (Parsons, 1996; Rhoads & Howard, 1998; Sachs & Clark, 2016). You may be surprised how much you have learned in many different areas of performance and knowledge on the job, from a better understanding of professional standards within your field of study to how to conduct onsite activities and complete a work shift (Kirby & Lawson, 2012; Kiser, 2000).

In addition to improvements in your onsite performance capabilities, you may find that you will exit from this field training with meaningful insights regarding your proficiency in working with others, personal beliefs of achievement, and your learning capability/motivation in social situations (Adler-Kassner, Crooks, Watters, American Association for Higher Education, & National Council of Teachers of English, 1997).

The content analysis process involved in reviewing your journaling is qualitative in approach and will reinforce the learning you have assessed to date (Ellis & Bochner, 1996; Emerson, Fretz, & Shaw, 1995; Wolcott, 2009). The practice of writing "in context" will assist you in further developing your contextual learning self-reflections and your associated writing strategies (Kostouli, 2005; Stevens & Cooper, 2009). As with most steps in this learning experience, it is important to engage in self-reflection as you examine all acquired KSAOs:

- Knowledge (K)—What did I gain in field related knowledge through my training?
- Skills (S)—What skills did I learn onsite through my field training?
- Abilities (A)—Which abilities improve through my onsite activities?
- Other (O)—What intangible, "other" learning did I experience that improved my performance (e.g., change in my work-related self-concept)?

You can apply Bloom's taxonomy to think about your onsite cognitive development, among other outcomes, as you begin the process of writing about your learning outcomes:

- *Knowledge*—knowledge of workplace practices, policies, and procedural details
- *Comprehension*—understanding the "who, what, why, when, and where" of the workplace
- *Application*—ability to apply what you know and understand to different situations and tasks
- *Analysis*—ability to review your activities in an objective, methodical manner for later evaluation
- *Evaluation*—assessing and making decisions based on your systematic review of the accumulated observations of your learning
- *Synthesis*—finally, based on the self-evaluations, creating conclusions and associated responses to learning outcomes to plan for future goals

Learning Goals for this Chapter

Chapter XII offers both informational resources and interactive exercises/activities to prepare you to:

→ Identify learning "themes" in your content analysis review of your journaling,
→ Develop a thematic structure to results with supporting, specific self observations of site-related experiences under each identifying learning theme, and
→ Brainstorm ideas of how your onsite learning contributes to your broader professional development.

Before beginning to discuss very specific training issues related to your field experience, let us explore some foundational concepts for this chapter:

Look It Up!

Define and Understand Important Concepts

In conducting an internship/field experience or service learning placement in your chosen field, you should have knowledge of specific learning concepts. Please consult the word glossary provided at the back of this manual, and look up the following terms discussed in the current chapter.

Learning Theme: _____
_____

Thematic Structure: _____
_____

Self Observation: _____
_____

Supporting Incident: _____
_____

Academic Training: _____
_____

Professional Development: _____
_____

Phase I: Learning "Theme" Identification Through Your Journal Review

Before you write up the results of your field training, you should understand that your outcomes relate to one *learning theme* or more across onsite and/or academic task accomplishments during your training hours. The shift in your analyses is from focusing on the completion of goal-related tasks to a more conceptual perspective in your learning accomplishments within and across training activities for both the workplace and in the classroom related to your field training experience.

The process of doing this qualitative content analysis does require some background knowledge on your part related to the methodology underlying this thematic analysis procedure.

Let us go through some general ideas of what you should do in preparing for this step in the process:

1. *Do your research*—Read a book(s) and/or scholarly articles regarding the process of conducting qualitative content analysis. There are many different approaches to conducting a content analysis, ranging from the "micro-level" analysis of frequency of words ideas to the more "macro-level" analysis of patterns of thought across areas of content in your journaling. The advantage of doing this process is that you're learning a new area of research analysis, in addition to better understanding the learning outcomes from your field training.

2. *Solicit an independent reviewer*—Make a second copy of your journaling, have an independent (i.e., unaware) reviewer examine sample contents of your journaling, and compare their own ideas regarding outcomes to your ideas. This process of having an independent person evaluate how you are conducting your thematic analysis is invaluable, prompting you to think more objectively about the analysis process and identified outcomes.

3. *Use thematic analysis software*—Utilize a thematic analysis software program to identify repeated words and/or phrases in your journal notes. This is a good "double check" to see if you and your independent reviewer are identifying the same patterns of words, phrases, and broader themes. The software program (e.g., Nudist) can, in effect, be the "third reviewer" in your qualitative content analysis process and may be a systematic way for you to glean supporting evidence of what you learned.

4. *Develop a matrix table*—Construct a matrix table presenting identified learning themes (first column), and then select supporting journal behavioral supporting incidents that exemplify these learning outcomes (second column). You have used this approach before in comparing goals and other content-related analyses of different steps in your field training process across chapters in this manual. This is a good strategy for organizing your thoughts regarding how you will ultimately write your final paper and/or other culminating project reflecting both your broad ideas of learning themes and specific behavioral and/or attitudinal examples to illiustrate your learning from your field training experiences.

5. *Compare notes*—Brainstorm your initial findings regarding your emergent learning themes with a group of peer interns in your academic program and/or onsite to see if they have similar ideas about their own learning. It is beneficial to check in with others who are doing very similar experiences to what you are doing to verify your assumptions of behavioral and/or attudinal training outcomes from others' perspectives.

Let us check in about your perceptions of the learning process at this point. The following are some important questions to ask yourself when preparing for your impending internship/field experience or service learning assignment:

What Do I Think About ... ?

1. Will I identify the same or similar learning-related themes as other independent reviewers and/or intern peers in a review of my journal content?
2. Do I share similar learning experiences onsite to other peer interns in my academic training program? Like other interns onsite?
3. Is it an easier process to identify and discuss task-related learning than broader learning themes when analyzing the results of my field training?
4. Are my subjective perceptions of personal learning outcomes potentially biased, and what might be the reason(s) if this is true?
5. "Writer's block" is an issue in most people's writing experiences over time. Will it be easier for me to write this type of paper in comparison to a more traditional research paper? Why, or why not?
6. If I use a content analysis software program, will it be a good assessment of my learning themes? Are there limitations to using this type of software in the analysis of journal content?
7. Will I recall more episodic information related to my onsite learning as I review my journal entries? Why might this happen?
8. What did I learn about myself through this introspective analysis of my journal content?

Before proceeding, you should review what you have learned so far! In the following, there will be a review exercise related to the information you learned through the activities suggested in Phase I.

"Let's Review!" Phase I Learning

1. What are important steps to follow when conducting a thematic analysis of written content? _____

2. Who or what is the best source of guidance in conducting qualitative analysis? Is it beneficial to have more than one source of information to follow? _____

3. What have you learned about yourself as an "objective" observer of your training outcomes? Are there areas for improvement in how you judge your own learning outcomes in comparison to others' perspectives toward what you learned? _____

4. What did you learn about your own metacognitive capabilities as you analyzed your thought processes through your journal entries? Give two examples. _____

Phase II: Thematic Structure with Supporting Site-related Experiences

Before you begin constructing the results section of your final paper and/or other final culminating work, you should learn how to create a meaningful thematic structure and associated transitions in thought ("flow") as you continue to document your learning outcomes. Let us go through some general ideas of what you should do in preparing for this step in the process:

1. Consult a qualitative research publication guide regarding how to effectively present thematic concepts in the results section of a paper or other publication/format (e.g., PowerPoint presentation).
2. As you did earlier in this process of working on your initial literature review, please meet with an on campus writing tutor to discuss ways to effectively and clearly present your written ideas regarding your resultant learning themes.
3. Using the matrix table you previously constructed, rank order the learning themes you identified according to their relative importance to your learning progress over time.
4. In addition to relative significance, also judge each identified learning theme's prioritization as it relates to the procedural sequencing of experiences during your training.
5. In addition to the above considerations, also think about starting with the learning theme that is associated with the most linkages to onsite learning incidents and so on, creating a thematic sequencing based upon this evidence-based criteria.
6. Develop an outline of your ranked themes across the different priortization approaches, and think about ways to construct transitional linkages between your learning themes, as they form a larger picture of your overall training experience.

FROM A SITE SUPERVISOR'S DESK

Dr. Selina Mushi, Northeastern Illinois University Coordinator of the Early Childhood Program:

Work closely with your supervisor. Your supervisor is an important link connecting key facets of your successful internship. Your supervisor has had similar internship experience, wants you to succeed, understands both your program of study and the field experience setting; knows what constitutes success throughout the internship period, and is aware of the unspoken rules of functioning successfully in a new evaluative situation. Verbal and written comments from your supervisor should always be taken as constructive feedback.

Internship is real-life work in a practical situation. The tasks assigned to you, such as teaching a lesson, working with a client, rescuing a survivor, attending a patient, counseling a family, interviewing research subjects, designing an experiment, etc., is real work to be done as would be done by a seasoned professional—it is not just for your practice! This means that theories, principles, or any guidelines you may have learned in class will be necessary background knowledge to help you execute the task at hand as expected. The background knowledge should be coupled with sound judgment that takes into consideration the sudden fire alarm in the building, the unexpected snow storm, the disruptive client/student/participant, your supervisor's unexpected visit, and even your alarm clock that malfunctioned the morning you needed to be very punctual. Enjoy the experience—this is your time to shine!

What Should I Do?
Putting Your Learning into Action

1. Develop an outline of the learning themes you have identified to date. Show your draft outline of learning themes to your faculty supervisor for editing feedback. They might also have suggestions for additional resources for this step in the writing process.

2. Schedule a meeting with the on-campus writing tutor to continue the previous discussion of writing a well-structured qualitative paper (or other culminating work) based upon your developed outline.

3. Discuss your outline ideas with a group of classmates who are also working on their culminating paper/project for their field training.

4. Identify any gaps in your supporting information from your journaling, and discuss ideas for filling in this missing information, as well as your onsite learning progress, with your site supervisor.

5. Talk to a reference librarian about ways to start the process of developing search terms from the outline you have created to help collect more research for your final paper/project. Schedule more than one meeting regarding the next library research steps for writing your final paper/culminating project.

Before proceeding, please review what you have learned in Phase II! The next section contains a series of review questions related to what you learned in doing the activities and exercises. To best help you with this ongoing learning process, please be accurate in your responses to assess what areas of learning may need further review.

"Let's Review!" Phase II Learning

1. What organizational approach worked best for you to prioritize your learning themes? Worked least well? _____
   _____
   _____
   _____
   _____
   _____
   _____

2. Did this process of reviewing the underlying meaning of the broad concepts related to your onsite learning help you think about associated research ideas for your final paper/culminating project? _____
   _____
   _____
   _____
   _____
   _____
   _____

3. In reviewing your journal content, did you find good examples of anectdotal information underlying your learning themes? How did you address any gaps in supporting evidence? _____
   _____
   _____
   _____
   _____
   _____

4. Do you feel that creating the outline and investigating ways to organize your learning themes in a meaningful manner will help you in your later writing for your paper and/or culminating project? Please explain. _____
   _____
   _____
   _____
   _____
   _____
   _____

Think About It!

Here are topics to consider as you identify areas for additional training needed to enhance your career viability and better prepare you for your entrance into the workforce as you complete your internship/field experience or service learning assignment:

1. Who would be a useful resource to assist you in better understanding trends and industry standards that you need to anticipate? Why? _____
   _____
   _____
   _____
   _____

2. Research how rapidly your specific industry changes in terms of training needs. What did you discover? Did your findings surprise you? _____
   _____
   _____
   _____
   _____
   _____

3. Regardless of how rapidly career updating may be characteristic of your specific field or discipline, do you think that that there are new areas of knowledge, skills, and abilities emerging which relate to your training needs, in general? Please explain. _____
   _____
   _____
   _____
   _____

Phase III: Onsite Learning Outcomes' Implications for Professional Development

In addition to identifying gaps between your initial learning goals and your resultant learning, you can also do a self observation analysis of what you see as the implications of your onsite training accomplishments for your long-term professional development based on a review of each collected experience (i.e., supporting incident). You might see areas of further training needs in both the classroom (i.e., academic training) and in the field as you compare your current knowledge, skills, and abilities (KSAs) to industry professional standards.

Preparing to find the entry-level job position to launch your career will benefit from these insights, because you will be able to anticipate your career viability and associated training needs (i.e., professional development). Here are some suggested activities:

- *Create a matrix table of acquired versus needed KSAs*—This is a draft document that you can show and discuss with both your supervisors at the end of your training.

- *Identify supplemental training resources*—As you identify needed training areas with your supervisors, it would be beneficial to also discuss available training resources to address your immediate training needs, in addition to possible long-term career training to supplement your professional development.

- *Interview an human resources (HR) manager*—In addition to consulting with your supervisors, schedule an appointment with an HR manager for the company for which you would like to be hired, or at least within your industry, and ask about supplemental training ideas to increase your career viability in the industry or discipline.

Apply Your Knowledge!

The following are some suggested ideas for you to consider when researching the projected training needs and career trends in your chosen field of professional training. These are attributes of effective career professionals across fields and industries:

1. *Be tech savvy*—Have the capability to work with different technology platforms and workplace software systems, as well as "virtual team" environments.
2. *Be culturally competent*—Be aware of demographic trends in the population and your specific industry/discipline. It is important to understand how population shifts in race, ethnicity, gender, and/or age can affect the workplace.
3. *Adapt and adopt to new situations*—Be flexible in diverse social situations. This relates to how easily you can "think outside the box" and adapt to what is needed for problem-solving and/or communication processes within social contexts.
4. *Communicate interdisciplinary thinking*—In addition to being flexible and adaptive, you can express insights as they apply to the workplace.
5. *Learn social intelligence*—Develop the skill to identify and effectively process social environment "cue" information to optimize your working and/or customer service performance can be trainable. Being adept in this skill will assist you in your career.
6. *Embrace data analysis*—Learn to collect and analyze industry-related data in an efficient and accurate manner. Be up-to-date in terms of data analysis trends within your industry/discipline to be "in demand" in your field.

Try It Out!
Social Media Posting Exercise

Social Media Posting Exercise Brief: Impression management is an important activity to engage in as you begin your career in your chosen field/discipline. Part of the impression you present to future employers relates to your social media presence. Think about your own history of social media postings and the elements of effective, career-oriented social media posting tasks. As part of this learning process, this exercise involves two different activities:

1. Review the content, if applicable, of your personal social media postings to date (e.g., Facebook postings) and judge how career relevant the content of your postings is to your career aspirations and how career-appropriate the social media posts are if reviewed by a potential future employer. This exercise is limited to 10 minutes.

2. Review a sample of LinkedIn profiles of peers and/or professionals in your area of study. Analyze the degree to which the content reflects career-relevant and career-appropriate messaging. This exercise is limited to 10 minutes.

The entire exercise is limited to 20 minutes.
After completion of the Social Media Posting Exercise, ask yourself the following:

1. What did you learn about a career appropriateness of your social media postings to date? What would you change about your future postings?

2. Based on this information, how does it compare to your sampling of peers' and/or professionals' social media postings in your field/discipline?

As you contemplate this next step in the process, even before you graduate, it is important for you to think about how to best communicate your training and consequence to a prospective employer for your post-graduation career. Impression management has been a concept you have encountered before in previous stages of this training process, and it equally applies here at this stage in your professional development.

Let us go through some general ideas of what you should do in preparing for this step in the process:

1. *Revisit your résumé*—Update the information on your résumé to reflect your latest career training accomplishments. Also, state your expanding career focus that reflects the breadth and depth of your recent onsite training experiences. Be sure to list job references who can speak to your current skill and knowledge training accomplishments. Remember to have a section detailing your field training and other career-relevant volunteer work. Lastly, make sure to mention your long-term career goals and aspirations.

2. *Conduct "mock" interviews*—Practice your verbal and nonverbal skills in "mock" interviews with your faculty supervisor and/or other peer interns. It helps you to prepare for possible interview questions, as well as the process steps in a typical job interview. Everything from the greeting/handshake to your closing remarks as you exit the interview are important to rehearse and refine.

3. *Write an effective cover letter*—"First impressions" are important to optmize in any social situation, and the cover letter is a form of a job-related social encounter. Be clear and concise in your written communication, using only formal and professional language (e.g., industry-appropriate jargon).

4. *Practice your e-mail correspondence*—Just as you need to express clear and concise language in your cover letter, you need to apply the same expectations of professionalism in your e-mail correspondence with prospective employers. Do not use texting-related abbreviations or other non-work stylistic communication approaches that would not correspond to the workplace expectations of prospective employers in your field.

5. *Post on career-related social media*—Social media is a reflection of its users, and impression management is equally, if not more so, applied here. It is important for you to evaluate the nature of your social media presence and edit your profile to present yourself as the emerging career professional you wish to be known as in your field. Evaluate both the imagery and words in your social media presence, and compartmentalize your social media usage to optimize your career-seeking efforts (e.g., use LinkedIn).

6. *Train on business etiquette*—Across career-related social situations, it behooves you to sign up for a workshop or engage in more extended training related to business etiquette. Business etiquette relates to all aspects of interacting with different constituents in the workplace and should not be taken lightly, because it can be a key part of your success and promotion within your chosen field (e.g., interacting with diverse clients/customers in a growing global economy).

Search the Web!
Learn About Creating an Effective Online Career Profile

Search the Internet for different websites regarding how to develop and maintain an effective online career profile. Check out at least three different websites pertaining to online career profiles within your area of study. As you review this information, please answer the following questions:

1. What were three helpful websites related to how (or why) to do targeted career postings using social media sources?

   a. _____
   b. _____
   c. _____

2. As much as you should understand *what to post* to help promote yourself in your emerging career, you should also be cognizant of what would not be "career relevant" to post? Is that difficult criteria to determine within your field/discipline? Why, or why not? _____
   _____
   _____
   _____
   _____
   _____
   _____
   _____

3. Can social media be a powerful tool for you in your job/career search? Please explain.
   _____
   _____
   _____
   _____
   _____
   _____
   _____
   _____

There is much to consider as you think about ways to effectively communicate your learning and accomplishments in an industry-appropriate and professional manner to future employers. Remember that impression management is important to reflect upon at many stages of your professional development. Discuss with your supervisors their experiences and advice regarding this critical factor related to your career training.

AN INTERN'S INSIGHTS

Siddharth Arya: Once you join the internship prove that you are a "team worker" intern and humbly develop a rapport with the team members. They will support you that will have a significant impact on your time spent interning. Show that you are committed to your work by coming on time and may be staying over time. Take internship seriously as it may promote you with an opportunity to be observed for a job in later stage. Socialization is most important during the internship training. It may help you to explore the expertness of others to broaden your scope. Never get disheartened by the initial feelings that you know nothing while undergoing internship. Making mistakes along the way do seem embarrassing as they may be, but they are also invaluable lessons. Learn from your mistakes. Do clarify questions with your supervisors.

It is important for you to dress, speak, write, and generally behave like a professional and show confidence. Focus on your communication skills, both written and verbal. When communicating with your co-workers, choose respectful, tactful, and professional language always. Internship training is like learning to drive. Remain in touch with the basic books of the subject you are internee of. Here are some more tips you should remember at the end of your internship. Always ask the contact number from the staff you think you might need for any later help and thank all staff for their time and for their help given to you. Do not dismiss feedback given by your supervisor. It will give you professional insights into yourself!

"Let's Review!" Phase III Learning

1. What did you learn about identifying your training needs? Will this be useful to you across your long-term career? _____
   _____
   _____
   _____
   _____

2. What is an effective approach to identifying your future career training needs? _____
   _____
   _____
   _____
   _____

3. How rapidly can a person become "obsolete" (i.e., not qualified to do the job) in your field? Why does it happen, and how can it be avoided? _____
   _____
   _____
   _____
   _____

4. How does impression management become a critical issue when you are beginning your job/career search process? Please explain. _____
   _____
   _____
   _____
   _____

Summary of the Chapter

This chapter reviewed information regarding how to identify learning themes from your journaling efforts over the time of your internship. You were guided in the process of conducting qualitative content analyses of your derived learning outcomes from your journaling. From those insights, you were shown how to document these themes by citing specific learning experiences exemplifying each of these learning outcomes. Finally, you were instructed in how to apply these learning insights to your broader career preparation steps. Understanding your career achievements helps you communicate your qualifications to future employers in a targeted and succinct manner.

What Did I Learn?

Self-reflection is a vital part of your learning process throughout the field experience. Without looking back in the chapter, please list what you feel were the main three points of learning that were personally relevant to you regarding the focus of the chapter (please explain why each is personally relevant to your learning):

1. _____
   _____
   _____

2. _____
   _____
   _____

3. _____
   _____
   _____

Discussion Questions

1. How does Bloom's Taxonomy apply in the analysis of your site-related learning outcomes?
2. What did you learn about the steps to conducting a content analysis of your learning outcomes?
3. Reflecting on your metacognitive skills, how have you improved in your analysis of your ongoing learning processes?
4. What are the learning "themes" you have identified through your journal analyses? Have your ideas developed over time? Why?
5. What did you learn about your personal learning style and/or capabilities as you reflected upon your training outcomes?
6. In reviewing your journaled observations, what onsite performance area(s) were indicated as needing further training development?
7. Communication is key to the process of becoming a professional. How has your writing style adapted over time during your field training to better communicate your personal career accomplishments and/or training needs?
8. What did you learn about how to best engage in impression management in this stage of your career preparation?
9. Who is the most useful mentoring resource for you at this step in your training? Why?
10. What advice would you offer someone who is approaching this same stage in his/her career development? Be detailed in your explanation.

Additional Information Links

- Carnegie Melon University website:
  http://www.cmu.edu/teaching/assessment/howto/basics/objectives.html
- Reference website:
  https://www.reference.com/education/write-observation-report-224afd3657c1aff4
- Brigham Young University's Dietetics website:
  https://dietetics.byu.edu/Dietetic Internship(DI)/InternLearningOutcomes

Fig. 13.1: Source: https://pixabay.com/african-descent-business-cheerful-247

CHAPTER XIII

Presenting the Results of Your Site-Related Learning

FIELD LEARNING FACTOID

"This is a tip from Guy Kawasaki of Apple. He suggests that slideshows should: (1) Contain no more than 10 slides; (2) Last no more than 20 minutes; and (3) Use a font size of no less than 30 point. This last is particularly important as it stops you trying to put too much information on any one slide. This whole approach avoids the dreaded 'Death by PowerPoint.' As a general rule, slides should be the sideshow to you, the presenter. A good set of slides should be no use without the presenter, and they should definitely contain less, rather than more, information, expressed simply. If you need to provide more information, create a bespoke handout and give it out after your presentation.

Source: Skills You Need (https://www.skillsyouneed.com/present/presentation-tips.html)

Introduction

As you have reviewed the meaning of your learning outcomes from the steps in the previous chapters, it is now time to create an overall "picture" of your learning and examine the broader implications toward your field preparation as an emerging professional (Bingham & Jeary, 2007; Malloch, Cairns, Evans, & O'Connor, 2010). This process of taking an overall assessment of the cumulative training results is a workplace skill itself, allowing you to see a more macro perspective of your learning achievements (Grand, 2000; Pincus, 2015).

When assessing what worked and what did not work as planned, you will need to assess both yourself and the training site—analyzing the "fit" correspondence between your training motivation and the resources provided onsite (Spikes, 1995; Swanson & Holton, 1999). If you recall, this issue of fit was first discussed regarding the need for you to carefully choose the training site that corresponded well to your training needs and/or career trajectory interests (Ichniowski, 2000). Presently, you are assessing how well this training site choice worked out for the completion of your field experience and what you understand to inform your future selection of training and/or career site opportunities (Prestoungrange, 1998; Wallwork, 2014).

In the most generalized perspective, you might judge the implications of this learning experience as it relates to your overall career plans or potential change to a different field. This self-evaluation of your ongoing career interests or aspirations is critical to engage in *before* you graduate and as you prepare to launch into your professional career (Melograno, 1998).

In addition to culminating your learning evaluation, you are also learning a whole new set of skills related to creating effective presentations about your learning outcomes, ranging from PowerPoint to multicultural communication (Atkinson, 2005; Kenton & Valentine, 1997; Kikoski & Kikoski, 1999). The learning of effective presentation skills will extend into your professional development over the course of your career (Jalongo & Machado, 2016; Manchester Open Learning, 1993; Morton, 2014).

Here are some suggestions regarding how to evaluate the outcomes of your field training. Ask yourself the following questions in reflection upon your culminating experience:

- Have you changed your long-term career goals? Short-term career goals?
- How do you view your professional field differently after your training? The same?
- If you could go back in time, would you approach the training experience differently?
- How has your approach to working with others in the workplace changed?
- What do you better understand about factors underlying personal work motivation from your training experience? What surprised you?
- What was the most significant, and unanticipated, learning about yourself during training?

Learning Goals for this Chapter

Chapter XIII offers both informational resources and interactive exercises/activities to prepare you to:

→ Review your initial theoretical literature review from your proposal, and compare it to the content of the results (i.e., learning "themes") to begin structuring the discussion section of your final paper/other culminating project;

→ Identify gaps in the theoretical explanation of your learning, and collect additional research sources (e.g., peer-reviewed, scholarly articles) to expand your discussion; and

→ Create a template of written and visual information to best convey your learning outcomes in light of available state-of-the-art field sources in a logical sequence according to field-appropriate presentation standards (e.g., American Psychological Association).

Before beginning to discuss very specific training issues related to your field experience, let us explore some foundational concepts for this chapter:

Look It Up!

Define and Understand Important Concepts

In conducting an internship/field experience or service learning placement in your chosen field, you should have a knowledge of specific learning concepts. Please consult the word glossary provided at the back of this manual, and look up the following terms discussed in the current chapter.

Theoretical Foundation: _____
_____
_____

Content Analysis: _____
_____
_____

Presentation Style: _____
_____
_____

Field-Relevant Standards: _____
_____
_____

Applied Learning Analysis: _____
_____
_____

Applied Discussion: _____
_____
_____

Phase I: Comparison of Initial Literature Review to Resultant Learning Themes

Before you begin to write your discussion and/or make associations between theories/concepts in your learning outcomes, it is important to develop a strong theoretical foundation for your paper or other culminating presentation. You will review the content of your journalled learning (i.e., content analysis) to guide you in this process. You should understand how to begin the process of analyzing the correspondence between your original research focus and what actually transpired as your learning evolved over the time of your field training (i.e., applied learning analysis).

Let us go through some general ideas of what you should do in preparing for this step in the process:

1. Review the content of your initial literature review you that you wrote several weeks ago.
2. Develop an outline of your learning outcomes related to the analysis of your themes, which has been ongoing for the past several weeks.
3. Schedule a meeting with an on-campus reference librarian to both revisit your colleted research to date on field relevant topics and to collect more recent research published since your last literature review.
4. Taking the concepts from this earlier theoretical examination of field-related concepts, do an initial comparison of these ideas and the outline you have developed already of your resultant learning.
5. Identify any new research "trends" reflecting topics related to your field training focus. You will utilize these new ideas to apply to the discussion of the results of your learning in your final paper/culminating final project.

Let us check in about your perceptions of the learning process at this point. The following are some important questions to ask yourself when preparing to present the results of your learning in the field training experience:

What Do I Think About ... ?

1. Have my learning outcomes, based on my original literature review, changed the focus of my subsequent conceptual analyses?
2. Are there unanticipated areas of learning that I will need to explain with additional theories and/or concepts?
3. Is my original theory or concept now limited in its coverage of what I subsequently learned during my field training?
4. How will I integrate information from multiple theories/concepts to explain my culminating field-related learning?
5. How have my library skills developed over time since I began this writing process across various stages of my field training?
6. What is the best approach to identifying gaps in theoretical/conceptual coverage in the explanation of my resultant training outcomes?
7. To date, what new insights do I have about myself as an emerging professional in the field?
8. Do I approach writing papers/culminating projects differently than I did before I began this learning experience? If so, how so?

"Let's Review!" Phase I Learning

1. What would you change about your initial literature review if you could go back in time and redo it? _____
_____
_____
_____

2. You recently began the process of revisiting your literature review. What do you see differently in the literature review process now that you may not have perceived when you wrote your learning plan? _____
_____
_____
_____

3. How have your self observation skills improved after viewing your learning gains during your training? _____
_____
_____
_____

4. What did you learn about yourself that was not expected through this self-evaluation process? Why? How does it relate to your broader professional development? _____
_____
_____
_____

Phase II: Starting to Conduct Research in Writing a Discussion Section

Before you begin the process of writing the discussion section of your final paper/other culminating work regarding your learning outcomes, you should learn how to integrate an expanded literature review into the discussion of what you have learned over time during the several weeks of your field training (i.e., applied discussion).

Let us go through some general ideas of what you should do in preparing for this step in the process:

1. Meet with a writing tutor about writing a discussion section for your final paper or project. As you did with the beginning literature review that you wrote several weeks ago, you should think about how you will both construct the structure of your discussion based upon your developing ideas and create appropriate transitions as you move from topic to topic within this section of your culminating final paper and/or project.
2. Develop a linkage chart of learning outcomes with associated theories/concepts to further investigate in your ongoing research.
3. Utilize the concepts identified as the basis for your research steps using field-appropriate search databases (e.g., PSYCInfo search database).
4. Set up an appointment with a Reference Librarian to continue your literature review search.
5. Develop a list of supporting theories/concepts to further explain the outcomes of your learning. Examine theories and concepts both within and outside your field/discipline to create a more expansive, interdisciplinary explanation of your learning processes over time.
6. Begin drafting your discussion with an expanded outline that presents the ordering of topics and sequencing of new theoretical content in response to new ideas about your learning.

FROM A SITE SUPERVISOR'S DESK

Dr. John Holton, Concordia University Chicago, Visiting Associate Professor of Gerontology and Director of the Center for Gerontology:

From my perspective as a former state director for the Illinois Department on Aging and currently a visiting professor of Gerontology and Director of the Center for Gerontology at Concordia University Chicago, I cannot stress enough the added value for employment for those students who successfully complete an internship during their academic careers. As much as professors labor to simulate challenging assignments for gerontology students in courses spanning the biologic, sociological, psychological, and life course developmental aspects of aging, the real-world experience contains invaluable information.

If becoming an administrator is your career objective, then, gain some experience in an administrator's office. You will learn about strategic planning, budgets, human resources, including the hiring and termination of employees, brokering relationships with the community, and most of all, what it takes to help those in care and/or in need of care at a facility, or in her/his residence. Most of all, you will make important contacts and resources with professionals in field during your internship. We succeed ultimately in the professional world based on the strength of our networks. Our networks are formed from relationships we establish during employment stints. Start building your network as soon as you are able, beginning with your instructors and continuing with professionals in a field placed internship.

What Should I Do?
Putting Your Learning into Action

1. Go online and review helpful websites regarding the process of analyzing learning outcomes for internships. Look for advice regarding writing effective learning-related discussions across different formats (e.g., PowerPoint presentation).

2. Review a book(s) or other training materials regarding effective writing techniques in your field of study (e.g., the American Psychological Association's writing style guidelines).

3. Beyond writing tips, collect information regarding the formatting of tables and/or figures (if applicable), which can further illustrate the results of your learning. For example, you might do a bar graph reflecting the frequency of different activities that you did onsite during your training. Here is an example bar graph:

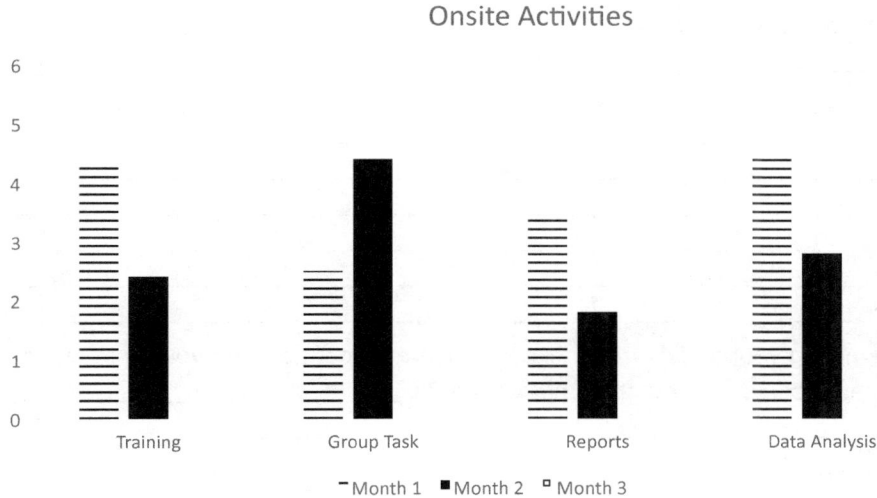

4. As you develop your ideas, ask a peer intern or another relevant feedback source to review the content of your writing regarding the clarity of the ideas expressed. As with any step in this process, it helps immensely to have another person(s) to give you constructive feedback on how to improve expressed ideas.

5. As you keep working on the sequencing of your ideas, developing a general "flow" in your writing that supports the expression of your learning outcomes. For example, as you transition from topic to topic in your paper, follow this writing "flow" template:

Topic #1: Fully describe your learning outcomes within a specific focus (e.g., "organization skills" focus). It is important to utilize multiple examples of your journaled learning. At the end of this section, relate this idea to the proceeding idea to be discussed.

Topic #2: Reiterate how the previous topic relates to the current topic to be discussed. Present multiple examples from your journaling process. At the end of this section, relate this idea to the proceeding idea to be discussed.

Before proceeding, please review what you have learned in Phase II! On the next page, there is a series of review questions related to what you learned in doing the activities and exercises.

"Let's Review!" Phase II Learning

1. After viewing your initial literature review and comparing it your resultant learning outcomes, what did you learn about writing a preliminary literature? How would you do it differently? _____
   _____
   _____
   _____
   _____
   _____
   _____
   _____

2. If you noticed a difference in the ability of initial literature review to your final learning-related topics, what were the "gaps" identified? _____
   _____
   _____
   _____
   _____
   _____
   _____
   _____

3. In examining your initial writing from the learning contract, do you feel that your writing has changed in style and/or format to date? _____
   _____
   _____
   _____
   _____
   _____
   _____

4. What concept(s) of field learning did you not anticipate but are evident and need to be addressed? _____
   _____
   _____
   _____
   _____
   _____
   _____
   _____

Phase III: Template to Examine Your Learning Outcomes

If done systematically, the identification of new research areas to be covered should be relatively straightforward for you as you take the next step in the writing process. As before, it is recommended that you utilize an outline or a linkage chart approach to plan the specific areas of research collected. These ideas can then be converted into conceptual search terms for use in library research databases.

An important aspect of this procedure is to be open to many different theoretical ideas to fully explain your learning-related thinking "outside the box" within and across disciplines/fields of study, as applicable. This experience may also help you see the relevance of different perspectives in everything from your initial field training preparation to your broader long-term career trajectory. Here is a way to think about drafting these analyses for your writing and follow research activities:

Onsite Learning:	Original Theoretical Coverage:	Additional Theories:
1. _____	_____	_____
2. _____	_____	_____
3. _____	_____	_____
4. _____	_____	_____
5. _____	_____	_____
6. _____	_____	_____
7. _____	_____	_____
8. _____	_____	_____
9. _____	_____	_____

Think About It!

Here are topics to consider as you think about writing your final analysis of your learning outcomes considering new research concepts since you began your field training:

1. How do your final learning observations reflect what you feel other interns in your field/program typically learn? How do you know? _____
   _____
   _____
   _____
   _____

2. How have your critical analysis skills improved through these ongoing comparative analyses in different areas of your writing? _____
   _____
   _____
   _____
   _____

3. It is important to think "outside the box" in analyzing concepts related to your learning. Give an example of you engaging in this process. _____
   _____
   _____
   _____
   _____

4. Did you find that some learning observations were not easily explainable through field-related theories or concepts? Why? _____
   _____
   _____
   _____
   _____

Apply Your Knowledge!

Beyond this aforementioned planning chart, here are some suggestions for you to follow. In developing this discussion section of your final paper/project, you should:

- Restate the original focus of your field training at the beginning of your applied discussion.
- Reiterate your goals for your training, but now them as "accomplishments" at the end of your training.
- In developing a template for this part of your writing, think about the structure moving from broader (macro) concepts for more specific (micro) topics in your analyses and application of your onsite field training outcomes.
- Review each of the outcomes presented in the results section of your paper/project, covering both the expected and potentially unexpected learning experiences.
- Next, analyze what you may consider to be unaddressed learning.
- Think about the need to apply what you personally learned to a broader cross-section of student interns within your field of study. What are the lessons learned that you would advise future intern to anticipate and plan for through their learning contract or other steps in the training process?
- Finally, reflect upon and develop ideas regarding both "limitations" and "future suggestions" of personal and situational factors (e.g., time scheduling conflicts to be avoided), which may curtail learning outcomes but, if anticipated, can assist in creating a successful field training experience.

Try It Out!
Work Scheduling Exercise

Work Scheduling Exercise Brief: Part of your ongoing learning involves critically analyzing details of the workplace and how it functions. In this task, you will use information from an employee workday availability sheet to complete a monthly work schedule. You will need to assign two people to each workday, but you can only assign one person twice a week.

Employee	Availability
Tom, Sarah, Emily	M, Th, F, every second W and every third Su
Josh, May, Sean	T, W, F, S, every first M
Maddie, Ally, Noah	M, Th, F, S, Su, every second T

Week	M	T	W	Th	F	S	Su
1							
2							
3							
4							

This exercise is limited to 20 minutes.

After completion of the Work Scheduling Exercise, ask yourself the following:

1. What did you learn from doing this critical analysis task?
2. What was the most challenging aspect of this exercise? Why?
3. How can you apply what you learned from doing this exercise to your learning outcomes?

By this time, you have realized that all steps in your field training differ from the cyclical process of seeking and responding to others' feedback. This also applies to the final writing process of your paper/culminating project. As you gather feedback, you should find information about determining an appropriate presentation style and field-relevant standards related to your presentation. The learning associated with soliciting others' perspectives on topics to be significant to you in your professional development in the field.

Let us go through some general ideas of what you should do in preparing for this step in the process:

1. Seek writing advice from an off-campus source (e.g., hire a professional editor).
2. Ask another intern to read your writing, maybe trading papers to both share ideas and see others' styles of writing.
3. Run your paper/writing content through a grammar editing program (e.g., Grammarly).
4. Utilize a spelling and plagiarism check software.
5. Read your paper out loud to double check that the paper has a good "flow" of ideas.
6. "Visualize" your learning to optimize the expressiveness in your writing process.
7. Deconstruct your text to reconstruct the sequencing of ideas in an optimal order.
8. Consult with a field-relevant expert to verify that your writing contains appropriate, field-relevant content (e.g., terminology).

There is much to consider as you finalize the presentation of your field learning outcomes. Consider the many different ways to express the accumulated self reflections of your field training and how multiple perspectives on topics can be incorporated through the aforementioned process of feedback seeking from multiple sources.

Search the Web!
Learn About Writing a Discussion

Search the Internet for different websites regarding how to write an effective discussion of your learning outcomes. Check out at least three different websites pertaining to summarizing your training outcomes within your area of study. As you review this information, please answer the following questions:

1. What were the three most helpful Internet sources for writing an effective discussion section for a final paper/culminating project?

   a. _____

   b. _____

   c. _____

2. When researching Internet information, how did the sources differentiate between writing a literature review and writing a discussion? _____

3. What was the best piece of online advice for writing a discussion section that you found? Why was it helpful? _____

AN INTERN'S INSIGHTS

Maria Marszalek: Internships are wonderful because they are an excellent way to get hands-on experience before entering the work environment. It gives you a "taste" of what that job entails and serves as a bit of a reality check. Moreover, an internship helps you discover yourself in ways you might not have thought about beforehand. It opens the door for you to network with diverse communities while interacting and learning about various cultures and giving you the opportunity to showcase your creativity and talents. Furthermore, they also greatly benefit the environment you are working in because of your challenging work and contribution to the site.

For whatever reason, you may choose to partake in an internship program to understand why you want the internship while also taking necessary steps prior to applying for the position. Whether you have control in picking a site or it has been preselected for you, a significant step would be to analyze the organization to better understand the organization's mission, culture, and goals. Not all agencies might be the perfect "fit" for you. This reality may affect your performance negatively, creating a less than optimal experience for you and the organization.

Therefore, it is imperative for you to research training sites and evaluate your level of openness regarding circumstances to which you may be exposed. Remember to be open to new experiences that might not always seem to "fit" your preferences, because this is when you discover your personal strengths, as well as weaknesses, that facilitate your unique path of learning into the future.

"Let's Review!" Phase III Learning

1. What have you learned about your field training as you finish this writing process? ____
   _____
   _____
   _____
   _____
   _____

2. In writing the results of your learning, was it more challenging to write conceptually or in an applied manner? ____
   _____
   _____
   _____
   _____
   _____

3. You have utilized feedback at all steps in your writing. Who or what was the most helpful source of feedback at this step in your analysis and writing process? Why? ____
   _____
   _____
   _____
   _____
   _____

4. If you are asked to give feedback to another intern about conducting this final analysis of field learning, what advice would you offer? ____
   _____
   _____
   _____
   _____

Summary of the Chapter

This chapter guided you through the steps of applying your learning outcomes to existing and new research areas, based on your self-reflections of onsite training experiences. Based on the activities and suggestions throughout this chapter, you should have expanded both your theoretical- and practitioner-focused perspectives about the culmination of your training in many ways (e.g., critical analysis of your skill development). Lessons learned extend meaningfully to your professional development as you graduate and enter your professional field.

What Did I Learn?

Self-reflection is a vital part of your learning process throughout the field experience. Without looking back in the chapter, please list what you feel were the main three points of learning that were personally relevant to you regarding the focus of the chapter (please explain why each is personally relevant to your learning):

1. _____
   _____
   _____

2. _____
   _____
   _____

3. _____
   _____
   _____

Discussion Questions

1. How has the conceptual focus of your learning evolved from its inception (learning contract) to the culmination (final paper/project/presentation) of this training experience?
2. You have engaged in several feedback-seeking activities over time. How have you improved in your communication skills related to this task over the past several weeks?
3. Do you think active listening is an important skill at this phase of your training? How so?
4. Perspective taking is an important part of this learning experience in several ways. Give two examples related to this point that were significant to your learning.
5. By this stage, you have consulted a variety of sources about your writing. What are two areas of your writing that have shown the greatest development? How?
6. There are different techniques that each writer develops to help achieve a proper flow in their writing. What is your favorite approach to sequencing ideas in your culminating paper/project/presentation?
7. What were new field(s) of study incorporated into your discussion that were not originally a part of your initial literature review? Why?
8. Were there good samples of papers online that guided your writing? Is searching for online sample papers a good strategy, or can it be counterproductive? Why?
9. You are encouraged to think "outside the box" and seek feedback sources beyond your two immediate supervisors. Why is this a beneficial learning process?
10. Finally, how can you generalize what you have learned in this chapter to your performance in the workplace?

Additional Information Links

- USC Libraries website:
  http://libguides.usc.edu/writingguide/oralpresentation
- EffectiveMeetings.com website:
  http://www.effectivemeetings.com/presenting/index.asp
- Community Tool Box website:
  http://ctb.ku.edu/en/table-of-contents/structure/training-and-technical-assistance/workshops/main
- Think Outside the Slide website:
  http://www.thinkoutsidetheslide.com/ten-secrets-for-using-powerpoint-effectively/
- Monash University website:
  http://www.monash.edu/it/current-students/resources-and-support/style-guide/analysing-and-presenting-results
- MindTools website:
  How Good are Your Presentation Skills? *https://www.mindtools.com/pages/article/newCS_96.htm*
- ProEdgeSkills website:
  https://www.proedgeskills.com/Presentation_Skills_Articles/difficult_questions.htm
- Free Management Library website:
  http://managementhelp.org/businessresearch/analysis.htm#anchor720320

Fig. 14.1: Source: https://pixabay.com/success-businesswoman-women-s-power-2073660/.

CHAPTER XIV

Reflection on Your Culminating Learning Experience and the Next Steps

FIELD LEARNING FACTOID

"First off, when you're applying to jobs, you need to tailor your résumé to the individual job descriptions by including relevant keywords. That way, you'll have a better chance at clearing the applicant tracking systems many companies use to prescreen résumés. For example, if you're pursuing a job as a book editor, be sure to use words like 'writers' and 'editing,' which likely appear in the job description. But also remember that a human is reading your résumé, so you want to also explain your accomplishments in various jobs and use numbers to quantify your achievements as much as possible. For all your résumés, make sure to highlight any previous internships and relevant coursework."

Source: Monster.com (https://www.monster.com/career-advice/article/what-to-do-after-graduation)

Introduction

The final, culminating phase of your onsite training experience has been reached, and it is time for you to reflect upon the accumulated meaning of your training time as it leads to your new career (Bravo & Whiteley, 2005; McCallum & Brooke, 2006; Waide, 2008). This culminating self-analysis will guide you as you transition from being a student to becoming a full-fledged professional (Zhang & Parsons, 2016).

Self-reflection is a skill you have used at almost every step during both your onsite and associated academic learning in this experience (Harr & Hess, 2010). These insights will become very helpful as you examine your overall learning and performance gains over time (Simeon, 2013; United States, 2004).

Your learning over time during the experience has hopefully guided your development of a field-relevant professional identity (Williams, 2013). You might be surprised by the amount of onsite learning you have accomplished by the end of your hours (Citrin, 2015). The self-reflection process is one of the many skills you developed over time, and this training-related skill will benefit you as you take the next important step in launching a career in your specific field/discipline (Asher, 2004; Collins, 1998; Kaputa, 2016; Leibman, 2015).

Learning Goals for this Chapter

Chapter XIV offers both informational resources and interactive exercises/activities to prepare you to:

→ Create culminating reflections on your learning by writing your thoughts about the general meaning of your learning onsite and in the classroom as they come together in one cohesive result,

→ Communicate your learning ideas to key stakeholders (i.e., site supervisor, faculty supervsor, other peer interns, and/or other constituents at the trainig site) in this training process, and

→ Construct a plan for the next steps in your professional development, based on your culminating onsite learning experiences.

Before beginning to discuss very specific training issues related to your field experience, let us explore some foundational concepts for this chapter:

Look It Up!
Define and Understand Important Concepts

In conducting an internship/field experience or service learning placement in your chosen field, you should have a knowledge of specific learning concepts. Please consult the word glossary provided at the back of this manual, and look up the following terms discussed in the current chapter.

Generalized Learning: _____
_____
_____
_____

Career Trajectory: _____
_____
_____
_____

Self Presentation: _____
_____
_____
_____

Written Communication Skills: _____
_____
_____
_____

Oral Communication Skills: _____
_____
_____
_____

Professional Developmental Plan: _____
_____
_____
_____

Phase I: Reflection on the Meaning of your Overall Training Experience

Before you achieve closure on your field training, you should understand the "take away" lessons from the training through your internship, or service learning placement. What was the resultant meaning from all that you learned in acquired knowledge, skills, and abilities in your field training? This is a critical time period for your professional development prior to entering the workforce and responding to the demands of your chosen field/occupation in which you will develop a generalized learning assessment to guide the next steps in your career trajectory. Let us go through some general ideas of what you should do in preparing for this step in the process:

1. *Reflect on your overall training*—Review your derived learning themes, and think about the general psychological, social, educational, and cultural outcomes from your field training over time. There are many learning outcomes that you received over your field instruction that you may not have directly anticipated but which may have had a meaningful impact on your training outcomes as a new professional in your field/discipline.
2. *Meet with a field practitioner*—Meet with a field-relevant expert about how to interpret and generalize the meaning of your onsite learning for your professional development.
3. *Discuss findings with your faculty mentor*—As with all previous steps in your learning process, consult with your faculty mentor about ideas to further explore related your overall learning from your training as they apply to your ongoing professional development after graduation.
4. *Talk with a field-relevant professional*—As you have regularly met with different key stakeholders involved in your field traiing, it is important conclude your learning experience through one or more meetings with a field-relevant professional to analyze your final learning as you prepare to enter the workforce.

Let us check in about your perceptions of the learning process at this point. The following are some important questions to ask yourself when preparing to finalize the assessment of your learning from the field assignment:

What Do I Think About ... ?

1. Have my perspectives about my career changed due to the training I received as an intern? If yes, how so?
2. What would I "do over" if I had a second chance at any step during the field training?
3. In retrospect, was I adequately prepared to fully engage in my field training? Why or why not?
4. Based upon my field training, have I experienced a meaningful change in how I engage with others in work-related tasks? If yes, how so?
5. Have the lessons I learned generalized to how I approach other learning situations?
6. Can this type of field training experience change a person's core values and beliefs? Does this apply to my learning outcomes in some way?
7. Who is the best source of feedback to help me with my ideas about learning outcomes?
8. What advice would I give a future intern at the same or a similar site to optimize his/her preparation?

"Let's Review!" Phase I Learning

1. What were the general lessons you learned from your field training? _____
   _____
   _____
   _____
   _____
   _____
   _____
   _____

2. How well did your self-reflected learning outcomes correspond to the initial insights/ advice of your supervisors? _____
   _____
   _____
   _____
   _____
   _____
   _____
   _____

3. What was an area of personal growth experience that you experienced but that you may not have anticipated? Why? _____
   _____
   _____
   _____
   _____
   _____
   _____
   _____

4. How have your personal learning insights from the completed training altered your professional self-concept? Please explain. _____
   _____
   _____
   _____
   _____
   _____
   _____
   _____

Phase II: Communication of Field-Related Learning to Key Stakeholders and Beyond

Before you conclude your training experience and graduate, you should communicate the outcomes of your field-related learning to the many different constituents who were involved in the process of your training and/or would benefit from the knowledge you can share. You will engage in an important self presentation of who you have become as an emerging professional, emphasizing development in both your written communication skills and oral communication skills. Please choose one of the following recommended actions and commit to it. Let us go through some ideas of what you should do in this step:

1. *Conduct an onsite presentation/workshop*—Supervisors, coworkers, and other onsite interns would benefit from the insights you have regarding being an intern onsite and any issues of adjustment that can be better planned for future interns.
2. *Share your learning in the classroom/department of your program*—Department faculty and other students would benefit from your learning.
3. *Do a conference presentation*—Submit your learning as a possible conference abstract for a poster presentation at a field-relevant professional conference. Your insights will contribute to the overall field and can certainly positively impact other students' expectations in how field-related training should be planned for.
4. *Write an article about your learning for an undergraduate field-related academic journal*—In addition to presenting, you can also reach professionals and/or students by publishing your paper/project in a student journal.
5. Begin an intern blog/vlog site about your learning—Share your thoughts and learning through social media to many different age groups and audiences.

FROM A SITE SUPERVISOR'S DESK

Dr. Julie Patrick, Professor of Psychology, West Virginia University:

Before your field work begins: It is important to know what the evaluation standards are, who will provide feedback, and how frequently the feedback will be given. If it is possible, ask at the beginning of your field experience for a rubric or a list of goals. You will also want to know whether you are being evaluated by someone who has contact with your day-to-day efforts or whether the evaluator only has access to information about large project outcomes. Finally, prepare for your performance review by completing a self-evaluation. Inventory your strengths, areas in which you think you have improved, areas in which you need support, and consider which experiences you would like to add to your field work.

During the feedback meeting: It can feel awkward or even threatening to sit face-to-face and receive feedback! But keep in mind that 1) a performance review is a conversation and you want to be able to contribute in meaningful ways and 2) everyone involved in your review wants you to succeed. Accept praise with grace; do not shrug it off or deflect. Similarly, be open to constructive feedback and ask for concrete ways to improve your performance. Finally, express your gratitude for the candid feedback. Rehearse something like, "Thank you for the feedback. I will think carefully about this and will continue to find ways to improve my work."

After the meeting: Reflect on the feedback and brainstorm ways to incorporate it. Ask for another meeting, if needed.

What Should I Do?
Putting Your Learning into Action

1. Research online resources about how to develop effective PowerPoint presentations (e.g., YouTube videos). Think about the best way to present your learning in short statements with imagery as supporting illustrations of your learning outcomes.

2. Meet with a speech/communication faculty member on your campus about tips for good oral presentation outcomes. Public speaking is a part of your field-related training, regardless of your specific field/discipline.

3. Have a discussion with your onsite supervisor about conducting the onsite presentation and associated logistics (e.g., arranging a meeting room and scheduling the event). Part of your learning associated with this task is organizational skills related to real work behaviors and arranging events that could be directly or indirectly related to your specific field or/discipline training.

4. Talk with your faculty supervisor about conducting a workshop and/or talk for intern students, and if permitted, learn how to arrange the event in your department or another on-campus location.

5. Edit your finalized field paper/project to create either an on-campus student conference presentation and/or to create a manuscript for submission to a journal.

Before proceeding, please review what you have learned in Phase II! The next section contains a series of review questions related to what you learned in doing the activities and exercises. To best help you with this ongoing learning process, please be accurate in your responses to assess what areas of learning may need further review.

"Let's Review!" Phase II Learning

1. What are different approaches to communicating insights from your field training experience? Is it important to understand the nuances of each option? _____
   _____
   _____
   _____
   _____
   _____
   _____
   _____

2. Do you anticipate that you may have different types of "audiences" for your presentation(s)? Why? _____
   _____
   _____
   _____
   _____
   _____
   _____
   _____

3. When thinking about presenting to potentially different types of audience members, what are some factors to consider in your presentation approach? _____
   _____
   _____
   _____
   _____
   _____
   _____

4. How will you know if your audience will understand the information you will be presenting? What presentation tools can you use in your presentation(s) to help assist in their comprehension based upon the research you have conducted? _____
   _____
   _____
   _____
   _____
   _____
   _____

Phase III: Plan for the Next Steps in Your Professional Training

The culmination of your training, and consideration of what this means to you, has the more immediate goal of summarizing your short- and long-term learning goals. Beyond that, create the next level of career planning (i.e., what you will do next in your professional development plan). There are two pragmatic ideas to think about at this stage of your career training. As you have recently evaluated that you learned about yourself in this career exploration process, you have most likely considered how this relates to (1) what motivates you as a professional in the field and (2) how you can maximize these types of motivational factor(s).

The following are some ideas about how to maximize what motivates you in your career trajectory both in the short and long-term. Choose a career that exemplifies the following ideas for you:

- What job would you do for free if you were a volunteer? Make that into a part of your career plan.
- What do others tell you that you are good at? For example, do others say that you are a great listener? Think about how you could make this a part of what you could do in your specific career field.
- What task-related responsibilities do you like to do, because you can become completely immersed in them and lose track of time? Those types of tasks should be, if possible, a part of the job and larger career search for you.
- Finally, what are job-related tasks in which you give 110% or more effort to complete, because they are personally meaningful topics that match your personal values and beliefs? Find a job and/or career that is personally meaningful on many levels for you.

Being proactive in your ongoing learning will need to continue as you enter this next stage of your career development. Think about these activities to engage in as you undergo this process:

- *Look forward*—Consider where you want to be in five or ten years, and research field-relevant anticipatory steps in your career training within your specific field or discipline. Anticipate career training trends—be proactive!
- *Be selective*—Find others in your training field who reflect your career values and beliefs. Seek their mentorship and advice as you begin your career, utilizing their knowledge and experience for the many stages of your professional development.
- *Make long-term connections*—Seek affiliations with different field-related professionals outside immediate training contacts but in associated areas to help as your career evolve.
- *To Facebook or not to Facebook*—Review your social media profile(s), and assess how your information presents you as a viable professional in your selected field/discipline. Realize that your current and future employers will be potentially review this information, so put your best "face" forward.

In addition to following the above suggestions, you should develop a structured plan to reflect all the factors you are assembling as you prepare to enter the workforce. When writing your career development plan, note the following factors to consider in this step-by-step process. It is important to identify "career viable" skills, knowledge, and abilities; supplemental coursework for further professional development; and additional educational degree(s)/professional training to complete for career advancement.

Think About It!

Here are topics to consider as you think about how to develop an effective career trajectory plan as you review many sources of information in constructing this document:

1. What is your primary career focus? State it as succinctly as possible. _____
   _____
   _____
   _____
   _____

2. Based upon your stated career focus, what are your short-term career goals? Long-term career goals? _____
   _____
   _____
   _____
   _____

3. With your short-term goals, what are current educational, volunteer, and/or employment activities that are helping you reach these intended career milestones? _____
   _____
   _____
   _____
   _____

4. Who should you consult about your developing career plan? Think of multiple support resources to have review your plan. _____
   _____
   _____
   _____
   _____

Apply Your Knowledge!

The following are some suggested ideas for you to consider when analyzing the next steps in your emerging career and how to ensure a successful beginning and continuation of your ongoing professional development:

1. *Join a career-related professional society*—This was recommended earlier as you began your learning contract writing, and it equally applies to this stage of your training. Examine support resources related to career guidance and/or training.
2. *Attend professional development seminars/training*—Through professional network connections in your program and/or school, attend training opportunities in your community or webinars to further supplement your career training.
3. *Research your desired long-term career*—Search the Internet for information related to trends in your field/discipline, ranging from new industry trends, consumer utilization patterns, and/or to emerging certification/licensure requirements.
4. *Seek advice from a career counselor/field expert*—Never miss the opportunity to acquire mentoring, because there is always information to learn and/or adapt to during your professional development.
5. *Go beyond required responsibilities*—Engage in extracurricular volunteer and/or job activities to further enhance your knowledge and skill bases. Be proactive in remaining current in your knowledge, skills, and abilities.

Try It Out!
Peer-to-Peer Mentoring Exercise

Peer-to-Peer Mentoring Exercise Brief: As you transition from being a trainee and mentoring recipient to an emerging professional in your field/discipline, you can apply what you have learned about being a good mentor through the activity of giving advice to intern peers. This exercise involves you practicing this mentoring role as a part of your ongoing experiential learning. Recruit a group of three to five (or more) peers in your academic program whom will be entering their field training in the coming one to two semesters.

Conduct a brief mentoring workshop/session utilizing different presentation "tools" (e.g., PowerPoint presentation), and answer any training-related questions from the attendees. Journal what you learned about your experience and apply your new learning to the role of becoming an emerging peer-to-peer mentor. This exercise is limited to one hour.

After completion of the Peer-to-Peer Mentoring Exercise, ask yourself the following:

1. How did you prepare to conduct your peer-to-peer mentoring session? What did you anticipate might be asked?
2. What presentation approach did you use to convey your advice (e.g., informal discussion, handouts, PowerPoint presentation)? Why?
3. What did you learn about your own breadth or depth of learning when you explained training-related concepts to others?

Mentoring is an important activity that is critical for you to pursue as a new emerging professional. You will become both a mentee and a mentor to newer field trainees—you benefited from mentoring, and now it is time for you to "give back" to others. Your role as a mentee is important to understand as this dynamic emerges in your ongoing mentoring activities.

Let us go through some general ideas of what you should do in preparing for this step in the process:

1. *Choose the ideal mentor*—Match your choice of mentor(s) based upon your core values and beliefs, in addition to field-specific qualifications. The mentor–mentee relationship is an interpersonal connection that requires a meaningful understanding of each other's perspectives and motivations to be effective and long-lasting in focus. This also applies to your choice of mentees in your expanded professional role within your field/discipline.

2. *Go outside your "comfort zone"*—This idea of engaging in mentoring outside of your daily activities will benefit all involved, because it will help both you and your mentor "stretch" beyond your typical knowledge and/or skills. You are learning more about your perceived (and actual) capabilities, as well as your thresholds (and limits) in selected performance areas. In turn, you are learning about your evolving mentoring role in the field.

3. *Be an active listener*—As with the many steps you have navigated through as an intern, you learned to develop your skills as an active listener. In your role as a career mentee, you are applying what you have learned for the purpose of developing both short- and long-term professional goals in correspondence with various mentoring resources.

4. *"Own" your goals*—You must see the task of goal setting as a daily/weekly/monthly/yearly time commitment that should guide your professional activities on a regular basis. If you find that your goals do not motivate you on some level (e.g., seeking a higher paying job, which may not reflect your value-based career motivation), you should quickly re-evaluate your goals and adjust your plan. You should also give this advice to those seeking your help.

5. *Always challenge yourself*—Do not immediately take "no" for an answer, and problem solve through possible obstacles to career opportunities. Be creative in your activities, think outside the box, and push yourself beyond your daily routine to achieve meaningful progress. This dynamic relationship with your mentor also means that he/she engage in the same process to optimize the mentoring exchange.

6. *Be realistic*—As much as there is the need to explore career possibilities, as both a mentee in as an emergent mentor, it is also important to understand that there will be situational constraints beyond your control (e.g., industry funding) that need to be knowledged as you develop realistic career plans and offer realistic mentoring advice to others.

CHAPTER XIV Reflection on Your Culminating Learning Experience and the Next Steps | 251

Search the Web!
Learn About Creating a Career Development Plan

Search the Internet for different websites regarding writing an effective career development plan. Check out at least three different websites pertaining to long-term career planning within your area of study. As you review this information, please answer the following questions:

1. What were three helpful websites for you to develop your career development plan?
    a. _____
    b. _____
    c. _____

2. What advice did you glean from the websites that meaningfully contributed to a career plan that was "above and beyond" the advice you received from other information sources?
   _____
   _____
   _____
   _____
   _____
   _____

3. Based on what you have learned, what do you think would be effective ways to assess the progress you will be making in your plan once you finalize and implement it? Be specific about possible self-assessment ideas (e.g., periodic meetings with a career mentor).
   _____
   _____
   _____
   _____

There is much to consider as you enter this exciting phase of your career development. Looking back at each of the steps you have completed along the way for the suggested activities in this manual, you should be well-prepared to reflect introspectively on your career aspirations and understand the resources to use to reach these goals. Contemplate how your ideas about a career in the field have evolved over the course of your field training. In addition to your ideas about possible career options changing, your professional self-concept has also grown over the same time period.

AN INTERN'S INSIGHTS

Glenda Sanabria: Obtaining your undergraduate degree is an excellent benefit when it comes to making yourself more employable, however; it's not the only asset that will allow you to stand out to potential employers. Amongst demanding and competitive workforces, students must be able to differentiate themselves between other applicants. Internships or field experiences will allow students to differentiate themselves and stand out against their competitors. Among hiring decisions, employers value and seek competitive advantage within their applicants. Field experiences/internships provides individuals with opportunities to apply classroom theory to "real world" scenarios. Students transition their knowledge and can apply it to reality within an organization. Throughout internships, students gain and develop organizational skills that cannot be taught within a classroom. Furthermore, field experiences/internships allow for network opportunities where students gain important contacts within the organization. Established connections within an organization will allow students to gain a competitive edge.

Nonetheless, selection of field experiences/internships is the most important process for students. Students must be aware of the qualifications gained and developed through the internship because the experience obtained must accentuate to the student's career path. Employers seek candidates with experiences, qualities and skills that are aligned to a job occupation. Therefore, students must choose a field experience/ internship that will strengthen their chances into landing a job in their career field.

"Let's Review!" Phase III Learning

1. What are some useful tips that you feel were especially relevant to your career planning in the short term? Long term? _____
   _____
   _____
   _____
   _____

2. Who have you identified as a good long-term career mentor, and how does their advice help you plan beyond your immediate situation? _____
   _____
   _____
   _____
   _____

3. Do you feel that the planned next steps in your career development is a natural extension of your field training to date? Why, or why not? _____
   _____
   _____
   _____
   _____
   _____

4. If you were to become a mentor for another student in your academic program tomorrow, what advice would you offer regarding writing a long-term career plan? _____
   _____
   _____
   _____
   _____

Summary of the Chapter

This chapter summarizes information to consider at this last step in your field training as you reflect upon what you have learned and how these acquired knowledge, skills, and abilities relate to your future career plans. Information was presented relating to how to make this planning process a well-articulated, methodical goal setting activity that should be reflected in your ongoing daily (or frequent) professional development initiatives. It was also explained how you can now apply all that you have learned to assume the new role of mentor and engage in the dynamic process of feedback-listening from a new perspective.

What Did I Learn?

Self-reflection is a vital part of your learning process throughout the field experience. Without looking back in the chapter, please list what you feel were the main three points of learning that were personally relevant to you regarding the focus of the chapter (please explain why each is personally relevant to your learning):

1. _____
   _____
   _____

2. _____
   _____
   _____

3. _____
   _____
   _____

Discussion Questions

1. What are three meaningful self-insights you have developed regarding your site-related learning over the past several weeks of your training?
2. Ultimately, did your ongoing journaling assist you in thinking about your learning outcomes as you finalize this experience?
3. Have you consulted with an expert in the field about the best way(s) to communicate the outcomes of your site training onsite? If so, what did you learn about workplace communication?
4. You have worked on your communication skills over the last several weeks of your field training. How did this help you in the onsite presentation of your learning outcomes?
5. As suggested in this chapter, there are many different options to share your learning outcomes with others. Which did you choose, and why?
6. How did you use your presentation "forums" to increase your career networking contacts?
7. When you consider your short-term career plans, what are the motivations underlying these decisions?
8. Do your personal values and beliefs more closely reflect your long-term career goals? Why, or why not?
9. Are your long-term goals too far into the future to be tangible? How can you make them more concrete?
10. Lastly, what have you learned about being a good career mentor? Be specific in your ideas, as they reflect upon your time as an intern seeking career mentoring advice from multiple sources over the course of your training.

Additional Information Links

- Psychology Today website:
  https://www.psychologytoday.com/blog/design-your-path/201507/10-best-career-advice-websites
- WiseBread website:
  http://www.wisebread.com/15-career-advice-sites-you-should-know-about
- Forbes.com website:
  https://www.forbes.com/sites/jacquelynsmith/2013/09/18/the-top-100-websites-for-your-career/#17428a8a2a02
- TheMuse website:
  https://www.themuse.com/#!
- Prospects website:
  https://www.prospects.ac.uk/careers-advice
- FlexJobs website:
  https://www.flexjobs.com/blog/post/10-career-advice-sites-millennials/
- EndlessJobOffers website:
  http://www.endlessjoboffers.com/18-best-career-blogs-to-read/
- TotalJobs website:
  https://www.totaljobs.com/careers-advice

References

Chapter I

Abuhusain, H., Chotirmall, S. H., Hamid, N., & O'Neill, S. J. (2009). Prepared for internship? *Irish Medical Journal, 102*(3), 82–84.

Bay, J. (2006). Preparing undergraduates for careers: An argument for the internship practicum. *College English, 69*(2), 134–141. doi: 10.2307/25472198

Brennan, M. D. (2010). Professionalism. *International Journal of Dermatology, 49*(10), 1210–1212. doi: 10.1111/j.1365-4632.2010. 04781.x

Clayton, J. K., & Myran, S. (2013). Content and context of the administrative internship: How mentoring and sustained activities impact preparation. *Mentoring & Tutoring: Partnership in Learning, 21*(1), 59–75. doi: 10.1080/13611267.2013.784059

Dotson, K. B., & Dotson-Blake, K. P. (2015). Factors of engagement: Professional standards and the library science internship. *Techtrends: Linking Research and Practice to Improve Learning a Publication of the Association for Educational Communications & Technology, 59*(3), 54–63. doi: 10.1007/s11528-015-0853-y

Fisher, J. W., Thompson, B. M., & Garcia, A. D. (2007). Integrative clinical experience: An innovative program to prepare for internship. *Teaching and Learning in Medicine, 19*(3), 302–307. doi: 10.1080/10401330701366788

Garman, A. N., Evans, R., Krause, M. K., & Anfossi, J. (2006). Professionalism. *Journal of Healthcare Management/American College of Healthcare Executives, 51*(4), 219–222.

Glazer, J. L. (2008). Educational professionalism: An inside-out view. *American Journal of Education, 114*(2), 169–189. doi: 10.1086/524314

Loh, K. Y., & Nalliah, S. (2010). Learning professionalism by role-modelling. *Medical Education, 44*(11), 1123. doi: 10.1111/j.1365-2923.2010.03827.x

Martimianakis, M. A., Maniate, J. M., & Hodges, B. D. (2009). Sociological interpretations of professionalism. *Medical Education, 43*(9), 829–37. doi: 10.1111/j.1365-2923.2009. 03408.x

McCord, M., Houseworth, M., & Michaelsen, L. K. (2015). The integrative business experience: Real choices and real consequences create real thinking. *Decision Sciences Journal of Innovative Education, 13*(3), 411–429. doi: 10.1111/dsji.12070

Miller, T. K. (1991). Using standards in professional preparation. *New Directions for Student Services, 53*, 45–62. doi: 10.1002/ss.37119915306

Phelps, L. A., & Swerdlik, M. E. (2011). Evolving internship issues in school psychology preparation. *Psychology in the Schools, 48*(9), 911–921. doi: 10.1002/pits.20602

Roth, M. T., Zlatic, T. D., & American College of Clinical Pharmacy (2009). Development of student professionalism. *Pharmacotherapy, 29*(6), 749–56. doi: 10.1592/phco.29.6.749

Stedman, J. M., & Hatch, J. P. (2000). Preinternship preparation in psychological testing and psychotherapy: What internship directors say they expect. *Professional Psychology: Research & Practice, 31*(3), 321–326. doi: 10.1037/0735-7028.31.3.321

Stedman, J. M., Hatch, J. P., & Schoenfeld, L. S. (2001). Internship directors' valuation of pre-internship preparation in test-based assessment and psychotherapy. *Professional Psychology: Research & Practice, 32*(4). 421–424. doi: 10.1037/0735-7028.32.4.421

Stephenson, G. J. (2005). An educational intervention to enhance preparation for internship. *Focus on Health Professional Education: A Multi-Disciplinary Journal, 7*(2), 75–87.

Varner, L. W. (2007). Preparation of future school leaders. *Journal of College Teaching & Learning, 4*(11), 31–40.

Wesley, S. C., & Bickle, M. C. (2005). Examination of a paradigm for preparing undergraduates for a career in the retailing industries: Mentors, curriculum, and an internship. *College Student Journal, 39*(4), 680–691.

Chapter II

Bajwa, N. M., Yudkowsky, R., Belli, D., Vu, N. V., & Park, Y. S. (2016). Improving the residency admissions process by integrating a professionalism assessment: A validity and feasibility study. *Advances in Health Sciences Education*, 1–21. doi:10.1007/s10459-0169683-8

Doran, J. M., & Cimbora, D. M. (2016). Solving the internship imbalance: Opportunities and obstacles. *Training and Education in Professional*

Psychology, 10(2), 61–70. http://psycnet.apa.org/doi/10.1037/tep0000113

Gherardi, S., Gherardi, S., Perrotta, M., & Perrotta, M. (2016). Re-thinking induction in practice: Profession, peer group and organization in contention. *Society and Business Review, 11*(2), 193–209. doi: 101108SBR-03-2016-0021

Hersh, J. B., & Poey, K. (1984). A proposed interviewing guide for intern applicants. *Professional Psychology: Research and Practice, 15*(1), 3–5.

Holsti, M., Hawkins, S., Bloom, K., White, R., Clark, E. B., & Byington, C. L. (2015). Increasing diversity of the biomedical workforce through community engagement: The University of Utah Native American summer research internship. *Clinical and Translational Science, 8*(2), 87–90. doi: 10.1111/cts.12258

Hutchinson, C., & Hyden, C. (2016). Student partnerships to build organizational capacity. *Health Promotion Practice, 17*(1), 9–12.

Jacob, M. C. (1987). Managing the internship application experience advice from an exhausted but content survivor. *The Counseling Psychologist, 15*(1), 146–155.

Keilin, W. G. (1998). Internship selection 30 years later: An overview of the APPIC matching program. *Professional Psychology: Research and Practice, 29*(6), 599–603. http://dx.doi.org/10.1037/0735-7028.29.6.599

Leversha, A., & Stewart, K. (2016). Factors influencing pharmacy students' internship site choice. *Journal of Pharmacy Practice and Research, 46*(3), 209–215. doi: 10.18549/PharmPract.2015.03.587

McHugh, P. P. (2016). The impact of compensation, supervision and work design on internship efficacy: Implications for educators, employers and prospective interns. *Journal of Education and Work*, online publication, 1–16. http://dx.doi.org/10.1080/13639080.-2016.1181729

McKenzie, D., Assaf, N., & Cusolito, A. P. (2016). The demand for, and impact of, youth internships: Evidence from a randomized experiment in Yemen. *IZA Journal of Labor & Development, 5*(1), 115. doi: 10.1186/s40175-016-0048-8

Merluzzi, J. (2016). How elite students get elite jobs. *Administrative Science Quarterly, 61*(2), NP13-NP16. doi: 10.1177/0001839216631490

Miloro, M. (2016). The perfect match. *Journal of Oral and Maxillofacial Surgery, 74*(10), 1905–1907. http://dx.doi.org/10.1016/j.joms.2016.07.004

Mitchell, S. L. (1996). Getting a foot in the door: The written internship application. *Professional Psychology: Research and Practice, 27*(1), 9–92.

Ransburg, D., Sage-Hayward, W., & Schuman, A. M. (2016). Selection. In *Human resources in the family business* (pp. 81–104). New York, NY: Palgrave Macmillan.

Rivero, S., Ippolito, J., Martinez, M., Beebe, K., Benevenia, J., & Berberian, W. (2016). Analysis of unmatched orthopaedic residency applicants: Options after the match. *Journal of Graduate Medical Education, 8*(1), 91–95. https://dx.doi.org/10.1007%2Fs11999-012-2471-8

Rodolfa, E., Haynes, S., & Kaplan, D. (1995). To apply or not to apply: That is the intern applicant's first question. *Professional Psychology: Research and Practice, 26*(4), 393–395.

Rodolfa, E. R., Vieille, R., Russell, P., Nijjer, S., Nguyen, D. Q., Mendoza, M., & Perrin, L. (1999). Internship selection: Inclusion and exclusion criteria. *Professional Psychology: Research and Practice, 30*(4), 415–419. http://psycnet.apa.org/doi/10.1037/0735-7028.30.4.415

Spencer, M. F., Atencio, I. J., McCullough, J. A., & Hwang, E. S. (2016, September). The AFRL Scholars Program: A STEM-based summer internship initiative. In *SPIE Optical Engineering+ Applications* (pp. 99460E–99460E). Wright-Patterson AFB, OH: International Society for Optics and Photonics.

Starineca, O. (2016). Human resource selection approaches and socially respons ble strategy. *Economics and Business, 28*(1), 106–114. https://doi.org/10.1515/eb-2016-0015

Stedman, J. M., Neff, J. A., Donahoe, C. P., Kopel, K., & Hays, J. (1995). Applicant characterization of the most desirable internship training program. *Professional Psychology: Research and Practice, 26*(4), 396–400. http://psycnet.apa.org/doi/-10.1037/0735-7028.26.4.396

Stein, L. (2016). Schools need leaders-not managers: It's time for a paradigm shift. *Journal of Leadership Education, 15*(2), 21–30. doi: 1012806/V15/I2/I3

Stewart, A. E., & Stewart, E. A. (1996). A decision-making technique for choosing a psychology internship. *Professional Psychology: Research and Practice, 27*(5), 521–526. http://psycnet.apa.org/doi/10.1037/07357028.27.5.521

Chapter III

Alpert, F., Heaney, J. G., & Kuhn, K. A. L. (2009). Internships in marketing: Goals, structures and assessment—Student, company and academic perspectives. *Australasian Marketing Journal, 17*(1), 36–45. http://dx.doi.org/10.1016/j.ausmj.2009.01.003

Angelique, H. L. (2001). Linking the academy to the community through internships: A model of service learning, student empowerment, and transformative education. *Sociological Practice, 3*(1), 37–53. doi:10.1023/A:1010143514585

Basow, R. R., & Byrne, M. V. (1994). Internship expectations and learning goals. *Journalism Educator, 47*(4), 48–54.

Beenen, G., & Rousseau, D. M. (2010). Getting the most from MBA internships: Promoting intern learning and job acceptance. *Human Resource Management, 49*(1), 3–22. doi: 10.1002/hrm.20331

Borzak, L., & Hursh, B. A. (1977). Integrating the liberal arts and preprofessionalism through field experience: A process analysis. *Alternative Higher Education, 2*(1), 3–16. doi: 10.1007/BF01079312

Calico, F. W. (1985). Multiple-level goals in clinical teaching. *Family Medicine, 17*(3), 114–116.

Compton, L., & Davis, N. (2010). The impact of and key elements for a successful virtual early field experience: Lessons learned from a case study. *Contemporary Issues in Technology and Teacher Education, 10*(3), 309–337.

Cunningham, W. G., & Sherman, W. H. (2008). Effective internships: Building bridges between theory and practice. In *The Educational Forum* (pp. 308–318). Batavia, IL: Taylor & Francis Group.

Curtis, R. C. (2000). Using goal-setting strategies to enrich the practicum and internship experiences of beginning counselors. *The Journal of Humanistic Counseling, 38*(4), 194–205.

Green, M. E. (1997). *Internship success: Real-world, step-by-step advice on getting the most out of internships.* New York, NY: McGraw Hill Professional.

Grow, G. O. (1991). Teaching learners to be self-directed. *Adult Education Quarterly, 41*(3), 125–149.

Johari, A., & Bradshaw, A. C. (2008). Project-based learning in an internship program: A qualitative study of related roles and their motivational attributes. *Educational Technology Research and Development, 56*(3), 329–359.

Kaufman, E. K., Israel, G. D., & Rudd, R. D. (2009). Exploring goal-setting as a tool for leadership development. *Journal of Leadership Studies, 1*(4), 51–61. doi: 10.1002/jls.20032

Kuiper, R. A. (2004). Nursing reflections from journaling during a perioperative internship. *AORN Journal, 79*(1), 195–218.

Ledoux, M. W., Thurlow, R., McHenry, N., Burns, M., & Prugh, E. (2007). Graduate students and field experience: Aligning curricular goals with multiple measures of assessment. *Journal of Social Studies Research, 3*(2), 12–19.

Li, S. T., Paterniti, D. A., Tancredi, D. J., Burke, A. E., Trimm, R. F., Guillot, ... Mahan, J. D. (2015). Resident self-assessment and learning goal development: Evaluation of resident-reported competence and future goals. *Academic Pediatrics, 15*(4), 367–373. http://dx.doi.org/10.1016/j.acap.2015.01.001

Little, M., & Robinson, S. (1997). Renovating and refurbishing the field experience structures for novice teachers. *Journal of Learning Disabilities, 30*(4), 433–441.

Nagle, L. M. (2014). Effects of an internship upon selected goals of the program. *The Journal of Educational Research, 48*(9), 711–714. http://www.jstor.org/stable/27529770

Noordzij, G., Hooft, E. A. J., Mierlo, H., Dam, A., & Born, M. P. (2013). The effects of a learning-goal orientation training on self-regulation: A field experiment among unemployed job seekers. *Personnel Psychology, 66*(3), 723–755. doi: 10.1111/peps.12011

Oettingen, G., Pak, H. J., & Schnetter, K. (2001). Self-regulation of goal-setting: Turning free fantasies about the future into binding goals. *Journal of Personality and Social Psychology, 80*(5), 736–753. http://dx.doi.org/10.1037/0022-3514.80.5.736

O'Neill, N. (2010). Internships as a high-impact practice: Some reflections on quality. *Peer Review, 12*(4), 4–8.

Ottesen, E. (2007). Teachers "in the making": Building accounts of teaching. *Teaching and Teacher Education, 23*(5), 612–623.

Phillion, J. A., Miller, P. C., & Lehman, J. D. (2005). Providing field experiences with diverse populations for preservice teachers: Using technology to bridge distances and cultures. *Multicultural Perspectives, 7*(3), 3–9. http://dx.doi.org/10.1207/s15327892mcp0703_2

Taing, M. U., Smith, T., Singla, N., Johnson, R. E., & Chang, C. H. (2013). The relationship between learning goal orientation, goal setting, and performance: A longitudinal study. *Journal of Applied Social Psychology, 43*(8), 1668–1675. doi: 10.1111/jasp.12119

Taylor, D. L. (2004). *Jumpstarting your career: An internship guide for criminal justice.* Upper Saddle River, NJ: Prentice Hall.

Weigand, D., Richardson, P., & Weinberg, R. (1999). A two-stage evaluation of a sport psychology internship. *Journal of Sport Behavior, 22*(1), 83–87.

Zimmerman, B. J., Bandura, A., & Martinez-Pons, M. (1992). Self-motivation for academic attainment: The role of self-efficacy beliefs and personal goal setting. *American Educational Research Journal, 29*(3), 663–676.

Chapter IV

Bansal, R. K. (1998). Research skills acquisition by interns: A case study. *Indian Journal of Medical Sciences, 52*(1), 8–15.

Bilimoria, D. (1998). From classroom learning to real-world learning: A diasporic shift in management education. *Journal of Management Education, 22*, 265–268.

Burgin, S. R., & Sadler, T. D. (2016). Learning nature of science concepts through a research apprenticeship program: A comparative study of three approaches. *Journal of Research in Science Teaching, 53*(1), 31–59. doi: 10.1002/tea.21296

Clark, S. C. (2003). Enhancing the educational value of business internships. *Journal of Management Education, 27*(4), 472–484.

Clark, S. C. (2001). *Self-directed learning manual* (2nd ed.). Upper Saddle River, NJ: Prentice Hall.

Downey, J. A., & Cobbs, G. A. (2007). "I actually learned a lot from this": A field assignment to prepare future preservice math teachers for culturally diverse classrooms. *School Science and Mathematics, 107*(1), 391–403. doi: 10.1111/j.1949-8594.2007.tb17762.x

Ducat, D. E. (1980). Cooperative education, career exploration, and occupational concepts for community college students. *Journal of Vocational Behavior, 17*(2), 195–203. http://dx.doi.org/10.1016/0001-8791(80)90004-4

Fleming, R. K. (1992). An integrated behavioral approach to the transfer of interpersonal leadership skills. *Journal of Management Education, 16*, 341–353.

Howard, J. P. (1998). Academic service learning: A counternormative pedagogy. *New directions for Teaching and Learning, 73*, 21-29. doi: 10.1002/tl.7303

Inkster, R. P., & Ross, R. G. (1995). *The internship as partnership: A handbook for campus-based coordinators and advisors.* Raleigh, NC: National Society for Experiential Education.

Kardash, C. A. M. (2000). Evaluation of an undergraduate research experience: Perceptions of undergraduate interns and their faculty mentors. *Journal of Educational Psychology, 92*(1), 191–201. http://psycnet.apa.org/doi/10.1037/0022-0663.92.1.191

Kolb, D. A. (1984). *Experiential learning.* Englewood Cliffs, NJ: Prentice Hall.

McCall, M. W., Jr., Lombardo, M. M., & Morrison, A. (1988). *The lessons of experience.* Lexington, MA: Lexington Books.

McCormick, D. W. (1993). Critical thinking, experiential learning, and internships. *Journal of Management Education, 17*, 260–262.

McGoey, J., & Ross, J. (1999). Research, practice, and teacher internship. *Journal of Research in Science Teaching, 36*(2), 117–120.

Mollica, M., & Hyman, Z. (2016). Professional development utilizing an oncology summer nursing internship. *Nurse Education in Practice, 16*(1), 188–192. http://dx.doi.org/10.1016/j.nepr.2015.07.001

Munodawafa, D. (2008). Communication: Concepts, practice and challenges. *Health Education Research, 23*(3), 369–370. https://doi.org/10.1093/her/cyn024

O'Sullivan, M., & Tsangaridou, N. (1992). What undergraduate physical education majors learn during a field experience. *Research Quarterly for Exercise and Sport, 63*(4), 381–392. http://dx.doi.org/10.1080/02701367.1992.10608760

Perry, W. G. (1970). *Forms of intellectual and ethical development in the college years.* New York, NY: Holt, Rinehart & Winston.

Prentice, M., & Garcia, R. M. (2000). Service learning: The next generation in education. *Community College Journal of Research & Practice, 24*(1), 19–26. http://dx.doi.org/10.1080/106689200264321

Rogan, J. M., & Anderson, T. R. (2011). Bridging the educational research-teaching practice gap: Curriculum development, Part 2: Becoming an agent of change. *Biochemistry and Molecular Biology Education, 39*(3), 233–241. doi: 10.1002/bmb.20509

Scholz, R. W., Steiner, R., & Hansmann, R. (2004). Role of internship in higher education in environmental sciences. *Journal of Research in Science Teaching, 41*(1), 24–46. doi: 10.1002/tea.10123

Schön, D. A. (1987). *Educating the reflective practitioner: Toward a new design for teaching and learning in the professions.* San Francisco, CA: Jossey-Bass.

Sims, R. R., & Lindholm, J. (1993). Kolb's experiential learning model: A first step in learning how to learn from experience. *Journal of Management Education, 17*, 95–98.

Stark, J. S., & Lattuca, L. R. (1997). *Shaping the college curriculum: Academic plans in action.* Boston, MA: Allyn & Bacon.

Stedman, J. M., & Schoenfeld, L. S. (2011). Knowledge competence in clinical and counseling training and readiness for internship.

Journal of Clinical Psychology, 67(1), 1–5. doi: 10.1002/jclp.20740

Taylor, M. S. (1988). Effects of college internships on individual participants. *Journal of Applied Psychology, 73*, 393–401.

Turunen, T. A., & Tuovila, S. (2012). Mind the gap. Combining theory and practice in a field experience. *Teaching Education, 23*(2), 115–130. http://dx.doi.org/10.1080/-10476210.2012.669751

Vaill, P. B. (1996). *Learning as a way of being.* San Francisco, CA: Jossey-Bass.

Whetten, D. A., & Clark, S. C. (1996). An integrated model for teaching management skills. *Journal of Management Education, 20*, 152–181.

Young, D. S., & Baker, R. E. (2004). Linking classroom theory to professional practice: The internship as a practical learning experience worthy of academic credit. *Journal of Physical Education, Recreation & Dance, 75*(1), 22–24. http://dx.doi.org/10.1080/07303084.2004.10608536

Chapter V

Alm, C.T. (1996). Using student journals to improve the academic quality of internships. *Journal of Education for Business, 72*(2), 113–115. http://dx.doi.org/10.1080/08832323.1996.10116837

Anderson, G., Boud, D., & Simpson, J. (1996). *Learning contracts.* London, England: Kogan Page.

Argote, L., & Miron-Spektor, E. (2011). Organizational learning: From experience to knowledge. *Organization Science, 22*(5), 1123–1137. http://dx.doi.org/-10.1287/orsc.1100.0621

Bailey, M. E., & Tuohy, D. (2009). Student nurses' experiences of using a learning contract as a method of assessment. *Nurse Education Today, 29*(7), 758–762. http://dx.doi.org/-10.1016/j.nedt.2009.03.012

Beard, F., & Morton, L. (1999). Effects of internship predictors on successful field experience. *Journalism & Mass Communication Educator, 53*(4), 42–53.

Boitel, C. R., & Fromm, L. R. (2014). Defining signature pedagogy in social work education: Learning theory and the learning contract. *Journal of Social Work Education, 50*(4), 608–622.

Boulert, A. (2012). Reflective practice, enhanced by a learning contract. *British Journal of Healthcare Assistants, 6*(11), 556–559.

Burke, L.A., & Miller, M.K. (1999). Taking the mystery out of intuitive decision making. *Academy of Management Executive, 13*(4), 91–99. doi: 10.5465/AME.1999.2570557

Callanan, G., & Benzing, C. (2004). Assessing the role of internships in the career-oriented employment of graduating college students. *Education+Training, 46*(2), 82–89. http://dx.doi.org/10.1108/00400910410525261

Coco, M. (2000). Internships: A try before you buy arrangement. *SAM Advanced Management Journal, 65*(2), 41–43.

Coy, P. G. (2014). Collective learning agreements as democratic practice and joint empowerment. *Conflict Resolution Quarterly, 31*, 229–256. doi:10.1002/crq.21087

Cutting, R. H., & Hall, J. C. (2008). Requirements for a workable intern/practicum in the environmental sciences: Experience for career and graduate. *Journal of Geoscience Education, 56*(2), 120–125.

Eyler, J. (2002). Reflection: Linking service and learning—Linking students and communities. *Journal of Social Issues, 58*(3), 517–534. doi: 10.1111/1540-4560.00274

Feldman, D. C., Folks, W. R., & Turnley, W. H. (1999). Mentor-protégé diversity and its impact on international internship experiences. *Journal of Organizational Behavior, 20*(5), 597–611. Retrieved from: http://www.jstor.org/stable/3100431

Freie, J. F. (1992). The individual learning contract. *Political Science & Politics, 25*(2), 230–234.

Friedman, B. D., & Neuman, K. M. (2001). Learning plans. *Journal of Teaching in Social Work, 21*, 123–138. http://dx.doi.org/10.1300/J067v21n03_10

Glennon F. (2008). Promoting freedom, responsibility, and learning in the classroom: The learning covenant a decade later. *Teaching Theology & Religion, 11*, 32–41.

Greenwood, S. C., & McCabe, P. P. (2008). How learning contracts motivate students. *Middle School Journal (j3), 39*(5), 13–22. http://dx.doi.org/10.1080/00940771.2008.11461649

Henry, J. S., Rehwaldt, S. S., & Vineyard, G. M. (2001). Congruency between student interns and worksite supervisors regarding critical elements of an internship experience. *Information Technology, Learning, and Performance Journal, 19*(1), 31–41.

Iverson, C. M. (1995). The power of the learning contract emerges once again: Applications in the military. *Adult Learning, 6*(3), 15–16.

Kim, E. B., Kim, K., & Bzullak, M. (2012). A survey of internship programs for management undergraduates in AACSB-accredited institutions. *International Journal of Educational*

Management, 26(7), 696–709. http://dx.doi.org/10.1108/09513541211263755

Lewis, J. J. (2004). The independent learning contract system: Motivating students enrolled in college reading courses. *Reading Improvement, 41*(3), 188–194.

Lubitsh, G., & Shaw, R. J. (2004). The learning contract: A behavioural approach to managing poor performance by consultants and preventing disciplinary action. *Clinician in Management, 12*(4), 181–186.

Miller, S. J., Hickson, D. J., & Wilson, D. C. (1996). Decision-making in organizations. In Clegg S. R., Hardy C., & Nord W. R. (Eds.), *Handbook of organization studies* (pp. 293–312). London, England: Sage.

Molseed, T. R., Alsup, J., & Voyles, J. (2003). The role of the employer in shaping students' work-related skills. *Journal of Employment Counseling, 40*(4), 161–171.

Moore, H. A., Mossop, R., & Simpson, J. M. (2003). Learning contract. *New South Wales Public Health Bulletin, 14*(5), 38–54.

Nelken, M. L. (2009). Negotiating classroom process: Lessons from adult learning. *Negotiation Journal, 25,* 181–194.

Rahmat, R. A., & Aziz, N. A. (2012). Stimulating learning ownership to engineering students via learning contract. *Asian Social Science, 8*(16), 57–64. http://dx.doi.org/10.5539/-ass.v8n16p57

Robinson, S., Kraatz M. S., & Rousseau, D. M. (1994). Changing obligations and psychological contract: A longitudinal study. *Academy of Management Journal, 37,* 137–152.

Rossman, M. H. (1983). The learning contract: Variation on a theme. *The Journal of Continuing Higher Education, 31*(1), 27–29. http://dx.doi.org/10.1080/07377366.1983.10401345

Rothman, M. (2007). Lessons learned: Advice to employers from interns. *Journal of Education for Business, 82*(3), 140–144. http://dx.doi.org/10.3200/JOEB.82.3.140-144

Rousseau, D. M., & Parks, J. M. (1993). The contracts of individuals and organizations. *Research in Organizational Behavior, 15,* 1–43.

Rye, K. J. B. (2008). Perceived benefits of the use of learning contracts to guide clinical education in respiratory care students. *Respiratory Care, 53*(11), 1475–1481.

Scott, S. V., Ray, N. M., & Warberg, W. (1990). The design and evaluation of off-campus internship and cooperative education programs. *Journal of Marketing for Higher Education, 3*(1), 121–39. http://dx.doi.org/10.1300/J050v03n01_09

Seymour, D. (1988). Staff development by negotiated learning contract. *Industrial and Commercial Training, 20*(6), 24–27. http://dx.doi.org/10.1108/eb004119

Shore L. M., & Tetrick L. E. (1994). The psychological contract as an explanatory framework in the employment relationship. In Cooper C., & Rousseau D. (Eds.), *Trends in organizational behavior* (pp. 91–109). New York, NY: John Wiley.

Stephenson J., & Laycock M. (Eds.). (1993). *Using learning contracts in higher education.* London, England: Kogan Page.

Taylor, M. S. (1988). Effects of college internships on individual participants. *Journal of Applied Psychology, 73*(3), 393–401. http://psycnet.apa.org/doi/10.1037/0021-9010.73.3.393

Tovey, J. (2001). Building connections between industry and university: Implementing an internship program at a regional university. *Technical Communication Quarterly, 10*(2), 225–239. http://dx.doi.org/10.1207/s15427625tcq1002_7

Vitton, J. J., & Butz, N. T. (2014). Adoption of a learning contract in higher education. *Journal of Cases in Educational Leadership, 17*(4), 96–110.

Wald, R. (1978). Confronting the learning contract. *Alternative Higher Education, 2*(3) 22–231. doi:10.1007/BF01080271

Watson, K. W. (1992). An integration of values: Teaching the internship course in a liberal arts environment. *Communication Education, 41*(4), 429–439. http://dx.doi.org/10.1080/03634529209378904

Chapter VI

Abraham, J. D., Burnett, D. D., & John, Jr, M. J. D. (2006). Feedback seeking among developmental assessment center participants. *Journal of Business and Psychology, 20*(3), 383–394. http://dx.doi.org/10.1007/s10869-005-9008-z

Abuhusain, H., Chotirmall, S. H., Hamid, N., & O'Neill, S. J. (2009). Prepared for internship? *Irish Medical Journal, 102*(3), 82–84.

Ashford, S. J., & Blatt, R. (2003). Reflections on the looking glass: A review of research on feedback-seeking behavior in organizations. *Journal of Management, 29*(6), 773–799.

Babbie, E. R. (2015). *The practice of social research.* Ontario, Canada: Nelson Education.

Badger, J. (2012). Analyzing levels of feedback delivered by cooperating teachers and supervisors in a teacher internship: A case study.

Georgia Educational Researcher, 9(1), 21–39. doi: 10.20429/ger.2012.090102

Basow, R. R., & Byrne, M. V. (1992). Internship expectations and learning goals. *The Journalism Educator, 47*(4), 48–54.

Bourland-Davis, P. G., Graham, B. L., & Fulmer, H. W. (1997). Defining a public relations internship through feedback from the field. *Journalism & Mass Communication Educator, 52*(1), 26–33.

Bok, H. G., Teunissen, P. W., Spruijt, A., Fokkema, J. P., van, B. P., Jaarsma, D. A., & van, V. C. P. (2013). Clarifying students' feedback-seeking behaviour in clinical clerkships. *Medical Education, 47*(3), 282–291. http://dx.doi.org/10.1111/medu.12054

Brooks, L., Cornelius, A., Greenfield, E., & Joseph, R. (1995). The relation of career-related work or internship experiences to the career development of college seniors. *Journal of Vocational Behavior, 46*(3), 332–349. http://dx.doi.org/10.1006/jvbe.1995.1024

Crommelinck, M., & Anseel, F. (2013). Understanding and encouraging feedback-seeking behaviour: A literature review. *Medical Education, 47*(3), 232–241. http://dx.doi.org/10.1111/medu.12075

Embo, M. P., Driessen, E. W., Valcke, M., & Van der Vleuten, C. P. (2010). Assessment and feedback to facilitate self-directed learning in clinical practice of midwifery students. *Medical teacher, 32*(7), e263–e269.

Harris, K. J., & Zhao, J. (2004). Industry internships: Feedback from participating faculty and industry executives. *International Journal of Contemporary Hospitality Management, 16*(7), 429–435. http://dx.doi.org/10.1108/09596110410559131

Hays, J. C., & Williams, J. R. (2011). Testing multiple motives in feedback seeking: The interaction of instrumentality and self-protection motives. *Journal of Vocational Behavior, 79*(2), 496–504. http://dx.doi.org/10.1016/j.jvb.2011.01.007

Krasman, J. (2011). Taking feedback-seeking to the next "level": Organizational structure and feedback-seeking behavior. *Journal of Managerial Issues, 23*(1), 9–30.

Major, D. A., & Kozlowski, S. W. (1997). Newcomer information seeking: Individual and contextual influences. *International Journal of Selection and Assessment, 5*(1), 16–28. doi: 10.1111/1468-2389.00042

Morrison, E. W., & Weldon, E. (1990). The impact of an assigned performance goal on feedback seeking behavior. *Human Performance, 3*(1), 37–50. http://dx.doi.org/10.1207/-s15327043hup0301_3

Park, G., Schmidt, A. M., Scheu, C., & DeShon, R. P. (2007). A process model of goal orientation and feedback seeking. *Human Performance, 20*(2), 119–145. http://dx.doi.org/10.1080/08959280701332042

Ren, R., Sun, J. Y., Zhang, Y., Chen, Y., & Liu, C. (2015). Can good impression and feedback-seeking behavior help Chinese graduates get a job? A mixed-methods study on a recruiting assessment center. *Journal of Chinese Human Resource Management, 6*(1), 14–32. http://dx.doi.org/10.1108/JCHRM-03-2015-0003

Roberson, L., Deitch, E. A., Brief, A. P., & Block, C. J. (2003). Stereotype threat and feedback seeking in the workplace. *Journal of Vocational Behavior, 62*(1), 176–188. http://dx.doi.org/10.1016/S0001-8791(02)00056-8

Rothman, M. (2007). Lessons learned: Advice to employers from interns. *Journal of Education for Business, 82*(3), 140–144. http://dx.doi.org/10.3200/JOEB.82.3.140-144

Subramony, M. (2000). The relationship between performance feedback and service-learnings. *Michigan Journal of Community Service Learning, 7*(1), 46–53. http://hdl.handle.net/2027/spo.3239521.0007.106

VandeWalle, D., Ganesan, S., Challagalla, G. N., & Brown, S. P. (2000). An integrated model of feedback-seeking behavior: Disposition, context, and cognition. *The Journal of Applied Psychology, 85*(6), 996–1003.

Williams, J., & Johnson, M. (2000). Self-supervisor agreement: The Influence of feedback seeking on the relationship between self and supervisor ratings of performance. *Journal of Applied Social Psychology, 30*(2), 275–292. http://dx.doi.org/10.1111/j.1559-1816.2000.tb02316.x

Chapter VII

Allen, S., Mims, C., Roberts, S., Kim, B., & Ryu, J. (2004). Internship experience: Engaging in the big discourse. *Techtrends: Linking Research and Practice to Improve Learning a Publication of the Association for Educational Communications & Technology, 48*(1), 44–48. http://dx.doi.org/10.1007/BF02784864

Baker, S. D., & Cotugna, N. (2013). Students entering internship show readiness in the nutrition care process. *Journal of Human Nutrition and Dietetics, 26*(5), 512–518. doi: 10.1111/jhn.12107

Baker, S. R., Romero, M. J., Geannette, C., & Patel, A. (2009). The value of the internship for radiation oncology training: Results of a survey of current and recent trainees. *International*

Journal of Radiation Oncology, Biology, Physics, 74(4), 1203–1206. http://dx.doi.org/10.1016/j.ijrobp.2008.09.024

Bay, J. (2006). Preparing undergraduates for careers: An argument for the internship practicum. *College English, 69*(2), 134–141.

Cannon, E. P., & Frank, D. (2009). Promoting ego development and multicultural competence during internship. *International Journal for the Advancement of Counselling, 31*(3), 199–211. http://dx.doi.org/10.1007/s10447-009-9078-0

Diambra, J. F., Cole-Zakrzewski, K. G., & Booher, J. (2004). A comparison of internship stage models: Evidence from intern experiences. *Journal of Experiential Education, 27*(2), 191–212.

Dilts, J. C., & Fowler, S. M. (1999). Internships: Preparing students for an entrepreneurial career. *Journal of Business and Entrepreneurship, 11*(1), 51–63.

Gerken, M., Rienties, B., Giesbers, B., & Könings, K. D. (2012). Enhancing the academic internship learning experience for business education: A critical review and future directions. In *Learning at the Crossroads of Theory and Practice* (pp. 7–22). New York, NY: Springer.

Gordon, G. H., Hubbell, F. A., Wyle, F. A., & Charter, R. A. (1986). Stress during internship. *Journal of General Internal Medicine, 1*(4), 228–231. doi:10.1007/BF02596188

Johari, A., & Bradshaw, A. (2008). Project-based learning in an internship program: A qualitative study of related roles and their motivational attributes. *Educational Technology Research and Development, 56*(3), 329–359. http://dx.doi.org/10.1007/s11423-006-9009-2

Kapoor, H., Tekian, A., & Mennin, S. (2010). Structuring an internship programme for enhanced learning. *Medical Education, 44*(5), 501–502. http://dx.doi.org/10.1111/j.1365-2923.2010.03681.x

Nutefall, J. E. (2012). Structuring a successful instruction internship. *College & Undergraduate Libraries, 19*(1), 80–94. http://dx.doi.org/10.1080/10691316.2012.652550

Stedman, J. M., & Schoenfeld, L. S. (2011). Knowledge competence in clinical and counseling training and readiness for internship. *Journal of Clinical Psychology, 67*(1), 1–5.

Tsang, W. K. (2003). Journaling from internship to practice teaching. *Reflective Practice, 4*(2), 221–240. http://dx.doi.org/10.1080/14623940308269

Welsh, J., Stanley, J., & Wilmoth, C. (2003). Competency based pre-internship supervision of school psychologists: A collaborative training model. *The Clinical Supervisor, 22*(1), 177–189. http://dx.doi.org/10.1300/J001v22n01_12

Zanchetta, M., Schwind, J., Aksenchuk, K., Gorospe, F. F., & Santiago, L. (2013). An international internship on social development led by Canadian nursing students: Empowering learning. *Nurse Education Today, 33*(7), 757–764. http://dx.doi.org/10.1016/j.nedt.2013.04.019

Chapter VIII

Bouldin, A. S., Holmes, E. R., & Fortenberry, M. L. (2006). "Blogging" about course concepts: Using technology for reflective journaling in a communications class. *American Journal of Pharmaceutical Education, 70*(4), 1–8. PMCID: PMC1636988

Coleman, K., & Flood, A. (2016). *Enabling reflective thinking: Reflective practice in learning and teaching.* Champaign, IL: Common Ground Publishing.

Collay, M. (1998). *Learning circles: Creating conditions for professional development.* Thousand Oaks, CA: Corwin Press.

Creede, C., Fisher-Yoshida, B., & Gallegos, P. V. (2012). *The reflective, facilitative, and interpretive practices of the coordinated management of meaning: Making lives, making meaning.* Madison, NJ: Fairleigh Dickinson University Press.

Ferrari, J. R., & Chapman, J. G. (1999). *Educating students to make-a-difference: Community-based service learning.* New York, NY: Haworth Press.

Harris, M. (2008). Is journaling empowering? Students' perceptions of their reflective writing experience. *Health SA Gesondheid, 10*(2), online.

Johns, C., & Burnie, S. (2013). *Becoming a reflective practitioner.* Chichester, West Sussex: Wiley-Blackwell.

Kirby, J. R., & Lawson, M. J. (2012). *Enhancing the quality of learning: Dispositions, instruction, and learning processes.* Cambridge, UK: Cambridge University Press.

Mezirow, J., & Taylor, E. W. (2009). *Transformative learning in practice: Insights from community, workplace, and higher education.* San Francisco, CA: Jossey-Bass.

Peery, A. B. (2005). *ARRIVE: Improving instruction through reflective journaling.* Englewood, CO: Advanced Learning Press.

Preis, J., & Stauder, E. (2014). *Reflective writing: From pedagogy to practice in a Jesuit university.* Jesuit Higher Education. Retrieved from: https://epublications.regis.edu/cgi/viewcontent.cgi?referer=https://www.bing.com/&httpsredir=1&article=1062&context=jhe

Rhoads, R. A., & Howard, J. (1998). *Academic service learning: A pedagogy of action and reflection.* San Francisco, CA: Jossey-Bass Publishers.

Stevens, D. D., & Cooper, J. E. (2009). *Journal keeping: How to use reflective writing for effective learning, teaching, professional insight, and positive change.* Sterling, VA: Stylus Pub.

Tsang, W. K. (2003). Journaling from internship to practice: Teaching. *Reflective Practice, 4*(2), 221–240. doi: 10.1080/14623940308269

feedback delivery. *Journal of General Internal Medicine, 23*(7), 969–972.

Tornow, W. W., London, M., & Center for Creative Leadership. (1998). *Maximizing the value of 360-degree feedback: A process for successful individual and organizational development.* San Francisco, CA: Jossey-Bass.

Ward, P. (1997). *360-degree feedback.* London, UK: Institute of Personnel and Development.

Zhang, N., & Parsons, R. D. (2016). *Field experience: Transitioning from student to professional.* Los Angeles, CA: Sage.

Chapter IX

Bracken, D., & Center for Creative Leadership (1997). *Should 360-degree feedback be used only for developmental purposes?* Greensboro, NC: Center for Creative Leadership.

Edwards, M. R., & Ewen, A. J. (1996). *360° feedback: The powerful new model for employee assessment & performance improvement.* New York, NY: AMACOM.

Fleenor, J. W., & Prince, J. M. (1997). *Using 360-degree feedback in organizations: An annotated bibliography.* Greensboro, NC: Center for Creative Leadership.

Hickok, C. (1995). *Improving performance with feedback: 51 practical strategies for using 360 degree feedback in training.* Washington, DC: Resources for Organizations.

Holmboe, E. S., & Hawkins, R. E. (2008). *Practical guide to the evaluation of clinical competence.* Philadelphia, PA: Mosby/Elsevier.

Kirkland, K., Manoogian, S., & Center for Creative Leadership (1998). *Ongoing feedback: How to get it, how to use it.* Greensboro, NC: Center for Creative Leadership.

Langdon, D. G., Whiteside, K. S., & McKenna, M. M. (1999). *Intervention resource guide: 50 performance improvement tools.* San Francisco, CA: Jossey-Bass/Pfeiffer.

Lepsinger, R., Lucia, A. D., & Lepsinger, R. (2009). *The art and science of 360-degree feedback.* San Francisco, CA: Jossey-Bass.

London, M. (2014). *The power of feedback: Giving, seeking, and using feedback for performance improvement.* Hoboken, NJ: Taylor and Francis.

Smith, J. (2012). *Using 360-degree feedback—what you need to know: Definitions, best practices, benefits and practical solutions.* Brisbane, Australia: Emereo Publishing.

Stark, R., Orenstein, D., & Karani, R. (July 01, 2008). Impact of a 360-degree professionalism assessment on faculty comfort and skills in

Chapter X

Bacal, R. (2004). *Manager's guide to performance reviews.* New York, NY: McGraw-Hill.

Echterling, L. G. (2016). *Thriving! A manual for students in the helping professions.* Los Angeles, CA: Sage.

Folkman, J. (2006). *The power of feedback: 35 principles for turning feedback from others into personal and professional change.* Hoboken, NJ: Wiley.

Garber, P. R. (2004). *Giving and receiving performance feedback.* Amherst, MA: HRD Press.

Hathaway, P. (1998). *Giving and receiving feedback: Building constructive communication.* Menlo Park, CA: Crisp Publications.

Kurtoğlu-Hooton, N. (2016). *Confirmatory feedback in teacher education: An instigator of student teacher learning.* London, UK: Palgrave Macmillan.

Maurer, R. (1994). *Feedback toolkit: 16 tools for better communication in the workplace.* Portland, OR: Productivity Press.

McCallum, D. (2016). *The feedback-friendly classroom: How to equip students to give, receive, and seek quality feedback that will support their social, academic, and developmental needs.* Markham, ON: Pembroke Publishers.

McKenzie, S., Burgess, A., & Mellis, C. (2017). *Interns reflect: The effect of formative assessment with feedback during pre-internship.* London, UK: Dove Press.

Miles, M. B. (1958). *Response to task-oriented and feeling-oriented feedback during training.* New York, NY: Columbia University.

Race, P. (2007). *How to get a good degree: Making the most of your time at university.* Maidenhead, England: McGraw Hill/Open University Press.

Seashore, C. N., Seashore, E. W., & Weinberg, G. M. (1997). *What did you say? The art of giving and receiving feedback.* Columbia, MD: Bingham House Books.

Seemiller, C. (2013). *The student leadership competencies guidebook: Designing intentional leadership learning and development*. San Francisco, CA: Jossey-Bass/Wiley.

Sutton, R. M., Douglas, K. M., & Hornsey, M. J. (2012). *Feedback: The communication of praise, criticism, and advice*. New York, NY: Peter Lang.

Chapter XI

Azevedo, R., & Aleven, V. A. W. M. M. (2013). *International handbook of metacognition and learning technologies*. New York, NY: Springer.

Bringle, R. G., Reeb, R. N., Brown, M. A., & Ruiz, A. I. (2016). *Service learning in psychology: Enhancing undergraduate education for the public good*. Washington, DC: American Psychological Association.

Eyler, J., & Giles, D. (1999). *Where's the learning in service-learning?* San Francisco, CA: Jossey-Bass.

Ferrari, J. R., & Chapman, J. G. (1999). *Educating students to make-a-difference: Community-based service learning*. New York, NY: Haworth Press.

Gordon, D. (2001). Tracking internship outcomes through comparative quantitative assessment. *Journal of Career Planning & Employment, 62*(2), 28–32.

Hatcher, J. A., Bringle, R. G., & Hahn, T. W. (2016). *Research on student civic outcomes in service learning: Conceptual frameworks and methods*. Ronks, PA: Stylus Publishing.

Heider, K. L. (2017). *Service learning as pedagogy in early childhood education: Theory, research, and practice*. New York, NY: Springer.

Martin, G., Wright, W., & Danzig, A. (2013). *School leader internship: Developing, monitoring, and evaluating your leadership experience*. Hoboken, NJ: Taylor and Francis.

Nadel, M., Majewski, V., & Sullivan-Cosetti, M. (2007). *Social work and service learning: Partnerships for social justice*. Lanham, MD: Rowman & Littlefield Publishers.

Newman, D. S. (2013a). *Demystifying the school psychology internship: A dynamic guide for interns and supervisors*. Hoboken, NJ: Taylor and Francis.

Newman, D. S. (2013b). *Transcending the hourly log: A guide to a dynamic school psychology internship*. Hoboken, NJ: Taylor and Francis.

Payne, D. A. (2000). *Evaluating service learning activities and programs*. Lanham, MD: Springer.

Russell-Chapin, L. A., & Ivey, A. E. (2004). *Your supervised practicum and internship: Field resources for turning theory into action*. Stamford, CT: Thomson/Brooks/Cole.

Chapter XII

Adler-Kassner, L., Crooks, R., Watters, A., American Association for Higher Education & National Council of Teachers of English (1997). *Writing the community: Concepts and models for service-learning in composition*. Washington, DC: American Association for Higher Education.

Cohen, A. (2014). *Speaking of learning: Recollections, revelations, and realizations*. Rotterdam, Netherlands: Sense Publishers.

Ellis, C., & Bochner, A. P. (1996). *Composing ethnography: Alternative forms of qualitative writing*. Walnut Creek, CA: AltaMira Press.

Emerson, R. M., Fretz, R. I., & Shaw, L. L. (1995). *Writing ethnographic fieldnotes*. Chicago, IL: University of Chicago Press.

Kirby, J. R., & Lawson, M. J. (2012). *Enhancing the quality of learning: Dispositions, instruction, and learning processes*. Cambridge, UK: Cambridge University Press.

Kiser, P. M. (2000). *Getting the most from your human service internship: Learning from experience*. Stamford, CT: Brooks/Cole.

Kostouli, T. (2005). *Writing in context(s): Textual practices and learning processes in sociocultural settings*. Boston, MA: Springer.

Parsons, M. H. (1996). *Promoting community renewal through civic literacy and service learning*. San Francisco, CA: Jossey-Bass.

Rhoads, R. A., & Howard, J. (1998). *Academic service learning: A pedagogy of action and reflection*. San Francisco, CA: Jossey-Bass Publishers.

Sachs, J., & Clark, L. (2016). *Learning through community engagement: Vision and practice in higher education*. Boston, MA: Springer.

Stevens, D. D., & Cooper, J. E. (2009). *Journal keeping: How to use reflective writing for effective learning, teaching, professional insight, and positive change*. Sterling, VA: Stylus Pub.

Wolcott, H. F. (2009). *Writing up qualitative research*. Los Angeles, CA: Sage.

Chapter XIII

Atkinson, C. (2005). *Beyond bullet points: Using Microsoft PowerPoint to create presentations that inform, motivate and inspire*. Redmond, WA: Microsoft Press.

Bingham, T., & Jeary, T. (2007). *Presenting learning*. Alexandria, VA: ASTD Press.

Grand, L. C. (2000). *The workplace skills presentation guide*. New York, NY: John Wiley & Sons.

Ichniowski, C. (2000). *The American workplace: Skills, compensation, and employee involvement*. Cambridge, UK: Cambridge University Press.

Jalongo, M. R., & Machado, C. (2016). *Making effective presentations at professional conferences: A guide for teachers, graduate students and professors*. New York, NY: Springer.

Kenton, S. B., & Valentine, D. (1997). *Crosstalk: Communicating in a multicultural workplace*. Upper Saddle River, NJ: Prentice Hall.

Kikoski, J. F., & Kikoski, C. K. (1999). *Reflexive communication in the culturally diverse workplace*. Westport, CT: Praeger.

Malloch, M., Cairns, L., Evans, K., & O'Connor, B. N. (2010). *The SAGE handbook of workplace learning*. London, UK: Sage Publications.

Manchester Open Learning. (1993). *Making effective presentations*. Manchester, UK: Kogan Page.

Melograno, V. (1998). *Professional and student portfolios for physical education*. Champaign, IL: Human Kinetics.

Morton, S. (2014). *The presentation lab: Learn the formula behind powerful presentations*. Hoboken, NJ: Wiley.

Pincus, A. (2015). *Presenting*. New York, NY: DK.

Prestoungrange, G. (1998). *The knowledge game: The revolution in learning and communication in the workplace*. London, UK: Cassell.

Spikes, W. F. (1995). *Workplace learning*. San Francisco, CA: Jossey-Bass.

Swanson, R. A., & Holton, E. F. (1999). *Results: How to assess performance, learning, and perceptions in organizations*. San Francisco, CA: Berrett-Koehler.

Wallwork, A. (2014). *Presentations, demos, and training sessions*. New York, NY: Springer.

Citrin, J. M. (2015). *The career playbook: Essential advice for today's aspiring young professional*. New York, NY: Crown Business.

Collins, S. (1998). *Getting into banking and finance: How to launch a rewarding career*. Oxford, UK: How to Books.

Fein, R. (1992). *First job: A new grad's guide to launching your business career*. New York, NY: Wiley.

Harr, J. S., & Hess, K. M. (2010). *Careers in criminal justice and related fields: From internship to promotion*. New York, NY: Wadsworth Cengage Learning.

Kaputa, C. (2016). *Graduate to a great career: How smart students, new graduates and young professionals can launch–Brand you*. Boston, MA: Nicholas Brealey Publishing.

Leibman, P. (2015). *Launch a teaching career: Secrets for aspiring teachers*. Lanham, MD: Rowman & Littlefield.

McCallum, V., & Brooke, A. (2006). *University wisdom: Discover the secrets of getting the most from your experience at university and use them as stepping stones to launch your life and career: A practical guide for all students*. Frankston, Victoria: Zermatt Press.

Simeon, R. (2013). *Working in the global economy: How to develop and manage your career across borders*. New York, NY: Routledge.

United States. (2004). *Launch a career in engineering*. Washington, DC: National Aeronautics and Space Administration.

Waide, L. (2008). *So you want to be a teacher? How to launch your teaching career*. London, UK: Continuum International Publishing Group.

Williams, J. (2013). *Constructing new professional identities: Career changers in teacher education*. Boston, MA: SensePublishers.

Zhang, N., & Parsons, R. D. (2016). *Field experience: Transitioning from student to professional*. Los Angeles, CA: Sage.

Chapter XIV

Asher, D. (2004). *How to get any job with any major: Career launch & re-launch for everyone under 30, or, how to avoid living in your parent's basement*. Berkeley, CA: Ten Speed Press.

Bravo, D., & Whiteley, C. (2005). *The internship advantage: Get real-world job experience to launch your career*. New York, NY: Prentice Hall Press.

Glossary of Terms

Academic Objective (Chapter 4): An academic objective relates to a learning-related task or goal to be accomplished. This is usually part of your broader learning goal plan (e.g., learning contract for a field training experience).

Academic Training (Chapter 12): Academic training involves both short- and long-term planning and accomplishment of onsite and classroom activities in coordination with supervisors from both institutions. There should be a clear correspondence between your academic training and your career development plans.

Actionable Goal (Chapter 3): An actionable goal is a planned activity, whether conceptual or applied in nature, which is doable in both its process and its outcome. An actionable goal also assists in the assessment of you and your learning outcomes.

Active Listening (Chapter 6): Active listening pertains to the process of a person both listening and responding to another person or group's communication in an accurate and responsive manner. Active listening has the benefit of increasing both your learning outcomes and communication effectiveness.

Adaptive Learning (Chapter 9): The process of adaptive learning relates to a person receiving information in the learning environment (e.g., task feedback) and adjusting their learning style and/or strategies within the learning situation. Your responsiveness to the many changes in your training underlies the successful completion of your career development experience.

Anchoring and Adjusting (Chapter 9): The anchoring and adjusting process entails the need to set a performance standard (i.e., anchor) with the expectation that your subsequent performance goals will shift (i.e., adjust) in response to performance feedback.

Applied Discussion (Chapter 13): An applied discussion involves the integration of your learning outcomes with relevant literature from a theoretical or applied perspective. The conceptual analysis of your field-relevant learning considering your original learning goals is a critical process in your ongoing career development.

Applied Learning Analysis (Chapter 13): An applied learning analysis approach incorporates your self-reflections on personal learning goals and their associated outcomes over time, as they relate to the theoretical foundation of your "micro" learning to the broader "macro" field perspectives of professional development within your field/discipline.

Business Etiquette (Chapter 1): Business etiquette reflects field-relevant norms of professional behavior and attitudes as reflected in both your professional work and your interactions with relevant "others" (e.g., clients). Your adherence to business etiquette standards in your field/discipline assists in your impression management tactics throughout your career.

Career Trajectory (Chapter 14): A career trajectory refers to the stages that a person experiences from the beginning stage through the middle and later stages of their career development. Planning for both short- and long-term goals related to this career development process will help you optimize outcomes at each of these stages.

Concept (Chapter 4): A concept is an idea or notion that can be applied in a learning context or task. From a research perspective, you will develop different concepts in your analysis of your ongoing learning goals and onsite learning accomplishments during your field training.

Content Analysis (Chapter 13): A content analysis involves a review of information conveyed through a specific communication format (e.g., written or oral information) to examine meaningful trends or "patterns" within the communication source for interpretation purposes.

Cooperative Agreement (Chapter 5): A cooperative agreement relates to an approved plan between multiple sources ("key stakeholders") related to a field-related learning experience. As applied to your field training, this may entail an agreement between you and your two faculty and site supervisors, at minimum, although it may involve more than those principal constituents.

Expectations (Chapter 7): Expectations relate to a person's anticipation of the self's or others' behavioral and/or attitude outcomes. Related to your onsite performance, your learning contract sets forth certain expectations of your training outcomes based upon the collaborative goals of your supervisors and yourself.

Feedback (Chapter 6): Feedback relates to environmental responses to our actions in the social environment and/or performance context. As a trainee, you will solicit and receive feedback from multiple sources both onsite and in the classroom to help you optimize your learning experience across the many weeks of your onsite skill development process.

360° Feedback (Chapter 9): The concept of 360° feedback refers to the process of soliciting performance feedback from multiple sources at various levels of observation, ranging from self to supervisors and, potentially, to those whom you may interact with as clients/customers.

Feedback Informant (Chapter 9): A feedback informant provides constructive performance information to a feedback recipient who would benefit from such information to adjust their task-related performance. As a field trainee, you will utilize multiple feedback informants to help you with multiple performance focuses.

Feedback Recipient (Chapter 9): The feedback recipient engages in active listening and clarifies the performance feedback received from feedback informants. You will engage in ongoing communication as a feedback recipient across many phases of your training process.

Feedback Responsiveness (Chapter 6): Feedback responsiveness relates to how well a person in the role of feedback percipient can analyze information for performance adjustment. Your supervisors, among other constituents, will evaluate you on your ability to respond to feedback in a perceptive and accurate manner.

Feedback Subgoal Planning (Chapter 10): Feedback subgoal planning refers to the idea of creating "doable" steps in your learning process to focus on performance improvement in response to ongoing feedback messages. You will find that segmenting your training tasks into subgoals will help you focus on specific goals over the course of your training area.

Field-Relevant Standards (Chapter 13): Field-relevant standards refer to the expectations of professional performance and associate the behaviors for such attitudes from experts in the field/discipline of your choosing. As an emerging professional in your field of training, you will benefit from this knowledge in many ways, from strategies in professional networking to the formatting of your written work.

Generalized Learning (Chapter 14): Generalized learning is when the trainee can extrapolate their field-related learning into broader themes that relate to professionalism in the chosen field/discipline. You will find that much of what you learned in your training can be applied to multiple contacts and task situations within your area of specialization.

Goal (Chapter 3): A goal is the focus of personal effort and/or performance achievement by a person or group within a performance context. In all phases of your field-related training, you will be setting, revising, and analyzing the outcomes of your performance goals (e.g., learning contract goals).

Goal Attainment (Chapter 10): Goal attainment refers to the accomplishment of established aims (goals) as it reflects on the self and others' expectations of performance. As you continue your training in your career, consider each attained goal as a "stepping stone" to the next performance level in your professional development.

Goal Follow-Up Assessment (Chapter 10): Goal follow-up assessment is a critical step in identifying the degree to which there has been progress made in accomplishing stated performance and/or learning aims (goals). You should actively seek out opportunities for the self and others' assessments of your progress to date to identify areas of needed assistance and/or patterns of learning adaptation over time.

Goal-in-Progress (Chapter 10): A goal-in-progress determination relates to the timing of assessments and the judgment of whether the goal has been properly implemented as planned. You will be performing goals at various stages of implementation across your training time, and it is important to be cognizant of these differential timing assessments.

Goal-Oriented Perspective (Chapter 11): A goal-oriented perspective refers to the practice of viewing task-related learning and performance outcomes is a series of goals with clearly defined steps and assessable outcomes. As you plan and implement your field training goals, you should keep in mind the different goals and subgoals underlying each of these broader field-related planned activities.

Goal Plan Responsiveness (Chapter 10): Goal plan responsiveness involves both the "person" and the "task situation" together as they dynamically interact and change over time, with the need to adjust accordingly. You will need to periodically review, and possibly revise, your goal plans (e.g., learning contract) more than once over the course of your field-related training experience.

Goal Relevance (Chapter 8): Goal relevance relates to how meaningful or pertinent a goal is to the overall aim of the training or learning context. You should be focused on planning, accomplishing, and building upon your training goals (and subgoals) as they relate to your overall training plan and your broader professional development trajectory.

Goal Review (Chapter 11): A goal review should be conducted periodically over the course of the field training process, reviewing your progress to date in accomplished, ongoing, and/or unaddressed field-training goals. You and your supervisors should meet on a regular basis to re-examine the focus of your training in your ongoing resolution of these aims.

Goal Setting (Chapter 3): Goal setting involves the process of establishing specific performance expectations with associated evaluation criteria for assessment purposes. You will develop goals in your learning contract, as well as engage in ongoing goal setting as your onsite and academic performance proficiency develops.

Goal-to-Outcome Discrepancy (Chapter 11): A goal-outcome discrepancy refers to the situation when an intended goal outcome may not correspond to the actual outcome from the goal-related activity. As an active learner onsite and in the classroom, you will need to be aware that not all goal outcomes are as expected and that you will need to adjust your performance goals accordingly over time.

Impression Management (Chapter 7): Impression management refers to the process of a person conforming to and behaviorally exemplifying the contextual, social, and cultural norms for his/her role in each social situation. As you will be interacting with different supervisors and other key stakeholders in your training, you will need to be aware of the impression you are making on others who may be judging your professionalism and performance capabilities.

Indoctrination (Chapter 7): Indoctrination is the process of a person or group to unconditionally adopting a set of beliefs conveyed by the larger "macro" group or culture (e.g., organizational culture of a company or institution). For your purposes, you will be expected to become indoctrinated with the rules and expectations of the training site in your role as a field trainee.

Integration (Chapter 6): Integration is the concept of bringing together various parts/aspects of a situation and/or a person into an integral, harmonious whole. Onsite and in the classroom, you will be integrating your learning experiences to gain a holistic perspective on your overall training outcomes.

Job Adaptation (Chapter 1): Job adaptation relates to the process of adjusting to the norms, expectations, and requirements of a specific job or job-related training position. You will be in the situation of adapting to your role and job as a trainee over the time of your field experience.

Job Analysis (Chapter 3): Job analysis is the process of reviewing the essential (required) and marginal functions of the job, based upon a variety of methodology (e.g., interviews, observations, and/or surveys). You will need to understand these job details as you train and learn onsite, bringing together conceptual and applied issues in your learning analyses.

Job Description (Chapter 3): A job description is a written document containing job-related information gathered during a job analysis. As a person learning a job position, it will be beneficial for you to review the job description(s) related to your training onsite.

Journaling (Chapter 5): Journaling is the process of recording self-observations, as well as task-related information, regarding ongoing learning in written form. You will benefit from this introspective self-analysis process in your journal writing, helping you to develop ideas regarding your personal learning processes, motivations, and performance outcomes over time.

Learning Achievement (Chapter 11): Learning achievement pertains to both the onsite and/or academic goal accomplishments of a person in a learning context. As you analyze the outcomes of your training, you will determine the number and degree of learning achievements you attained in reflection upon your initial learning-related goals.

Learning Analysis (Chapter 11): A learning analysis is a review of both personal learning processes (e.g., learning context preferences) and learning progress, based on established goals from a learning plan (e.g., learning contract). You will undergo an ongoing analysis of your training outcomes across the hours and weeks of your training experience, deriving an enhanced understanding of your specific learning style, motivations, and needs.

Learning Contract (Plan of Action) (Chapter 5): A learning contract is an agreement between the trainee and their supervisors (i.e., site, faculty, and relevant others) related to your commitment to onsite training times, dates, and learning goals, as well as any "deliverables" at the conclusion of the training. You will utilize this plan as a guide at all stages of your training.

Learning Goal (Chapter 3): A learning goal is a designated outcome for the learning experience. You will utilize goals for both your onsite and classroom (academic) learning activities in your learning plan or contract.

Learning Outcomes (Chapter 6): Learning outcomes are measurable, assessable results from agreed-upon learning goals from a learning plan or contract. Although most outcomes can be anticipated, you may also note that you have additional unexpected learning outcomes from the vast array of learning benefits you will derive through your onsite training in combination with your academic instruction.

Learning Theme (Chapter 12): A learning theme relates to the idea of examining the content of the journal notes and identifying patterns of behavior and/or attitudes about the field training. You will identify these themes as part of your learning outcomes, creating a conceptual framework for your culminating paper, project, and/or site-related presentation.

Lift Goal (Chapter 11): A lift goal is a type of goal focused on improving personal performance and/or status in a social situation. As an emerging professional in your field/discipline, it is important for you to set these types of goals in your early career development, as well as in an ongoing manner throughout your long-term career trajectory.

Literature Review (Chapter 4): A literature review entails researching, collecting, reviewing, and synthesizing both theoretical and empirical research information. You will write a field-relevant literature review in support of your training focus and proposed learning outcomes.

Needs Analysis (Chapter 3): A needs analysis is one procedural step within a full job analysis process, with this step focused on the training-related needs of an incumbent in a specific job position. This focus is beneficial to you as you determine the gap between your existing knowledge, skills, and abilities, and the requirements of your job-related training position onsite for additonal training recommendations, if appropriate.

Oral Communication Skills (Chapter 14): Oral communication skills are a critical part of information exchanges between people in different social contexts (e.g., the workplace). As a field trainee, you will utilize and further hone your communication skills in collaboration with multiple site-related participation involved directly or indirectly with your training activities onsite or in the classroom.

Organizational Analysis (Chapter 2): Organizational analysis is a macro-level examination of workplace productivity and functioning (e.g., organizational culture and communication "paths"). You will benefit from understanding this information to further optimize organizational socialization and associated training outcomes throughout your experience.

Organizational Culture (Chapter 1): Organizational culture refers to the workplace's norms, values, and beliefs, which affect workplace participants' behaviors and/or interactions onsite. As a new entrant in your training site, you will need to learn and adapt to the training site's organizational culture and expectations of you as a participant in the workplace.

Organizational Fit (Chapter 2): Organizational fit is the degree to which a person's values, beliefs, performance standards, and other job-relevant characteristics match the same criteria from the perspective of the organization. The degree to which you can optimize your training experience can be influenced by how well you match the expectations of the site on different levels of evaluation criteria (e.g., leadership style).

Organizational Norms (Chapter 7): Organizational norms are the workplace's expectations of employees' behaviors and attitudes in the execution of job-related duties. You will be expected to adhere to these site-related expectations as a trainee in the workplace, but this also has implications toward your broader career development and professionalism training.

Organizational Socialization (Chapter 1): Organizational socialization is the process of becoming socialized within the workplace and, among other outcomes, attaining social acceptance among organizational peers and supervisors. Although a site placement is more short-term in duration, you should seek out ways to become integrated into the organization's social network during your training time.

Organizational Values (Chapter 7): Organizational values reflect the core beliefs of the organization in terms of their expectations of employees' behavioral and attitudinal conduct in response to others inside, and possibly outside, the workplace. You will benefit from understanding the training site's values as they resonate with your own training evaluations and/or outcomes, either directly or indirectly.

Performance Review (Chapter 10): A performance review is conducted within an organization on a periodic basis and should be grounded in establishing performance standards for each employee, based on ongoing training opportunities and job-relevant qualifications from well-documented job descriptions. As a field trainee, you will undergo more than one performance review with your site supervisor, as well as with your facultly supervisor, over the time period of your field-related experience.

Person Analysis (Chapter 2): A person analysis examines the characteristics (e.g., training background) of an effectively-performing job incumbent in a specific job position. This information can assist you in better understanding the characteristics of the person you need to emulate in conducting your job training duties.

Perspective Taking (Chapter 8): Perspective taking refers to the ability to understand others' viewpoints on an issue or task. Learning how to acquire and understand others' perspectives will benefit you in processing performance feedback in the workplace and/or classroom during your field-related training.

Plagiarism (Chapter 4): Plagiarism is a concern in writing when a person may utilize text directly from published sources without giving appropriate authorship citations and not fully rewording the text into a new text form. As you write the text for your culminating paper, project, and/or presentaton, ensure that you create your own original written work, and properly cite all reference content used.

Presentation Style (Chapter 13): Presentation style refers to field-relevant standards of presentation content and format (e.g., American psychological Association format). This knowledge is an important practical issue in support of your professional training as you engage in multiple opportunities to present your learning outcomes in different professional contexts.

Professional Development (Chapter 12): Professional development is the process of learning all aspects of field-relevant standards of performance and behavior as they relate to success within the industry/discipline. In an ongoing manner, you will engage in professional development activities related to your planned learning goals as well as more informal activities onsite and in the classroom.

Professional Developmental Plan (Chapter 14): A professional development plan is associated with your learning plan (e.g., learning contract) but may be broader in focus and relate to both short- and long-term professional goals. You should consult with both your site and faculty supervisors in constructing your personalized development plan in light of specific career goals and associated field-related standards of performance.

Revision (Editing) Process (Chapter 6): The revision (editing) process should be a systematic, step-by-step procedure involving the analysis and problem-solving response for each received feedback point. You will receive revision feedback from multiple informants at every stage of your training and post-training at the time of presenting the results of your learning.

Scholarly Research (Chapter 4): Scholarly research refers to published articles and/or books, which are peer-reviewed during the publication process, suggesting meaningful field relevance in the approval of the associated content. In your training, you should utilize scholarly, peer-reviewed research sources to create your own scholarly written work.

Self Analysis (Chapter 8): Self analysis involves the ability to be introspective in examining personal ongoing progress in knowledge and/or skill development. The journaling activity helps assist in this self-analysis process as you reflect upon your daily accomplishments in light of your approved learning goals (e.g., learning contract).

Self-Directed Learning (Chapter 8): Self-directed learning is when a person adapts their learning goals to achieve specific knowledge and/or skills to best optimize the training experience. Your learning goals, as well as subsequent learning activities, should be self-directed as much as they can match your career plans and your internalized goals, values, and beliefs.

Self Observation (Chapter 12): Self observation is the ability to be aware of and record personal performance processes and outcomes, as well as associated attitudes underlying processes. You will utilize this skill during your journal notetaking and develop this further as your training proceeds to its completion.

Self Presentation (Chapter 14): Self presentation refers to presenting learning outcomes in reflection upon personal growth and professional accomplishments in an ongoing manner and at the completion of the field training. The purpose of this activity is to optimize your continuing professional development as you learn onsite.

Self Reflection (Chapter 5): Self reflection is the procedural step between observation and analysis in your journal notetaking. Across your field training, you will undergo self-reflection to best understand your internalized needs and motivations in response to the many different activities of your training experience.

Self-Regulatory Learning (Chapter 9): Self-regulatory learning is the idea that a person's learning should be responsive to the feedback presented in the learning environment, adapting to the changing learning standards and skill and knowledge levels as they continue to become more sophisticated in functioning. You will find that you become more attuned to your self-regulatory learning processes over time as you further enhance your professional and career development outcomes.

Self-Regulatory Process (Chapter 8): Self-regulatory process is an "anchoring and adjusting" experience of receiving and responding to feedback from a performance context. As a trainee onsite, you are going to engage in ongoing self-regulatory processes as an effective onsite learner and future career professional.

Supporting Incident (Chapter 12): A supporting incident is a specific learning event underlying or exemplifying a thematic outcome of training. In your journaling, it is beneficial to take note of specific learning contexts or situations to help you best analyze, in detail, your learning outcomes.

Task Analysis (Chapter 2): A task analysis reviews the needed knowledge, skills, and/or abilities to accomplish the specific job tasks. As you engage in many onsite training tasks, you will benefit from analyzing each task in determining how to best accomplish it in an effective and time-efficient manner.

Task Statement (Chapter 5): A task statement is a part of the job description and conveys the exact duties to be accomplished, as well as possible underlying knowledge, skills, and/or abilities entailed in completing the job task. In learning your training role, it's helpful to review the task statements related to your onsite training duties.

Teamwork (Chapter 7): Teamwork pertains to the motivation to work well with others in a short-term, focused project. You will likely be faced with being involved in team-based projects, and you will need to contribute to the effort as a "team player" in the workplace during your training.

Thematic Structure (Chapter 12): Thematic structure refers to the general outcomes, and the interdependent factors underlying these outcomes, from the journaled self-observations of learning. As you begin the process of reviewing your field training, you will identify a "structure" (e.g., priority sequencing of learning outcomes) to your learning themes as they relate to your conceptual ideas of learning.

Theoretical Foundation (Chapter 13): Theoretical foundation pertains to the idea that any analysis of outcomes, ranging from research to learning on a personal basis, should be grounded in a theoretical framework (e.g., Social Learning Theory) for interpretation purposes. As you write the results of your learning for your culminating paper, project, and oral presentation, they should be presented within a conceptual foundation or "framework" for interpretation purposes.

Theory (Chapter 4): A theory encapsulates multiple factors and uses generalized principles to explain a conceptual or applied phenomenon. You will use a theory to help guide the conceptual analysis of your ongoing field training outcomes through the writing of your final paper, project, and/or onsite presentation.

Time Management (Chapter 8): Time management relates the ability to be efficient in the utilization of time in conducting task-related activities. Onsite, you will be faced with multitasking different assignments, and you will learn how to best manage your time in accomplishing multiple task deadlines within an allotted time.

Work Professionalism (Chapter 1): Work professionalism reflects the behaviors and attitudes of a select profession's standards, as embodied by its representatives within a field/discipline. Part of your planned subsequent onsite training will focus on you developing a keen sense of work professionalism.

Work Role (Chapter 7): A work role is the assigned duties in a job. Your work role is defined by your established learning goals (e.g., learning contract), but realize that your training may cover different work roles to create a breadth of training.

Writing "Flow" (Chapter 4): Writing "flow" relates to how well the written topics create a logical sequence and rationale from the beginning to the end. You will work on this writing skill as you develop your written correspondence during your training.

Written Communication Skills (Chapter 14): Written communication skills are a key part of conveying ideas in the workplace, especially for the benefit of enhancing workplace productivity through effective communication between and among levels of an organization. As an intern, you will utilize your written communication to convey your learning outcomes to your supervisors and other key stakeholders involved in your learning experience.

Appendix A

List of Suggested Supplemental Book Readings by Chapter

Chapter I Optimizing Socialization, Learning, and Professionalism in the Workplace

Kramer, M. (2010). Organizational socialization: Joining and leaving organizations (1st Edition). Cambridge, UK: Polity. ISBN-10: 0745646352

Nicolson, P. (2015). Gender, power and organization: A psychological perspective on life at work (2nd Edition). London, UK: Routledge. ISBN-10: 1848723237

Wanberg, C. (Editor). The Oxford handbook of organizational socialization (1st Edition). London, UK: Oxford University Press. ISBN-10: 0199763674

Wanous, J. P. (1991). Organizational entry: Recruitment, selection, orientation, and socialization of newcomers (2nd Edition). Upper Saddle River, NJ: Prentice Hall. ISBN-10: 020151480X

Chapter II Identifying the Community Site and Your "Fit" Within It

Berger, L. (2012). All work, no pay: Finding an internship, building your resume, making connections, and gaining job experience. Berkeley, CA: Ten Speed Press. ISBN-10: 1607741687

Russell, M. A. (2013). Finding your internship: What employers want you to know. Indianapolis, IN: Dog Ear Publishing. ISBN-10: 1457520109

Williams-Nickelson, C., Prinstein, M. J., & Keilin, W. G. (2012). Internships in Psychology: The APAGS workbook for writing successful applications and finding the right fit (3rd Edition). Washington, D.C.: American Psychological Association. ISBN-10: 143381210X

Woodard, E. (2015). The ultimate guide to internships: 100 steps to get a great internship and thrive in it. New York, NY: Allworth Press. ISBN-10: 1621534383

Chapter III Creating Site-Related Goals for the Field Experience

Blackett, K. (2015). Career achievement: Growing your goals (student success) (2nd edition). Chicago, IL: McGraw-Hill Education. ISBN-10: 0077831888

Fleming, K. J. (2016). (Re)defining the goal: The true path to career readiness in the 21st century. Seattle, WA: CreateSpace. ISBN-10: 1532912587

Murphy, W., & Kram, K. (2014). Strategic relationships at work: Creating your circle of mentors, sponsors, and peers for success in business and life. Chicago, IL: McGraw-Hill Education. ISBN-10: 0071823476

Scott, S. J. (2014). S.M.A.R.T. goals made simple: 10 steps to master your personal and career goals. Seattle, WA: CreateSpace. ISBN-10: 1496154061

Chapter IV Creating Academic Objectives for the Field Experience

Bateman, B. D., & Herr, C. M. (2006). Chapter IV Creating Academic Objectives for the Field Experience. In Writing, measurable IEP goals and objectives. Verona, WI: Attainment Co Inc. ISBN-10: 1578611490

Cumming, A. (2006). Goals for academic writing: ESL students and their instructors (language learning & language teaching). Amsterdam, Netherlands: John Benjamins Publishing Company. ISBN-10: 9027219710

Singh, A. A., & Lukkarila, L. (2017). Successful academic writing: A complete guide for social and behavioral scientists (1st edition). New York, NY: The Guilford Press. ISBN-10: 1462529399

Steenburgen, F. (1981). Practical guide to writing goals and objectives. Novata, CA: Academic Therapy Publications. ISBN-10: 0878792740

Chapter V Creating a Learning Contract or "Plan of Action"

Fabricant, F., Miller, J., & Stark, D. (2013). Creating career success: A flexible plan for the world of work (1st edition). Belmont, CA: Wadsworth Publishing. ISBN-10: 1133313906

Lattuca, L.R., & Stark, J. S. (2009). Shaping the college curriculum: Academic plans in context (2nd edition). San Francisco, CA: Jossey-Bass. ISBN-10: 0787985554

Marzano, R. J. (2009). Designing and teaching learning goals and objectives: Classroom strategies that work perfect. Denver, CO: Marzano Research Laboratory. ISBN-10: 0982259204

Zmuda, A., Curtis, G., & Ullman, D. (2015). Learning personalized: The evolution of the contemporary classroom (1st edition). San Francisco, CA: Jossey-Bass. ISBN-10: 1118904796

Chapter VI Getting Feedback about Your Learning Contract and Associated Approvals

Bossidy L., Charan R., & Burck C. (2009). Execution: The discipline of getting things done (Kindle edition). New York, NY: Crown Business.

Dye, D. (2008). The effect of specific feedback on critical reflection of students: Affecting critical reflection of healthcare professional students during clinical internships. Sarrbrucken, Germany: VDM Verlag. ISBN-10: 3639045815

London, M. (2003). Job feedback: Giving, seeking, and using feedback for performance improvement (2nd edition). East Sussex, UK: Psychology Press. ISBN-10: 0805844953

Seashore, C. N., Weinberg, G. M., & Seashore, E. W. (2013). What did you say? The art of giving and receiving feedback (Kindle Edition). Boston, MA: Weinberg & Weinberg.

Chapter VII Contacting Your Site Supervisor and Beginning Your Site Activities

Blayney, M. (2017). Your first job: How to make a success of starting work and ensure your first year is the launch of a successful career (Kindle edition). Northumberland, UK: The Work Press.

Crane, M. (2013). Starting work: For interns, new hires, and summer associates (100 things you need to know). New York, NY: Mary Crane & Associates. ISBN-10: 0989066401

Crane, M. (2014). 100 things you need to know: Business etiquette: for students and new professionals. New York, NY: Mary Crane & Associates. ISBN-10: 0989066444

Druce, E. (2015). This is where to start: Find superstar mentors, master all they know, and get ahead in your career (Kindle edition). Seattle, WA: Amazon Digital Services.

Chapter VIII Starting the Site-Related Journaling Process: Introspection in Action

Shea, L. (2015). Journaling basics—Journal writing for beginners. North Charleston, SC: CreateSpace. ISBN-10: 1507730195

Sy, A. (2016). ABC's of journaling (Kindle edition). Chicago, IL: Summit Publishing Co., Inc.

Totoro, M. (2017). Journaling toward wholeness: 28-day plan to develop a journaling practice. North Charleston, SC: CreateSpace. ISBN-10: 154693538X

Zahn, C. S. (2017). Discover the art of bullet journaling (Kindle edition). Seattle, WA: Amazon Digital Services.

Chapter IX Seeking Performance Feedback: Utilize 360 Degree Feedback Opportunities

Cooper, J. (2015). How to discuss 360 feedback: The essential guide (Kindle edition). Banbury, UK: Careertrain Publishing.

Edwards, M. R., & Ewen, A. J. (1996). 360 degree feedback: The powerful new model for employee assessment & performance improvement. New York City, NY: AMACOM. ISBN-10: 0814403263

Jones, J. E., & Bearley, W. L. (1996). 360-degree feedback: Strategies, tactics, and techniques for developing leaders. Pelham, MA: Human Resource Development Press. ISBN-10: 087425356X

Tornow, W. W., & London, M. (1998). Maximizing the value of 360-degree feedback: A process for successful individual and organizational development (1st edition). San Francisco, CA: Jossey-Bass. ISBN-10: 0787909580

Chapter X Receiving and Adjusting to Performance Feedback: Be Open to the Process

AlAdl, A. (2016). Using corrective feedback to develop writing attitude and performance. Saarbrucken, Germany: LAP LAMBERT Academic Publishing. ISBN-10: 365989446X

Bristow, N. J. A. (2010). Where's the gift? Using feedback to work smarter, learn faster and avoid disaster. Elk Grove Village, IL: LCI Press. ISBN-10: 0974140937

London, M. (2003). Job feedback: Giving, seeking, and using feedback for performance improvement (2nd edition). New York, NY: Psychology Press. ISBN-10: 0805844953

Ruiz-Primo, M. A., & Brookhart, S. M. (2017). Using feedback to improve learning (1st edition). London, UK: Routledge. ISBN-10: 1138646571

Chapter XI Analyzing the Results of Your Site-Related Learning

Lindsey, D. B., Lindsey, R. B., Hord, S. M., & Frank, V. V. (2015). Reach the highest standard in professional learning: Outcomes (1st edition). Thousand Oaks, CA: Corwin. ISBN-10: 1452291950

McDonald, M. E. (2013). The nurse educator's guide to assessing learning outcomes (3rd edition). Burlington, MA: Jones & Bartlett Learning. ISBN-10: 1449687679

Stone, R. (2011). The real value of training: Measuring and analyzing business outcomes and the quality of ROI. Chicago, IL: McGraw-Hill Education. ISBN-10: 0071759972

Verma, G., & Pumfrey, P. (2017). Educational attainments: Issues and outcomes in multicultural education (1st edition). London, UK: Routledge. ISBN-10: 1138071323

Chapter XII Writing the Results of Your Site-Related Learning

Barrio Minton, C. A., Gibson, D. M., & Wachter Morris, C. A. (2016). Evaluating student learning outcomes in counselor education. Alexandria, VA: American Counseling Association. ISBN-10: 1556203373

Dufour, R., DuFour, R., Eaker, R., & Many, T. (2010). Learning by doing: A handbook for professional communities at work–a practical guide for PLC teams and leadership. Bloomington, IN: Solution Tree. ISBN-10: 1935542095

Marzano, R. J., McTighe, J., & Pickering, D. (1993). Assessing student outcomes: Performance assessment using the dimensions of learning model. Alexandria, VA: Association for Supervision & Curriculum Development. ISBN-10: 0871202255

Suskie, L. (2009). Assessing student learning: A common sense guide (2nd edition). San Francisco, CA: Jossey-Bass. ISBN-10: 0470289643

Chapter XIII Presenting the Results of Your Site-Related Learning

Bowden, M. (2013). How to present: The ultimate guide to presenting your ideas and influencing people using techniques that actually work. Hoboken, NJ: Wrightbooks. ISBN-10: 1118476247

Jones, F. C (2008). How to wow: Proven strategies for presenting your ideas, persuading your audience, and perfecting your image. Crawfordsville, IN: Ballantine Books. ISBN-10: 0345501780

Nicol, A. A. M., & Pexman, P. M. (2010). Presenting your findings: A practical guide for creating tables (6th edition). Washington, D.C.: American Psychological Association. ISBN-10: 143380705X

Sarnoff, D. (1983). Make the most of your best: A complete program for presenting yourself and your ideas with confidence and authority. New York, NY: Henry Holt & Co. ISBN-10: 0030623766

Chapter XIV Reflection on Your Culminating Learning Experience and the Next Steps

Asher, D. (2009). How to get any job: Life launch and re-launch for everyone under 30. Emeryville, CA: Ten Speed Press. ISBN-10: 158008947X

Beal, M. (2017). 101 lessons they never taught you in college: The essential guide for students and recent graduates to launch their careers. Charleston, SC: CreateSpace. ISBN-10: 1545362750

Bravo, D., & Whiteley, C. (2005). The internship advantage: Get real-world job experience to launch your career. Upper Saddle River, NJ: Prentice Hall. ISBN-10: 0735203911

White, W. J. (2005). From day one: CEO advice to launch an extraordinary career. Upper Saddle River, NJ: FT Press. ISBN-10: 0132206862

Appendix B

List of Career Training Resources by Focus/Field of Study

Overview: National Association of Colleges and Employers (NACE) Criteria for an Effective Field Training Experience:

Overview: One of the best resources related to you finishing your field training relates to your understanding of what is a good and effective training experience. A source from the National Association of Colleges and Employers (NACE) relates different criteria for this evaluation. Your field training should:

- Exemplify clearly-defined learning objectives/goals that directly relate to the professional goals of the student and his/her academic program.
- Involve field-relevant resources, equipment, and facilities to support the learning related to establishing student learning objectives/goals.
- Have opportunities for supervision by a professional(s) with relevant expertise and educational and/or professional background.
- Advance the learning of "real world" work that a regular employee would routinely perform.
- Be transferable to other employment settings.
- Reflect the major work behaviors of a job description within the structure of the field training.
- Offer opportunities for constructive and routine feedback by the experienced supervisor(s).

Cross-Cultural and International Training

Field Training in Cross-Cultural and International Training

Connect123
The Connect123 internship program has an international network of organizations across many different disciplines/fields pertaining to training and work related to, among other foci, human rights, journalism, education, business consulting, entrepreneurship, healthcare, engineering, and sustainable development. You are encouraged to customize your internship experience to best satisfy your personal and/or professional goals. Start dates are based on your availability. Please contact:

> Connect123
> 37 Roeland St
> Cape Town City Centre, Cape Town, 8001, South Africa
> +27 21 462 5968
> Organization internship weblink: https://www.connect-123.com/programs/internships/

Cross-Cultural Solutions
The Cross-Cultural Solutions internship program is designed for students and emerging professionals ages 18 and older who wish to explore and better understand critical social issues impacting communities around the world. You will train in locations from Ghana, Guatemala, and India to Peru, Tanzania, and Morocco. You will be involved in a myriad of guided training activities and have opportunities for independent exploration. Please contact:

>Cross-cultural Solutions
>2 Clinton Place
>New Rochelle, NY 10801
>(914) 632-0022
>Organization internship weblink: https://www.crossculturalsolutions.org/international-internships/

Internships Down Under
The Internships Down Under internship program focuses interns on helping others needing assistance with health problems, economic hardship, mental problems, addictions, legal problems, and family conflict, among other issues. All internships are unpaid, but they involve hands-on training and supervision critical to professional development. Please contact:

>Internships Down Under
>Ste. 102, 282 Oxford St.
>Bondi Junction NSW 2022
>+61 2 9386 5441
>Organization internship weblink: http://www.internshipsdownunder.com/category/internships/industry/social-work/

World Endeavors
The World Endeavors internship program places interns with nonprofits, government agencies, or international social agencies in South America, Ireland, England, Mexico or Asia. Interns may help counsel clients and provide them with resources, prepare reports for funding agencies, update and manage client files, or help develop and deliver public awareness programs. Some research and administrative support work may also be part of interns' responsibilities. Please contact:

>World Endeavors
>3015 E Franklin Ave.
>Minneapolis, MN 55406
>(612) 729-3400
>Organization internship weblink: https://www.worldendeavors.com/programs/social-work-internships-abroad

World Internships
The World Internships program has a U.S. office in Northampton, Massachusetts, and they work with partners around the world in twenty countries to coordinate customized internship programs for people ages eighteen to thirty. This is a good training experience for you if you are seeking a professional career in an international setting across different disciplines/areas of specialization. Please contact:

World Internships—U.S. office location
17 New South St., #302
Northampton, MA 01060
(970) 797-5616
Organization internship weblink: https://www.worldinternships.org/why-world-internships/

Education

Field Training Resources in Education

- A Composite Estimator of Effective Teaching – With the support of the Bill and Melinda Gates Foundation, the Measures of Effective Teaching (MET) project was created by Mihaly and colleagues to develop and test multiple measures of teacher effectiveness. Among other types of professional feedback during field training, this would be helpful for you to gain clarity in your ability to convey information in a clear and concise manner to your students. Downloadable PDF: http://k12education.gatesfoundation.org/resource/a-composite-estimator-of-effective-teaching/

- Better Feedback for Better Teaching: A Practical Guide to Improving Classroom Observations – With the support of the Bill and Melinda Gates Foundation, this book by Archer and colleagues offers you practical guidance for improving self and "other" assessment of teaching educators through more systematic strategies for teaching observations for accurate and "actionable" feedback. Downloadable PDF: http://k12education.gatesfoundation.org/resource/better-feedback-for-better-teaching-a-practical-guide-to-improving-classroom-observations/

- National Geographic Teaching Resources – This website presents instructional resources designed to support the teaching of courses related to geography and other related subjects. This would be a good instructional tool for you as either a student teacher and/or a new teacher entering the educational field. Website: http://k12education.gatesfoundation.org/resource/a-composite-estimator-of-effective-teaching/

- National Science Foundation Instructional Resources – The website offers a variety of instructional resources derived from information provided by teachers, their students, and the students' families. Primarily provided by the National Science Digital Library, the instructional resource materials are arranged by subject area to help you easily locate support materials in your teaching area to create your lesson plans.
Website link: https://www.nsf.gov/news/classroom/

- Resources for Formatting of Research Papers – These websites offer guidelines for teachers in how to teach students to write their research and literature review papers in different paper formatting styles (Modern Language Association (MLA) and American Psychological Association (APA) style).
MLA Style website links: https://style.mla.org/teaching-resources/
APA Style website links: https://owl.english.purdue.edu/owl/section/3/

- Scholastic Teaching Resources and Lesson Plans – This website offers a variety of instructional support resources for teachers and educational interns, ranging from lesson plans to articles and informational blogs. The information will help you tailor your instructional activities to best match the education level of your students and the learning goals of the classroom. Website link: https://www.scholastic.com/teachers/home/

Field Training in Education

American Federation of Teachers
The American Federation of Teachers internship program trains interns on issues of labor unions in education. You may be conducting research, writing, and attending meetings and conferences. Your internship can be selected from a variety of departments, ranging from human rights and community relations to business, legal, and communications, among others. You might also work on American Educator, a quarterly professional magazine by the union. Please contact:

American Federation of Teachers
555 New Jersey Ave N.W.
Washington, D.C. 20001
(202) 879-4439
intern@aft.org
Organization internship weblink: https://www.aft.org/careers/internship-opportunities#sthash.FWCZWF3i.dpuf

Breakthrough Collaborative
The Breakthrough Collaborative internship program offers an internship with rigorous training and supervision processes. The teaching training program involves a two-week training program with lesson planning, curriculum templates, classroom behavior methods, and peer-related collaborations. After the training is complete, you will apply your newly acquired skills in school systems (and with students) needing your expertise in creating a fair and balanced educational experience for high-need populations. Please contact:

Breakthrough Collaborative
P.O. Box 71420
Oakland, CA 94612
(579) 335-1706
Organization internship weblink: http://www.breakthroughcollaborative.org

Children's Defense Fund
The Children's Defense Fund internship program creates opportunities for teaching a group of ten students at the Freedom Schools. The philosophy of the Freedom Schools program is to enhance students' academic achievement and help connect students and their families to community resources. You would undergo a week-long training program before you would begin teaching at the schools. Please contact:

Children's Defense Fund
25 E St., N.W.
Washington, D.C. 20001
(800) 233-1200
Organization internship weblink: http://www.childrensdefense.org/programs-campaigns/freedom-schools/participate/servant-leader-interns.html

Study Abroad—Teaching

The Study Abroad—Teaching internship program presents great opportunities for teaching abroad through your university's study abroad office. Not only does teaching abroad allow you to learn about another education system, but it provides clearer insight into the strengths and weaknesses of education in the US. Depending on the country you choose, you could also learn another language in the process or sharpen the skills of a language you are currently studying. Please contact:

StudyAbroad.com
3803 West Chester Pk., Ste. 125
Newtown Square, PA 19073
(800) 266-4441
Organization internship weblink: http://www.globalinksabroad.org/programs_by_major/education_and_teaching/

Teach for America

The Teaching for America internship program gives many training opportunities that will prepare you to begin your career in the education field. You will be challenged to think creatively, make a difference in students' lives, and lead boldly. You will be taught how to make a real difference in the educational system, facing the challenges of educational systems in urban and rural regions of the country. Please contact:

Teach for America
300 W Adams St.
Chicago, IL 60606
(312) 254-1000
Organization internship weblink: https://www.teachforamerica.org/get-involved/college-students

Teaching for Change

The Teaching for Change internship program focuses on educational reform rather than teaching in a classroom. Students participating in this internship will be a part of making a real-world impact for current and future students through education reform and mobilizing multiple constituents (i.e., parents, children, administrators, teacher, and community activists) involved in the educational experience to make real and long-lasting reforms (Students First program). Please contact:

Teaching for Change
P.O. Box 73038
Washington, D.C. 20056
(202) 588-7204
Organization internship weblink: http://www.teachingforchange.org/about/internships

Psychology and Social Sciences

Field Training Resources in Psychology and Social Sciences

- Health Insurance Portability and Accountability Act of 1996 (HIPAA) Rules and Related Mental Health Sharing Information Resources – A website that provides information for professionals in the fields of counseling and applied psychology in how to work with diverse populations. Website: https://www.hhs.gov/ hipaa/for-professionals/special-topics/mental-health/index.html
- Multicultural Training Resources for Working with Diverse Populations – A website that provides information for professionals in the fields of counseling and applied psychology on how to work with diverse populations. Website: http://www.apa.org/pi/oema/resources/multicultural-training.aspx
- Professional Development Resources – A website that provides information for professionals in the fields of counseling and applied psychology on how to work with diverse populations. Website: http://www.cpa.ca/professionaldevelopment/webcourses/
- Resources for Early Career Professionals in Psychology/Social Services Field – A website that provides information for professionals in the fields of counseling and applied psychology on how to work with diverse populations. Website: http://www.apa.org/careers/early-career/index.aspx

Field Training in Psychology and Social Sciences

American Psychological Association
The American Psychological Association (APA) internship program is coordinated through the APA Education Directorate, and your training will help you improve the quality of your teaching and research practices. The internship training will change your perspective on the science of psychology and enhance your high school, undergraduate, graduate, or post-graduate experience through academic training and development. Please contact:

American Psychological Association
750 First St. NE
Washington, D.C. 20002-4242
(800) 374-2721
Organization internship weblink: http://www.apa.org/careers/internships/index.aspx

Feminist Majority Foundation
The Feminist Majority Foundation internship program gives opportunities for interns from monitoring press conferences, research, Web and social media outreach and writing, event and community organizing, public policy analysis, organizational networking, media relations, and monitoring Congressional hearings. Each intern works closely with a staff member to learn directly from hands-on experience and to contribute to substantive projects. All who are interested are encouraged to apply. Please contact:

Feminist Majority Foundation
1600 Wilson Blvd., Ste. 801
Arlington, VA 22209
(703) 522-2214
Organization internship weblink: http://jobs.feminist.org/feminist-majority-foundation-jobs/

Johns Hopkins Laboratory for Child Development
If you are interested in developing a better understanding of child development for the purposes of research and/or client work with young children and their families, this might be the field training experience for you. The Johns Hopkins Laboratory for Child Development allows you to investigate children's cognitive development (e.g., language learning and reasoning). Paid summer internship positions are available and entail approximately 40 research hours per week. Please contact:

Johns Hopkins University
Zanvyl Krieger School of Arts & Sciences
Department of Psychological & Brain Sciences
3400 N. Charles St.
Baltimore, MD 21218
(410) 516-7055
Organization internship weblink: http://www.psy.jhu.edu/%7Elabforchilddevelopment/pages/join.html

Points of Light
The Points of Light organization is affiliated with 250 cities and associated non-profit and service organizations. This field training opportunity will give you great real-world opportunities to interact with many diverse groups in need in society and see what are truly areas that need further assistance above programmatic and public policy levels. Please contact:

Points of Light
600 Means St., Ste. 210
Atlanta, GA 30318
(404) 979-2900
Organization internship weblink: http://www.pointsoflight.org

Art, Fine Arts, and Museum Science

Field Training Resources in Arts, Fine Arts, and Museum Science

- Museum Resource Board—This is a very helpful website for young professionals such as yourself beginning to enter this field/discipline. You can review information such as job openings and internships. You can also post your résumé for free on this website to attract potential employers and/or internship supervisors. Website: http://seeing2020.com/museums/jobs.html
- The Library of Congress—This website resource provides a searchable database of an online collection of art as part of its American Memory project. Website:

http://memory.loc.gov/cgi-bin/ query/Shammed/collections:@field%28COLLID+ndlcoll%29:heading=All+Collections

- National Gallery of Art—In addition to the Library of Congress online collection, you can access more than 4,000 digitalized images of various art collections. Website: http://www.nga.gov/collection/collect.htm
- The Fine Arts Museums of San Francisco—This website offers a great searchable database of approximately more that 50% of the museums' art collections. You can even zoom in on the images for a closer inspection of the art objects. Website: http://www.thinker.org/fam/virtual-gallery.html
- Smithsonian Institution—This informative website of museum artifacts and information at the Smithsonian is an impressive online resource for you as either a practitioner or educator in this field. Website: http://educate.si.edu/
- San Francisco's Exploratorium—This is an interesting online resource for you as someone utilizing information about "art in motion" through your professional activities. This website provides wonderful interactive activities related to sound and motion. Website: http://www.exploratorium.edu/
- Art Museum Image Consortium—There is a lot of educational information on this website, derived from collections available online of 25 major American art museums. You can search a catalog of pictures, and some data is available for research purposes. Website: http://www.amico.org/
- Canadian Museum of Civilization—This website offers valuable information related to collections of art objects from Canada. Information presented on this website can give you important cultural background on both the history and current trends in artistic expression within the Canadian culture. http://www.civilization.ca/collect/csintroe.html

Field Training in Arts, Fine Arts, and Museum Science

American Folk-Art Museum
A field-related training opportunity is available through the American Folk Art Museum in New York City. The purpose of this internship program is to help interns such as yourself to be exposed to diverse cultures within the topic of folk art instruction and seminal pieces over the decades. You will have training in different departments within the museum, conducting research utilizing the museum library and archives, assisting in the development and/or maintenance of library publications and website, and collaborating with the curator in cataloging and/or maintaining the collections within museum. Please contact:

American Folk-Art Museum
2 Lincoln Sq.
New York, NY 10023
(212) 265-1040
Organization internship weblink: http://www.folkartmuseum.org/internships

Disney Animation
As an intern, you will have the unique opportunity to work directly with a Disney mentor as you explore all aspects of art, storytelling, and filmmaking. Your internship will also allow you to meet and collaborate with a talented group of students from around the globe and become part of a multi-disciplinary team focused on both individual and group projects. Please contact:

Disney
500 South Buena Vista St.
Burbank, CA 91521
(818) 560-1000
Organization internship weblink: https://www.disneyanimation.com/careers/interns-apprentices

George O'Keeffe Museum
If you appreciate the collected works of this artist, this internship experience would be for you. Every year, they have a variety of internship opportunities, combination of both unpaid and paid positions. There are various departments within the museum that you can be trained within based upon availability of opportunities and your specific interests within this onsite experience. You will develop paperwork reflecting your goals between you, your university, and the museum site. Please contact:

George O'Keeffe Museum
217 Johnson St
Santa Fe, NM 87501
(505) 946-1000
Organization internship weblink: http://www.okeeffemuseum.org/paid-internships.html

Guggenheim Museum
The world-famous Guggenheim Museum provides a variety of training experiences for students interested in this area of specialization. You will be assigned to a specific division or department within the museum based upon your specific academic background, existing skills, career plans, and interests in the fields of art, and/or Museum science. Interns are given the opportunity to engage in field trips to other institutions for an appreciation of art and the conduction of museum activities. Each internship opportunity is approximately three months long. Please contact:

Guggenheim Museum
1071 5th Ave.
New York City, NY 10128
(212) 360-4355
Organization internship weblink: http://www.guggenheim.org/new-york/education/internships

J. Paul Getty Trust
The Getty Foundation created the Multicultural Undergraduate Internship program in Los Angeles to provide opportunities for diverse college undergraduates who do not have the resources within the community be trained in the field of art and/or museum science and are underrepresented in this area of training. The goal of this program is to create a more diverse, well-educated body of professionals who work within the field of art and museum science to broaden the cultural backgrounds and expertise of those who work in this industry. Please contact:

J. Paul Getty Trust
1200 Getty Center Dr.
Los Angeles, CA 90049
(310) 440-7360
Organization internship weblink: http://www.getty.edu/about/opportunities/intern_opps.html

Museum of Contemporary Art, Chicago
The Museum of Contemporary Art in Chicago offers hands-on experiences for you at different areas within the institution. You will have the opportunity to work with the museum curators, educators, and/or program/exhibit planners, among other activities, during your training experience. You will help promote using events and possibly even create text museum materials. You will work closely with the museum staff, and actively engage in various levels of functioning within the institution process. Please contact:

Museum of Contemporary Art, Chicago
220 E Chicago Ave
Chicago, IL 60611
(312) 280-2660
Organization internship weblink: http://www2.mcachicago.org/employment/internships

National Endowment for the Arts
Unpaid internship positions at the National Endowment for the Arts are available throughout the year. As an accurate intern onsite you would be involved in assisting staff in the federal grant funding processes. For your activities onsite under supervised conditions, you will be exposed to a variety of resources and educational experiences during your training time (e.g., attendance at advisory meetings) that will assist you in your ongoing educational and skill training within this area of expertise. At the end of your training experience, you will have a much clearer understanding of the grant funding process for many different projects and programs within the arts. Please contact:

National Endowment for the Arts
Office of Human Resources
400 7th St., SW
Washington, D.C. 20506
(202) 682-5400
Organization internship weblink: https://www.arts.gov/about/jobs/internships
Organization internship weblink: https://www.nga.gov/content/ngaweb/opportunities/interns-and-fellows/graduate.html

National Endowment for the Humanities
The National Endowment for the Humanities promotes an appreciation of the arts. Based upon the ideology that these efforts will enhance social knowledge and educational quality within society, you might be involved in a variety of activities, including educational initiatives, the development of cultural exhibits, and the preservation of manuscripts and other artifacts in museums and libraries. In addition to these activities, you will also have opportunities to gain valuable experience interacting with staff and administrators in the administrative offices of the institution. Applications for internships are encouraged any time during the year. Please contact:

National Endowment for the Humanities
400 7th St. SW
Washington, D.C. 20506
(202) 606-8400
Organization internship weblink: https://www.neh.gov/about/human-resources/neh-internship-program

National Gallery of Art

The National Gallery of Art has offered professional museum training to candidates from all backgrounds through a variety of internship and volunteer programs. Interns such as yourself can come from a variety of backgrounds and interests related to the appreciation of art and education involving the dissemination of information in society. You can work with staff and administrators in conducting daily activities and long-term planning related to the institution's programming. In addition to the Gallery's paid internships and fellowships, many unpaid internships and research assistantships are available. Please contact:

> National Gallery of Art
> Department of Academic Programs
> Division of Education
> 2000B South Club Dr.
> Landover, MD 20785
> (202) 737-4215
> Organization internship weblink: https://www.nga.gov/content/ngaweb/education/interns-fellows.html

Nickelodeon Animation

If you are interested in becoming an illustrator and/or wish to understand the process of animation in an established animation studio, an internship at Nickelodeon Studios may be for you. Nickelodeon animation produces well-known cartoons like SpongeBob SquarePants and Teenage Mutant Ninja Turtles. "Nickterns" have the opportunity to learn about all aspects of animation and programming, as well as experiences such as attending free movie screenings, working with animation artists and potentially networking the studio executives in different projects. An internship at Nickelodeon can launch you on an exciting, fun-filled career in children's entertainment. Please contact:

> Nickelodeon Animation
> 231 W Olive Ave.
> Burbank, CA 91502
> (818) 736-3000
> Organization internship weblink: https://www.nickanimationstudio.com/nickelodeon-internship-program

Smithsonian Institution

The Smithsonian is world renowned as an educational institution and offers wonderful training opportunities for intern such as yourself interested in cultural information and history. Interns can come from different backgrounds and career interests. The internship can cover a lot of different fields of study, ranging from art and education to business and public administration. It is a competitive process to be an intern at this institution, so it is recommended that you apply for more than one opportunity at a time. At the Smithsonian, you can apply to be an intern in a specific department or apply for a general internship across different units within the institution. Please contact:

> Smithsonian Institution
> 1000 Jefferson Dr. SW
> Washington, D.C. 20560
> (800) 521-5330
> Organization internship weblink: http://www.smithsonianofi.com/internship-opportunities/

The Jewish Museum
The Jewish Museum offers primarily unpaid internships year-round for college students and emerging professionals. As an intern, you would have the opportunity to work with staff and/or administrators related to curatorial tasks, museum membership, collections, marketing, and program development. Among other tasks accomplished, you will learn much about cultural beliefs and the historical background of the Jewish people, which relates to broader appreciation of diversity in our society. Please contact:

The Jewish Museum
1109 5th Ave
New York, NY 10128
(212) 423-3200
Organization internship weblink: http://www.thejewishmuseum.org/Internships

The Metropolitan Museum of Art
As an intern, you will participate in weekly museum activities, programming projects, and staff meetings across divisions within the institution. Through unpaid internships at The Met Fifth Ave., you will work at least twelve hours per week for a minimum of ten weeks. Academic credit may be arranged for interns at their schools' discretion. You will be given the opportunity to engage in behind-the-scenes tours, staff meeting lunches, and other networking opportunities during your training. You will learn much about the cultural event planning, exhibition programming, and associated tasks (e.g., fundraising) of an institution within the larger museum system of New York City. Please contact:

The Metropolitan Museum of Art
1000 Fifth Ave. at 81st St
New York, NY 10028
(212) 535-7710
Organization internship weblink: http://www.metmuseum.org/research/internships-and-fellowships/internships/internships-for-college-and-graduate-students

The Museum of Fine Arts, Boston
The Museum of Fine Arts in Boston offers many opportunities for internship training all year-round. As an intern, you can participate in a broad range of activities for your professional development. Museum training activities for internships entail, but are not limited to, activities related to writing publications, handling intellectual property, engaging in curatorial activities, engaging in public relations tasks, creating materials or engaging in situations for educational activities, utilizing information technology for the dissemination of museum information, and/or learning about human resource activities. Please contact:

The Museum of Fine Arts, Boston
465 Huntington Ave
Boston, MA 02115
Phone: (617) 267-9300
Organization internship weblink: http://www.mfa.org/employment/internship-opportunities

The Museum of Fine Arts, Houston

The Museum of Fine Arts in Houston offers opportunities for academic credit and unpaid internships to train college students to enter the field of art and museum science. You will be exposed to a variety of cultural information and artifacts during your training, working with museum staff and administrators in the day-to-day activities of museum planning, events, and exhibitions. Please contact:

> The Museum of Fine Arts, Houston
> 465 Huntington Ave
> Boston, MA 02115
> (617) 267-9300
> Organization internship weblink: http://www.mfah.org/programs-for/page/about-internship-program/

The Museum of Modern Art

The Museum of Modern Art, or MoMA, offers you a significant opportunity to work with curators and educators in a world-renowned museum environment. You will learn about the process of curating and presenting museum collections and the broader organizational systems related to the functioning of the institution over time. You will also work closely with MoMA staff on various tasks, attend weekly lectures on different museum-related programming activities, and be invited to attend curator talks related to museum initiatives. Please contact:

> The Museum of Modern Art
> 11 West 53 St.
> New York City, NY 10019
> (212) 708-9700
> Organization internship weblink: http://www.moma.org/learn/courses/internships#about

United States Holocaust Memorial Museum

The United States Holocaust Memorial Museum offers both paid and unpaid internships during the year, with the duration of an internship typically being about one semester. Flexible scheduling of internship hours is done, as possible. As an intern, you will learn about the topic of the Holocaust, as well as the functioning of the museum in conveying information about this event in history. The museum encourages diverse applicants and U.S. citizenship is not a requirement to be an intern. Please contact:

> United States Holocaust Memorial Museum
> 100 Raoul Wallenberg Place
> Washington, D.C. 20024-2126
> (202) 488-0400
> Organization internship weblink: http://www.ushmm.org/museum/volunteer_intern/intern/

Whitney Museum of American Art

Regarded as one of New York City's most popular museums, the Whitney offers an intern program that provides training and hands-on experience in many different activities within the museum's day-to-day operations. You would be involved in engaging in activities with the public, conducting museum research, assisting professional staff and administrators, and/or supporting the planning and/or execution of educational events. Diverse applicants interested in learning how the museum works from different academic backgrounds, cultural interests, and career planning initiatives are encouraged to apply. Please contact:

Whitney Museum of American Art
945 Madison Ave. at 75th St.
New York City, NY 10021
(212) 570-3600
Organization internship weblink: http://www.whitney.org/About/Internships

Social Work

Field Training Resources in Social Work

There are many national and international social work organizations dedicated to enhancing professional growth, advancing social policies, and creating a just society. Annual membership fees often apply, but most of the organizations listed below also offer membership discounts to inquiring social work students and professionals.

- National Association of Social Workers—Since 1955, the National Association of Social Workers (NASW) has provided unique opportunities for networking among social workers in different areas of specialization. With over 123,000 members in the professional network, you can gain valuable career information through networking events, opportunities for peer-to-peer mentoring, access to social work publications, and online forum discussions. You can also participate in discounted career training workshops and attend annual conferences for free or discounted continuing education (CE) credits. Website: http://www.naswdc.org/
- Clinical Social Work Association—The Clinical Social Work Association (CSWA) gives valuable information regarding legislative policies, advocacy opportunities, and ongoing trends in the field through media coverage and newsletters. Best clinical practices are routinely communicated to members. Members can receive free legal advice and a discounted liability insurance for professional practice.
Website: http://www.clinicalsocialworkassociation.org/
- American Clinical Social Work Association—The American Clinical Social Work Association (ACSWA) offers online opportunities for professional networking and resources regarding professional trends in clinical social work. Through online resources provided through membership, individuals can engage in online discussions of field-related issues (e.g., discussion boards, chats/blogs) and review posted field information through a variety of social media. Student members may also apply for clinical scholarships and/or become a liaison for ACSWA through their educational institution.
Website: http://www.acswa.org/
- Society for Social Work and Research—The Society for Social Work and Research (SSWR) supports the continuing education of field-related advocates, professionals, and students. Members benefit from receiving field-relevant publication discounts, access to job postings, and a discounted rate for the annual SSWR conference, which provides opportunities for professional networking with professionals from various locations and backgrounds. Website: http://sswr.org/

- School Social Work Association of America—The School Social Work Association of America (SSWAA) gives members several field-relevant resources through periodic newsletters, webinars, and professional publications. The aim of the association is to promote students' academic achievement and social/emotional balance for both current and future practitioners. Website: http://www.sswaa.org/

Field Training in Social Work

Green Chimneys
The Green Chimneys internship program gives interns hands-on experience in working with children and their families. Interns are responsible for being a facilitator for at least one group of eight children, as well as conducting individual and family therapy and being a case manager for two to three children. Interns are also to create and administer a short-term psychological education, clinical-specific, or behavior change group. Residential interns are expected to attend clinical seminars, conferences, and staff meetings. Please contact:

Green Chimneys
400 Doansburg Rd., Box 719
Brewster, NY 10509
(845) 279-2995
Organization internship weblink: http://www.greenchimneys.org/careers/swintern/

National Council for Adoption
The National Council for Adoption internship program offers interns the opportunity to work with children needing a lovely home through adoption, but it is not an adoption agency. This is an unpaid intern position and relates to training in child advocacy. Interns can choose to work in one of several departments related to government relations and public policy, development and general administration, and/or social work. Please contact:

National Council for Adoption
225 N. Washington St.
Alexandria, VA 22314-2561
(703) 299-6633
Organization internship weblink: https://www.adoptioncouncil.org/who-we-are/internships

Southern California's Geriatric Social Work Education Consortium
The Southern California's Geriatric Social Work Education Consortium internship program offers placement in sites representing a multi-association consortium. Interns are trained in geriatric-focused health centers around the greater Los Angeles area. According to the U.S. Department of Veteran Affairs, there is a growing need for geriatric-trained social workers in the U.S., and there is a remarkable success rate of the interns being hired after graduation by their training sites. Please contact:

Partners in Care Foundation
732 Mott St. Ste. 150
San Fernando CA 91340
(818) 837-3775
Organization internship weblink: http://www.losangeles.va.gov/grecc/socialwork.asp

U.S. Army–Social Work Internship Program
The U.S. Army – Social Work Internship Program is a two-year internship that takes place at a medical treatment facility. The internship program trains students to both become a licensed Clinical Social Worker and attain the level of 73A area of concentration (AOC) as a commissioned officer. Please contact:

> U.S. Army
> 1500 Defense Pentagon
> Washington, D.C. 20310
> Organization internship weblink: https://www.hrc.army.mil/Milper/14-186

Youth Villages
The Youth Villages internship program provides training in working with troubled children and their families, with more than 22,000 children and families helped each year across 20 states and Washington, D.C. The goal of your training would be to help you learn how you work with families and children to improve the possibilities of keeping families together in a safe and accountable manner. Interns are welcome from diverse training areas, from social work, psychology and related social service fields. Please contact:

> Youth Villages
> P.O. Box 368
> Marylhurst, OR 97036
> (901) 251-5000
> Organization internship weblink: http://www.youthvillages.org/join-our-team/internships/paid-summer-internship-program.aspx#sthash.TKDraA87.dpuf

Business Management

Field Training Resources in Business Management

The National Association of Business Management Professionals—The National Association of Business Management Professionals is a resource for professionals at all levels of business management and offers information related to professionalism in conducting ethical and quality practices within the business management industry. Membership in the professional society provides valuable opportunities for industry-wide networking and professional development. Through this professional association, you can complete a Certified Business Management Professional Certification Program, which is designed to certify you at a level of professional competency, so you can be recognized within the industry. Website: http://nabmpro.com/

Field Training in Business Management

Boeing
The Boeing internship program offers a 12-week training program in which you will work on projects with a global focus in areas of specialization like Finance, Supply Chain Management, Business Operations, and Human Resources. You, as an intern, will be active contributing members to projects and important business decisions, from analyzing areas of profitable growth to managing ongoing projects. You will also be involved in site tours, community involvement,

networking events, and seminars to further your development. Finally, you will also be assigned an onsite career mentor. Please contact:

    Boeing
    100 North Riverside
    Chicago, IL 60606
    (312) 544-2000
    Organization internship weblink: http://www.boeing.com/careers/college/business-internships.page

BP America

The BP America internship program has paid internship opportunities for undergraduate, business school, and law students. You, as an intern, will have a variety of work-related training foci at various levels and departments within the organization. You will network and work with geologists, engineers, and business executives during your training process. Please contact:

    BP America, Inc.
    501 Westlake Park Blvd
    Houston, TX 77079
    (281) 366-2000
    Organization internship weblink: http://www.bp.com/en/global/bp-careers/students-and-graduates/student-opportunities/business-students.html

Capital One

The Capital One internship program provides onsite intern training incorporating issues of critical business decision making and situations for collaborative teamwork with industry professionals. As an intern, you will build your career-related knowledge and skills for success. The internship program offers paid finance, information technology, brand/marketing, and analyst internships to undergraduates (Juniors). By the end of your training, you may have the opportunity to present the results of your training to the management in your training department. Please contact:

    Capital One
    1680 Capital One Dr.
    McLean, VA, 22102-3491
    (888) 810-4013
    Organization internship weblink: https://campus.capitalone.com/intern

Deloitte

The Deloitte's Pioneer internship program, designed for Freshman-level summer interns, provides training for interns to acquire industry-related knowledge and skills needed to succeed in the global marketplace. During this six-week extensive experience, you will have the opportunity to engage in "hands on" workplace activities and learn from Deloitte professionals. Please contact:

    Deloitte
    111 S. Wacker Dr.
    Chicago, IL 60606
    (312) 486-1000
    Organization internship weblink: https://www2.deloitte.com/us/en/pages/careers/articles/join-deloitte-pioneer-internship.html

Northwestern Mutual
The Northwestern Mutual financial representative internship program offers interns training experiences in local network offices. As an intern, you will be guided in how to create personalized financial solutions for each client's needs. Through the onsite training, you will be mentored in your professional development in coordination with your academic instruction. The company works with students' academic schedules to best arrange onsite training during the academic fall-spring or summer schedules of student interns. Please contact:

Northwestern Mutual
720 E. Wisconsin Ave.
Milwaukee, WI 53202
(414) 271-1444
Organization internship weblink: https://www.northwesternmutual.com/careers/about-our-financial-representative-internship

Plante Moran
The Plante Moran internship program is from a company that has been one of the 100 best companies to work for over the past approximately 15 years. The program offers more than 100 internships annually to both undergraduate and graduate students from different educational backgrounds in business, law, and related degrees. You as an intern will work closely with different departments within the organization to have a well-rounded training experience. Please contact:

Plante Moran
10 S Riverside Plaza #900
Chicago, IL 60606
(312) 207-1040
Organization internship weblink: http://www.plantemoran.com/careers/campus/pages/opportunities.aspx

PricewaterhouseCoopers LLP
The PricewaterhouseCoopers LLP internship ("Start") program offers opportunities for students to learn the various aspects of this industry and help you plan a successful career. You as an intern will be a part of professional development opportunities, and get experience related to research, knowledge management, auditing projects, and other related work assignments across departments. You will have opportunities to work with staff from the internal firm services group, which can include, but are not limited to, areas of human resource development, marketing and sales, and learning and development projects. Please contact:
PricewaterhouseCoopers
601 South Figueroa St., Ste. 900
Los Angeles, CA 90017
Telephone: (213) 356-6000
Organization internship weblink: https://www.pwc.com/us/en/careers/campus/programs-events/start.html

<u>The Boston Consulting Group</u>
The Boston Consulting Group internship program offers opportunities for interns to be part of a "case team" and work with a variety of staff members to gain experience in how to become a consultant on projects. You as an intern will engage in a 10-week training experience and opportunities across the globe and is open to business school students and other related undergraduate majors. Please contact:

The Boston Consulting Group
300 N LaSalle Dr.
Chicago, IL 60654
(312) 993-3300
Organization internship weblink: https://www.bcg.com/careers/path/internships/default1.aspx

Healthcare/Nursing

Field Training Resources in Healthcare/Nursing

- Association for Healthcare Administrative Professionals – The Association for Healthcare Administrative Professionals is the premier organization for healthcare professionals dedicated to those who support our nation's top healthcare leaders. You will be a part of a dynamic group and have opportunities to join various committees and participate in leadership activities within the industry. You can also attend the association-related annual conference, which will assist in your professional development and networking within the field. Website: http://www.ahcap.org/
- HealthIT.gov's Guide to Privacy and Security of Electronic Health Information – The HealthIT.gov's guide website provides an overview of information related to HIPAA Rules and has links to security training games, risk assessment tools, and other aids. Website: https://www.healthit.gov/providers-professionals/guide-privacy-and-security-electronic-health-information

Field Training in Healthcare/Nursing

<u>Abbott Laboratories</u>
The Abbott Laboratories internship program gives opportunities for interns to have hands-on experience within the healthcare field and illustrious career preparation as a young professional entering the industry. You, as an intern, will have the benefit of a flexible ten- to twelve-week paid summer experience that will allow you to both balance school and work and gain invaluable experience within the healthcare industry. Please contact:

Abbott
100 Abbott Park Rd.
Abbott Park, IL 60064-3500
(224) 667-6100
Organization internship weblink: https://www.abbott.com/careers/students/internships.html

Actavis

The Actavis internship program reflects joining a pharmaceutical manufacturing company that is well recognized across the globe as being a leader within the healthcare industry. You as an intern will be given "hands-on" experience working with other healthcare professionals and staff in a dynamic workplace. Please contact:

Actavis
Morris Corporate Center III
400 Interpace Pkwy
Parsippany, NJ 07054
(862) 261-7000
Organization internship weblink: http://www.actavis.com/careers/university/internships-and-programs/internship-programs

Alcoa

The Alcoa internship program provides opportunities for students interested in joining the healthcare industry and gives them invaluable experience in terms of how you can work with industry leaders on creating innovative healthcare products and services. You as an intern will be part of the global force that is concerned with various aspects of sustainability products in serving the global population. Please contact:

Alcoa
201 Isabella St.
Pittsburgh, PA 15212
(412) 553-4131
Organization internship weblink: http://www.alcoa.com/global/en/careers/campus/internships.asp

Biogen Idec

Biogen Idec has the distinction of being one of the oldest independent biotechnology companies and offers "hands-on" opportunities for interns related to various aspects of training within this specific area of healthcare services. You as an intern will hone your skills and develop your career or goals through the many different mentoring and training experiences within the company. Internship programs and related co-op programs are offered at their facilities in North Carolina and Massachusetts. Please contact:

Biogen Idec
225 Binney St.
Cambridge, MA 02142
(617) 679-2000
Organization internship weblink: http://www.biogenidec.com/careers_university_internships.aspx?ID=5840

Bio-Rad Laboratories

The Bio-Rad Laboratories internship program provides opportunities for interns to work with state-of-the-art equipment and instruments within the company's facilities. You, as an intern, can train from June to August in a full-time internship, and paid internships can be applied for in the departments of accounting quality control and assurance, microbiology, technology, and other areas within the corporation. Please contact:

Bio-Rad Laboratories
875 Alfred Nobel Dr. Ste. M
Hercules, CA 94547
(847) 699-2217
Organization internship weblink: http://www.bio-rad.com/en-us/corporate/summer-internship

Bristol-Myers Squibb

The Bristol-Myers Squibb internship program offers both undergraduate and graduate summer training experiences involving working on real world state-of-the-art projects and presenting the results of the projects to management. You as an intern will work with experienced staff, professionals, and mentors within the industry and can also apply for a six-month co-op educational program, if available. Please contact:

Bristol-Myers Squibb
345 Park Ave.
New York, NY 10154
(212) 546-4000
Organization internship weblink: http://www.bms.com/careers/university_recruitment/internships_co-ops/pages/graduates_undergraduates.aspx

Boston Scientific

The Boston Scientific internship program provides interns with unique learning experiences regarding global health-related issues through the work they will do onsite across different departments and working with different professionals in the field. You, as an intern, will be trained in a tailored 12-week summer training program designed to best meet students' educational and career goals. You may also be a part of longer four- to six-month co-op assignments that focus on training and operations, regulatory affairs, and/or research and development. Please contact:

Boston Scientific
300 Boston Scientific Way
Marlborough, MA 01752-1234
(800) 876-9960.
Organization internship weblink: http://www.bostonscientific.com/en-US/careers/students/internships-co-ops.html

Cardinal Health Group

Cardinal Health Group offers paid internships for students interested in learning real world career skills related to human resources, public affairs, engineering, finance, and related areas of training. You, as an intern, will be given opportunities to work with industry professionals in healthcare and have the benefit of ongoing mentoring related to your career aspirations in the healthcare industry. The company also offers a unique leadership development program called "Emergence" for those who qualify. Please contact:

Cardinal Health Group
7000 Cardinal Place
Dublin, OH 43017
(614) 757-5000
Organization internship weblink: http://www.cardinal.com/us/en/careers/collegestudents/internships

CareFusion
The CareFusion internship program trains interns in key areas of healthcare services, focusing on reducing costs and improving safety for the population. You as an intern will have the opportunity to work in several locations across many different disciplines related to healthcare issues of infection prevention, medication management, device interfaces, and other key areas of safety within the healthcare field for clients. Please contact:

> CareFusion
> 3750 Torrey View Ct.
> San Diego, CA 92130
> (858) 617-2000
> Organization internship weblink: http://www.carefusion.com/careers/internship-development-opportunities.aspx

Cerner
The Cerner internship program provides 12-week summer internships for seniors interested in training within pharmacy and engineering, among other programs. You as an intern will work alongside industry professionals on real world projects related to state-of-the-art technology and investigation of healthcare-related issues. You will have the benefit of ongoing career mentorship as you complete this training. Please contact:

> Cerner
> 2800 Rockcreek Pkwy
> Kansas City, MO 64117
> (816) 221-1024
> http://www.cerner.com/about_cerner/careers/students/summer_internships/

Covance
The Covance internship program is for students interested in working in animal science laboratories and/or medical technology field work. You, as an intern, will have the benefit of engaging in entry-level opportunities. Working with executives and staff will allow you to gain valuable career path training in the healthcare and technology fields. Please contact:

> Covance
> 210 Carnegie Center
> Princeton, NJ 08540
> (609) 452-4440
> Organization internship weblink: http://careers.covance.com/university/internship_placements.php

CVS Caremark
The CVS Caremark internship program provides a full-time internship for students who are interested in healthcare administration and/or business information training within the healthcare industry over a period of 10 weeks. You, as an intern, who provided with comprehensive and mentoring training within the healthcare field related to what the organization does, and you'll receive opportunities for networking with industry professionals. Please contact:

CVS Caremark
One CVS Dr.
Woonsocket, RI 02895-6146
(401) 765-1500
Organization internship weblink: http://jobs.cvscaremark.com/texas/intern/jobid4714753-undergrad-intern-it-pharmacy-claims-jobs

Dentsply International
The Dentsply International internship program focuses on training interns in the growing area of dental healthcare. You as an intern would be given "hands-on" experience related to planning, development, and implementation in the delivery of dental equipment supplies on a global basis with the organizational aim of improving the quality of dental health for diverse groups around the world. Please contact:

Dentsply International
221 W. Philadelphia St.
York, PA 17401
(717) 845-7511
Organization internship weblink: https://www.dentsply.com/en-aa

Eli Lilly
Eli Lilly provides internship opportunities for students May through September who are interested in training to help them successfully launch their careers within the healthcare industry. You will be given opportunities to work with industry professionals on many different projects reflecting healthcare industry trends. You will have financial support through a paid internship and possible support funding for housing and/or transportation if you need to relocate to the Indianapolis, Indiana, location for training purposes. Please contact:

Eli Lilly
1 Lilly Corporate Center
Indianapolis, IN 46285
(317) 276-2000
Organization internship weblink: http://www.lilly.com/careers/student-opportunities/Pages/internships.aspx

Forest Laboratories
The Forest Laboratories internship program gives interns "hands-on" experience and training within the pharmaceutical industry through involvement in state-of-the-art research and development projects related to drug manufacturing focused on treating chronic diseases. You will have the benefit of ongoing hands-on career training and mentoring, as well as potential networking opportunities, within this company. Please contact:

Forest Laboratories
13600 Shoreline Dr.
Earth City, MO 63045
(314) 493-7000
Organization internship weblink: http://www.frx.com/pdf/careers/Fellowship_brochure.pdf

HealthSouth

The HealthSouth internship program offers training programs for both undergraduate and graduate students who are interested in speech pathology, physical therapy, occupational therapy, and/or nursing and wish to gain clinical training hours during their career training. You will be working with experts in the field will guide you in specific areas of clinical training, and you might even have the possibility of having additional training and rehabilitative services, a growing area within the healthcare industry. Please contact:

> HealthSouth
> 3660 Grandview Parkway, Ste. 200
> Birmingham, AL 35243
> (800) 765-4772
> Organization internship weblink: http://www.healthsouth.com/en/careers/clinical-opportunities/healthsouth-on-campus

Hologic

The Hologic internship program trains interns across industry topics of different growing healthcare-related concerns in women's health. You, as an intern, will be exposed to different healthcare-related strategic planning initiatives, program development, and service plans in response to issues of women's quality of health across the life span. You will be trained in women's healthcare-related population trends and be mentored by professionals within the field to better prepare you for a successful launch. Please contact:

> Hologic
> 290 S. Main Pl.
> Carol Stream, IL 60188
> (630) 653-3700
> Organization internship weblink: http://www.hologic.com/careers/apprentice-program

Johnson and Johnson

The Johnson and Johnson internship program provides internship training for students interested in medical technology and healthcare-related career development. You, as an intern, will be given opportunities to work on projects and be involved in planning teams' cutting-edge research and product development intended for improving the health of many groups in society. You have great opportunities for networking and mentoring with industry professionals. Please contact:

> Johnson and Johnson
> 4545 Creek Rd.
> Cincinnati, OH 45242
> (513) 337-7000
> Organization internship weblink: http://careers.jnj.com/sites/default/files/ldp/pdf/RALDPSell Sheet-2013.pdf

Kindred Healthcare

The Kindred Healthcare internship program represents opportunities to train with a network of healthcare professionals with a range of backgrounds and experience with acute-care, hospital care, rehabilitative care, and/or assisted living healthcare support. You, as an intern, will be trained in conducting clinical research and engage in educational training related to various aspects of healthcare programming and service provision. Please contact:

Kindred Healthcare
680 South Fourth St.
Louisville, KY 40202-2412
(502) 596-7300
Organization internship weblink: http://www.kindredhealthcare.com/careers/

Magellan Health Services
The Magellan Health Services internship program offers training for students interested in finance and/or information technology from May to August or possibly forty hours per week for ten to twelve weeks. You as an intern will receive the benefits of compensation as well as in-depth training related to advanced healthcare techniques. Please contact:

Magellan Health Services
1291 Shermer Rd.
Northbrook, IL 60062
(847) 509-6900
Organization internship weblink: http://www.magellanhealth.com/join-our-team/magellan-careers/magellan-internship-program.aspx

Mead Johnson Nutrition
The Mead Johnson Nutrition internship program has a thirteen-week summer internship, which gives interns an opportunity to train in different areas of the healthcare industry within the corporation. You as an intern will have opportunities to work in different departments ranging from global marketing, research and development, and information technology to finance, marketing, and supply chain operations as each relates to the broader healthcare industry practices and future trends. Please contact:

Mead Johnson Nutrition
225 N. Canal St., 25th Floor
Chicago, IL 60606 USA
(312) 466-5800
Organization internship weblink: http://www.meadjohnson.com/careers/joining-mead-johnson#internshipprograms

Medical Mutual of Ohio
The Medical Mutual of Ohio internship program provides opportunities for interns to work in a corporation reflecting operations in response to a changing and dynamic healthcare system. You, as an intern, will be given real-world, onsite training experiences through both online and classroom education, networking events, and other "hands-on" training opportunities. Please contact:

Medical Mutual of Ohio
2060 E. 9th St.
Cleveland, OH
(800) 382-5729
https://www.medmutual.com/About-Medical-Mutual/Careers/College-Internship-Program.aspx

Molina Healthcare
The Molina Healthcare internship program presents training opportunities for interested interns related to training and human relations, marketing and communications, and information technology healthcare systems. You as an intern will have great opportunities working with healthcare or related industry professionals in all aspects of organizational functioning in the service and provision of healthcare operations to clients. Please contact:

>Molina
>222 W. Adams St. #450
>Chicago, IL 60606
>(888) 858-2156
>Organization internship weblink: http://www.molinahealthcare.com/members/common/en-US/abtmolina/compinfo/careers/ pages/Internshipprogram.aspx

Mosaic
The Mosaic internship program provides unique training opportunities to interns who are interested in quality of care from the perspective of supporting the human spirit. You, as an intern, will be given the opportunity to be trained in healthcare policies and provisions from more of a "holistic," dignity-emphasized perspective on healthcare services. Please contact:

>Mosaic
>Atria Corporate Center, Ste. E490
>Plymouth, MN 55441
>(763) 577-2700
>Organization internship weblink: http://mosaicservices.org/who-we-are/employment/

Mylan
The Mylan internship program offers opportunities for interns who are interested in pharmaceutical manufacturing and product development related to serving a global market. You will work with different divisions across the company in terms of your training to better understand the different operations underlying pharmaceutical product development, marketing, and service provisions. Please contact:

>Mylan
>1000 Mylan Blvd
>Canonsburg, PA 15317
>(724) 514-1800
>Organization internship weblink: https://mylan.taleo.net/careersection/2/jobdetail.ftl

NBTY
The NBTY internship program provides interns for training related to organizational operations in the production of nutritional supplements to a variety of consumers. You, as an intern, may be involved in various aspects of training pertaining to distribution, manufacturing, and/or marketing of products across the world. Please contact:

NBTY
2100 Smithtown Ave
Ronkonkoma, NY
(631) 200-2000
Organization internship weblink: https://hub-nbty.icims.com/jobs/search?ss=1&searchKeyword=intern&searchCategory=&searchLocation=&latitude=&longitude=&searchZip=&searchRadius=20

OmniCare University Relations
The OmniCare University Relations internship program offers training related to pharmaceutical studies, accounting, and other organizational-related operational divisions in healthcare. The company is committed to training students to better understand healthcare-related issues to both further their education and healthcare itself. You as an intern will benefit from a collaborative relationship between the organization and colleges/universities across the U.S. and Canada to optimize your career development within the industry. Please contact:

OmniCare
2313 S Mt Prospect Rd
Des Plaines, IL 60018
(847) 635-3000
Organization internship weblink: http://www.omnicare.com/careers/university-relations.aspx

Perrigo
The Perrigo internship program offers summer, fall, and winter internships ranging from marketing and media trends, information technology auditing, and data collection and analysis. You as an intern will gain practical, real-world experience related to industry-based strategic planning and implementation in healthcare service provision. Please contact:

Perrigo
515 Eastern Ave
Allegan, MI 49010
(269) 673-8451
Organization internship weblink: http://perrigocareers.com/locations/new-jersey/new-jersey-location-and-internships/new-jersey-student-internship-services/

Pfizer
The Pfizer internship program offers opportunities for interns to train in their medical research–related divisions with the aim of advancing global health. You as an intern may have the opportunity to work in summer internship programs focused on the delivery of products and related services that support quality of health in the population. Please contact:

Pfizer
235 East 42nd St.
New York, NY 10017
(212) 733-2323
Organization internship weblink: http://pfizercareers.com/university-relations

St. Jude Medical
The St. Jude Medical internship program provides training to interns related to electrical engineering, mechanical engineering, and/or biomedical instruction to develop cutting edge devices in the treatment of life-threatening diseases. You will be trained in various aspects of healthcare treatments related to life-threatening illnesses and the need for effective medical interventions. Please contact:

St. Jude Medical Inc.
One St. Jude Medical Dr.
St. Paul, MN 55117-9983
(651) 756-2000
Organization internship weblink: http://www.sjm.com/corporate/careers/for-university-students/internships-co-ops

Target
The Target internship program provides interns with the opportunity to work in the company's pharmacy and clinic divisions. Training involves ten weeks of real-world training related to organizational services and practices in the pharmacy and clinic. You will benefit from having multiple mentors within the team to work with. Please contact:

Target
1000 Nicollet Mall
Minneapolis, MN 55403-2542
(612) 304-6073
Organization internship weblink: https://corporate.target.com/careers/college-students

UnitedHealth Group
The UnitedHealth Group internship program offers a wide variety of training opportunities that relate to the healthcare industry. You will be trained in various aspects of healthcare services and products as they relate to quality of care for clients. Please contact:

UnitedHealth Group
13625 Technology Dr.
Eden Prairie, MN 55344
(800) 765-6713
Organization internship weblink: http://careers.unitedhealthgroup.com/college/college-internships

Universal Health Services
The Universal Health Services internship program offers both paid and unpaid internships for interns in Sudan training in human relations, nursing, social work, psychology, and other related health services fields. You, as an intern, will be exposed to a variety of healthcare-related services training in clinical treatment. Please contact:

Universal Health Services
367 S. Gulph Rd.
King of Prussia, PA 19406
(610) 768-3300

Organization internship weblink: http://jobs.uhsinc.com/tulsa/rehabilitation/jobid3653872-internship-%28graduate-unpaid%29-jobs

Varian Medical Systems

The Varian Medical Systems internship program provides interns with the opportunity to be trained in the planning, development, and implementation of technology-related products including equipment and software that help to fight against cancer and other health-related conditions, which necessitate radiosurgery, radiotherapy, and brachytherapy. You, as an intern, will be trained in various aspects of designing and producing technology-related healthcare products. Please contact:

Varian Medical Systems
3100 Hansen Way
Palo Alto, CA 94304
(650) 493-4000
Organization internship weblink: http://www.varian.com/us/corporate/careers/job_search_us.htmlCerner

Walgreens

The Walgreens internship program teaches interns all areas of operation within a company, from retail to product distribution. The ten-week program opportunities allow interns to be involved in meaningful projects and networking with experienced management within the corporation. You will be trained in many different areas related to pharmaceutical and/or healthcare supply products and/or services. Please contact:

Walgreens
P.O. Box 4024
Danville, IL 61834
(217) 443-0410
Organization internship weblink: http://careers.walgreens.com/students/internships-programs/#.U2Zq61cVdHo

Zimmer Holdings

The Zimmer Holdings internship program offers both students and recent graduates training opportunities to gain real world experience focused on musculoskeletal healthcare products and services. You will have the opportunity to engage in mentored training with industry professionals in healthcare, in addition to be a part of the leadership development program with Master of Business Administration-related interns. Please contact:

Zimmer Holdings
345 E. Main St.
Warsaw, IN 46580
(574) 267-6131
Organization internship weblink: http://www.zimmer.com/en-US/careers/internships.jspx

Political Science/Public Policy

Field Training in Political Science/Public Policy

Congressional Black Caucus Foundation
The Congressional Black Caucus Foundation internship program presents opportunities for interns to work on projects and interact with various professionals within the field for personal educational and leadership development in furthering understanding of the Black culture and associated public policy initiatives to better support this population. You, as an intern, will have opportunities to be trained and engage in mentoring and supervision from professionals/practitioners working in public policy to successfully launch you within this area of expertise. Please contact:

> Congressional Black Caucus Foundation
> 413 New Jersey Ave., S.E.
> Washington, D.C. 20003
> (202) 785-3634
> Organization internship weblink: http://www.cbcfinc.org/internships/

Congressional Hispanic Caucus Institute
The Congressional Hispanic Caucus Institute internship program gives training opportunities for students interested in furthering Hispanic students' awareness of governmental practices, public policy, and leadership skill development. You as an intern will have opportunities to work on governmental policy projects, in addition to developing a better understanding of the workings of the U.S. government in response to issues of a growing Hispanic population and its culture. Please contact:

> Congressional Hispanic Caucus Institute
> 1128 16th St. N.W.
> Washington, D.C. 20036
> (202) 543-1771
> Organization internship weblink: http://www.chci.org/internships/

Ford Motor Company/Congressional Hispanic Leadership Institute
The Ford Motor Company/Congressional Hispanic Leadership Institute internship program provides opportunities for students interested in learning about D.C.-based think tanks, the federal government, United States Congress, and/or any international-related governmental organizations. You as an intern will have invaluable opportunities related to team-based work and networking opportunities to better understand the functioning of the U.S. government and its associated public policy and programmatic outcomes. Please contact:

> Ford Motor Company/Congressional Hispanic Leadership Institute
> 734 15th St., N.W. Ste. 620
> Washington, D.C. 20005
> (202) 347-8280
> Organization internship weblink: http://www.chli.org/?page=Internship

Hispanic Association of Colleges and Universities
The Hispanic Association of Colleges and Universities internship program opportunities for Hispanic students will be trained in Washington, D.C., as well as other locations across the nation, and

focuses on issues related to the Hispanic culture and the associated education needed regarding this group. You will have multiple opportunities to engage in real world events and projects working with professionals on educational and public policy issues for Hispanic populations. Please contact:

Hispanic Association of Colleges and Universities
One Dupont Circle N.W.
Ste. 430
Washington, D.C. 20036
(202) 261-5080
Organization internship weblink: http://www.hnip.net/intern/

Morris K. Udall Foundation Native American

The Morris K. Udall Foundation Native American internship program gives interns the opportunity to be trained on governmental proceedings and legislative processes in congressional matters. You as an intern will have the benefit of working with public policy makers and experts within this area of expertise will mentor you in your career development within this very important in developing the areas of social and public policy. Please contact:

Morris K. Udall Foundation—Native American
130 S. Scott Ave.
Tucson, AZ 85701
(520) 901-8500
Organization internship weblink: https://www.udall.gov/OurPrograms/Internship/AboutInternship.aspx

National Academy of Social Insurance

The National Academy of Social Insurance internship program promotes training opportunities for students, which are challenging in nature and offer experience in understanding the nuances of social insurance and what it means for a changing population. You will receive real world experience related to various aspects of this public policy focus and the multiple constituents involved in decision-making and implementation. Please contact:

National Academy of Social Insurance
1776 Massachusetts Ave. N.W.
Washington, D.C. 20036
(202) 452-8097
Organization internship weblink: http://www.nasi.org/info-url_nocat3815/info-url_nocat.htm

Public Policy and International Affairs Program

The Public Policy and International Affairs Program internship program presents opportunities for interns to work in public administration, public policy, and other public service roles. You as an intern can be involved in a seven-week summer program that focuses on national and international affairs-related public policy. You will have opportunities to work with different constituents in the areas of functioning related to public service and public policy. Please contact:

Public Policy and International Affairs Program
130 Humphrey School
301 19th Ave. S.
Minneapolis, MN 55455
(877) 774-2001
Organization internship weblink: http://www.ppiaprogram.org/programs/jsi.php

Fund for American Studies
The Fund for American Studies internship program exposes interns to the experience of being involved in, or working with, media outlets, think tanks, nonprofit organizations, policy groups, government agencies, and/or the Congressional office. You will have the opportunity to take a class through George Mason University, as well as engage in thirty to thirty-five hours of training per week related to governmental functioning across various levels and areas of focus. Please contact:

The Fund for American Studies
1706 New Hampshire Ave. N.W.
Washington, D.C. 20009
(202) 986-0384
Organization internship weblink: http://www.dcinternships.org/

U.S. Department of State
The U.S. Department of State internship program offers interns the opportunity to engage in training in the U.S. government and potentially in over 270 U.S. embassies, missions, and consulates across the world, if available. The internships are unpaid and intensive in focus, giving interns real-world experience and insights into the daily operation of U.S. national and foreign governments. You as an intern will gain vast knowledge and experience related to ongoing governmental policies and practices across many different departments and organizations operating within the government. Please contact:

U.S. Department of State
2201 C St. N.W.
Washington, D.C. 20520
(202) 647-4000
Organization internship weblink: https://careers.state.gov/work/opportunities/vacancy-announcements/dos-student-internship-unpaid

Information Technology/Computer Science

Field Training Resources in Information Technology/Computer Science

- International Association for Computer Science and Information Technology – The International Association for Computer Science and Information Technology professional society has a diverse membership of professionals, ranging from research scientists and experienced software development directors to technology students. The mission of the professional society is to support and engage in industry-wide collaborations among professionals and students using state-of-the-art approaches and research-driven outcomes. Website: http://www.iacsit.org/

- Institute of Electrical and Electronics Engineers – The Institute of Electrical and Electronics Engineers professional society offers a wide range of learning and career-enhancement opportunities within the engineering sciences, research, and other technology areas. The goal of these training programs is to ensure the growth of skill and knowledge among professionals and to foster individual commitment to continuing education. Website: http://www.ieee.org/index.html
- Microsoft Virtual Academy – Microsoft Virtual Academy offers courses in information technology, cloud computing, and other areas of technology trends. Website: http://www.microsoftvirtualacademy.com/
- CodeAcademy – CodeAcademy is designed to help you learn code, starting with the basics of HTML if needed. Website: http://www.codecademy.com/

Field Training in Information Technology/Computer Science

Agilent Technologies
The Agilent Technologies internship program provides opportunities for training related to technical consulting, hardware, design, supply chain engineering, and/or software design engineering. You, as an intern, will benefit from multi-faceted training across many different areas of technology under the guidance and supervision of experts within the technology area training. Please contact:

Agilent Technologies
5301 Stevens Creek Blvd.
Santa Clara, CA 95051
(408) 345-8886
Organization internship weblink: http://www.jobs.agilent.com/students/usa.htmlActavis

Allstate
The Allstate internship program offers training experiences to qualified information technology interns, related to everything from claims adjustment and customer service to actuarial analysis and policy sales. You as an intern will have opportunities to engage in experiences across many business units within the corporation as you learn about technology usage within its operations and customer service. Please contact:

Allstate
2775 Sanders Rd. Ste. F7
Northbrook, IL 60062
(877) 810-2920
Organization internship weblink: http://www.allstate.com/careers/students-and-new-grads.aspx

Apple
The Apple internship program offer interns in the U.S. and across the world training experiences related to corporate information technology software development and/or hardware engineering. You will have opportunities to work on major product launches and team-based work related to specific skill and knowledge development. You can also engage in leadership networking opportunities to further enhance your career development experience. Please contact:

Apple
70 Oakbrook Center
Oak Brook, IL 60523
(630) 481-3470
Organization internship weblink: http://www.apple.com/jobs/us/students.html#internship

AT&T
The AT&T internship program offers training opportunities for interns interested in technology, learning, and development opportunities within this industry. You will work in their network and/or emerging technology departments, and you will learn industry trends and innovative ways to engage in anticipatory analyses and strategic planning associated with this area of specialization. Please contact:

AT&T
208 S. Akard St.
Dallas TX 75202
(210) 821-4105
Organization internship weblink: http://att.jobs/careers/college/internships/technology-internships

Boeing IT
The Boeing information technology internship program offers training experiences to interns who are interested in a broad range of information technology–related career development, pertaining to project management, application architecture, security, and network design, among other areas of focus. The future of technology is the focus of the corporation, and this anticipation of future trends relates to what you will be doing as an intern in your work with other professionals in the corporation. You will engage in different activities related to engaging in community involvement, networking, mentoring, training, and site-related tours. Please contact:

Boeing
100 N. Riverside
Chicago, IL 60606
(312) 544-2000
Organization internship weblink: http://www.boeing.com/boeing/careers/collegecareers/ITintern.page

Booz Allen Hamilton
The Booz Allen Hamilton internship program provides opportunities for students to be trained in all aspects of information technology functioning related to malware analysis, cloud computing, network security, analysis, systems engineering, and other related tasks with the focus of solving client issues in consulting. You as an intern will be exposed to many different areas of consulting work related to solving client issues and anticipating future trends related to business functioning. Please contact:

Booz Allen Hamilton
8283 Greensboro Dr.
McLean, VA 22102
(703) 902-4109

Organization internship weblink: http://www.boozallen.com/media/file/BAH-internship-program.pdf

Chevron

The Chevron internship program offers opportunities for interns to train in information technology roles related to the development of applications, database management, and the utilization of business analysis tools through applications such as UNIX O/S and SAP. You as an intern will hone your career-related skills in project management, analysis, consulting, and/or programming. Please contact:

Chevron
6001 Bollinger Canyon Rd.
San Ramon, CA 94583
(925) 842-1000
Organization internship weblink: http://careers.chevron.com/disciplines/index_of_disciplines/information_technology/it_internships.aspx

Cigna

The Cigna internship program offers a variety of positions related to training through its Technology Early Career Development Program (TECDP) summer program. You will have opportunities for engaging in mentoring, networking, panel discussions, and executive speaker series events. Your training may encompass a wide range of challenging onsite experiences related to quality assurance, policy operations, and/or applications. Please contact:

Cigna
900 Cottage Grove Rd.
Bloomfield, CT 06002
(860) 226-6000
Organization internship weblink: http://careers.cigna.com/CIGNAPage.aspx?page=102

Comcast

The Comcast internship program involves eleven weeks of mentoring, networking opportunities, training, and development for qualified interns. You as an intern will benefit from direct supervision from industry leaders related to the entertainment and Internet fields, in addition to having multiple opportunities for engaging in career development experiences with experts across many different disciplines and backgrounds. Please contact:

Comcast
1 Comcast Center
Philadelphia, PA 19103
(215) 286-1700
Organization internship weblink: http://jobs.comcast.com/Campus-Programs/Internships-and-rotational-programs/Comcast-Internship-Program

Dell

The Dell internship program provides ten- to twelve-week information technology internship training programs, which provide real-world projects working with managers in assisting with different ongoing projects. You will have supervised training and can present the findings of your training outcomes in front of mentors, managers, and other interns. Please contact:

Dell
1 Dell Way
Round Rock, TX 78682
(512) 338-4400
Organization internship weblink: http://www.dell.com/learn/us/en/uscorp1/internships

Devon Energy
The Devon Energy internship program provides trainees with opportunities to engage in information technology team-based work with senior technical analysts, software developers, database architects, and other professionals within the corporation. You as an intern will be immersed in real-world, "hands-on" training tasks under the supervision of experienced managers, and you will be working with subject matter experts and diverse teams of professionals within the field. Please contact:

Devon Energy
333 West Sheridan Ave.
Oklahoma City, OK 73102-5015
(800) 583-3866
Organization internship weblink: http://www.devonenergy.com/Careers/Pages/Students.aspx#terms?disclaimer=yes

Dow Chemical
The Dow Chemical internship program offers training opportunities for students who are interested in cutting-edge technology regarding agriculture, infrastructure, and energy production on a global basis. You as an intern will be involved in various aspects of strategic planning, product analysis and associated industry-related problem solving. Please contact:

Dow Chemical
2030 Dow Center
Midland, MI 48674
(989) 636-1000
Organization internship weblink: http://www.dow.com/careers/programs/student.htm

Ecolab
The Ecolab internship program provides interns with training for creating Web-based solutions and engaging in fiscal management initiatives, among other areas, related to keeping healthcare and other service-related public venues safe and clean. You as an intern will have the opportunity to work on real-world projects within cross-functional work teams. Please contact:

Ecolab
370 Wabasha St.
St. Paul, MN 55102
(651) 293-2233
Organization internship weblink: http://www.ecolab.com/careers/learn-more-about/campus-recruiting/undergraduate-internships

First Energy

The First Energy internship program provides training for interns related to supply chain management, engineering, computer science, technology, information technology, and other business-related and information technology areas of training. You will have the benefit of broad-based training in various aspects of organizational strategic planning and implementation within this industry. Please contact:

    First Energy
    341 White Pond Dr., Building B3
    Akron, OH 44320
    (888) 254-4769
    Organization internship weblink: https://www.firstenergycorp.com/content/fecorp/careers/student_opportunities/co-op_intern.html

General Electric

The General Electric internship program presents opportunities for students to learn across multiple divisions within the corporation, with a special information technology focus of training in software technology, information systems security, and global software development. You will have a variety of opportunities for mentored supervision across different training areas, as well as opportunities for career-related networking with management. Please contact:

    General Electric
    3135 Easton Turnpike
    Fairfield, CT 06828
    (203) 373-2211
    Organization internship weblink: https://www.ge.com/careers/culture/university-students/information-technology-leadership-program/united-states

General Motors

The General Motors internship program trains interns through its EXCEL (Exploring Careers through Experiential Learning) program, offering students real-world, "hands-on" opportunities to learn about vehicle energy sources and the associated manufacturing of automobile technology utilizing these energy sources. You will receive opportunities to engage in networking with various leadership constituents and engaging community service events. Please contact:

    General Motors
    300 Renaissance Center
    Detroit, MI 48265-3000
    (313) 556-5000
    Organization internship weblink: http://careers.gm.com/student-center.html

Halliburton

The Halliburton internship program offers training opportunities for students interested in information technology-related project management, engineering, and project development. You will be actively engaged in many aspects of company functioning related to product development and analysis relevant to a dynamically changing industry. Please contact:

Halliburton
3000 N. Sam Houston Pkwy E.
Houston, TX 77032
(281) 871-4000
Organization internship weblink: http://www.halliburton.com/en-US/careers/students-and-recent-graduates/internships.page?node-id=hgeyxtcl

Hewlett-Packard
The Hewlett-Packard internship program supplies real-world opportunities for information technology interns interested in engaging in transformational technology, which meaningfully changes how people work and live. You, as an intern, will assist in data analysis, project management, research and development, and/or server administration, under the supervision of experiments from the field. Research and development interns may also assist managers with project development and/or the analysis of future technology trends. Please contact:

Hewlett-Packard
3000 Hanover St.
Palo Alto, CA 94304
Organization internship weblink: http://h30631.www3.hp.com/careers/it-students-and-graduates-jobs

Humana
The Humana internship program provides training opportunities for interns who are interested in application development, among other applied industry initiatives. You as an intern, through the Specialized College Programs, will work with industry professionals on real-world projects, and you will gain experience under the supervised guidance of experienced developers. You will also have opportunities to network with corporation executives. Please contact:

Humana
500 West Main St.
Louisville, KY 40202
(502) 580-1000
Organization internship weblink: https://www.humana.com/about/careers/college-programs/specialized-college-programs

IBM
The IBM internship program offers training for interns through its well-respected Extreme Blue intern program. You will have experience in working on business plans related to developing open source code, creating client solutions, and developing modern technologies. Computer programming and/or advanced business training (i.e., MBA) would be beneficial in applying. Please contact:

IBM
1 New Orchard Rd.
Armonk, NY 10504
(914) 765-1900
Organization internship weblink: http://www-01.ibm.com/employment/us/extremeblue/

Intel
The Intel internship program offers training opportunities for students who are interested in software engineering and is primarily targeted for first- and second-year computer science majors. You will benefit from engaging in professional development training through the Intel University, having first-hand exposure to and experience in working with the latest hardware and software products, engaging in ongoing professional development, and networking with corporate executives. Please contact:

    Intel
    2200 Mission College Blvd.
    Santa Clara, CA 95054-1549
    (408) 765-8080
    Organization internship weblink: http://www.intel.com/content/www/us/en/jobs/locations/united-states/ students/internships/intel-early-internship-software-engineering.html

John Deere
The John Deere internship program offers thirteen-week summer internship positions, which cover training in server administration, project management, systems analysis, and/or project development, among other opportunities. You, as an intern, will work on real-world projects and engage in anticipatory onsite problem-solving with management in the field. Please contact:

    John Deere
    One John Deere Place
    Moline IL 61265-8098
    (800) 537-8233
    Organization internship weblink: https://www.deere.com/wps/dcom/en_US/corporate/our_company/careers/students/college/college.page

Kellogg
The Kellogg internship program provides training to students who are interested in information technology-related positions ranging from enterprise architects, digital marketers analysis applications developers, business analysts, and/or security analysts. You as an intern would benefit from various networking opportunities with management, tailored orientation training, engagement in community events, and professional feedback from two performance reviews. Please contact:

    Kellogg
    1 Kellogg Square
    Battle Creek, MI 49016
    (269) 961-2000
    Organization internship weblink: https://www.kelloggcareers.com/global/grow-with-us/career-opportunities/career-opportunities-students-new-grads.html

Marathon Petroleum
The Marathon Petroleum internship program provides opportunities for information technology interns related to training and systems analysis, business analysis applications, and/or infrastructure. You, as an intern, will gain invaluable workplace-related training, experience, and networking

opportunities with executives and supervisors in the workplace that will help you successfully launch your career within this competitive industry. Please contact:

Marathon Petroleum
539 South Main St.
Findlay, OH 45840
(419) 421-2121
Organization internship weblink: http://www.marathonpetroleum.com/Careers/College_Graduate_Intern_or_Coop/Looking_to_be_a_Coop_or_Intern/Campus_Recruitment/Information_Technology/

Microsoft

The Microsoft internship program welcomes freshmen and sophomores interested in learning about software development as a career field. You as an intern may work with industry professionals related to software design, hardware engineering, and/or product testing if you have a background in C++ and/or Java programming, among other programming skills. Please contact:

Microsoft
One Microsoft Way
Redmond, WA 98052
(425) 882-8080
Organization internship weblink: http://careers.microsoft.com/careers/en/us/internships.aspx

Morgan Stanley

The Morgan Stanley internship program will give students the opportunity to work in the financial business industry using cutting-edge technology for client interface, trading, risk assessment, and system security operations. You will have the opportunity to be a technology analyst, working on team-based projects with professionals on business analysis, infrastructure, and/or development. Please contact:

Morgan Stanley
1585 Broadway Ave.
New York, NY 10036
(212) 761-4000
Organization internship weblink: http://www.morganstanley.com/about/careers/programs/articles/282955423.html

Nationwide

The Nationwide internship program offers summer internships in information technology for students interested in training within this field. You, as an intern, will be exposed to different learning opportunities community service events, a tailored intern orientation, and general networking opportunities. Please contact:

Nationwide
1 Nationwide Plaza
Columbus, OH 43215
(614) 249-7111
Organization internship weblink: http://www.nationwide.com/about-us/careers-college.jsp

Oneok
The Oneok internship program offers opportunities for students to learn from one of the country's largest energy companies that manufactures and delivers natural gas. You, as an intern, will have the experience of working with professionals within the field in a wide range of activities covering design, coding, testing, and development of software, as well as managing existing technologies and other related tasks. Please contact:

    Oneok
    100 W. 5th St. Fl. 5
    Tulsa, OK 74103
    (918) 588-7000
    Organization internship weblink: http://www.theonetoworkfor.com/~/media/ONEOK/Careers/PositionProfiles/Recruiting Insert IT 2011.ashx

Oracle
The Oracle internship program provides opportunities for interns related to learning about database management and cloud computing with a variety of products for business consumers. You, as an intern, will be involved in working on real world products and will have the opportunity to network with other interns, experienced developers, and executive management. Please contact:

    Oracle
    500 Oracle Pkwy
    Redwood Shores, CA 94065
    (650) 506-7000
    Organization internship weblink: http://www.oracle.com/us/corporate/careers/college/intern-at-oracle/product-development/index.html

Publix Supermarkets
The Publix internship program is internship training for students who are interested in various aspects of food supply. Internships are ten to twelve weeks during the summer and occur at the company's Lakeland, Florida, headquarters. You will learn various aspects of organizational functioning within this industry, ranging from customer service support to infrastructure analysis and planning. Please contact:

    Publix Supermarkets
    3300 Publix Corporate Pkwy
    Lakeland, FL 33811-3311
    (863) 688-1188
    Organization internship weblink: http://corporate.publix.com/careers/support-areas/internships

Raytheon
The Raytheon internship program provides interns with training related to cutting edge cyber security and defense systems technology. Internships occur during all times of year and are both part time and full time. You will have the opportunity to work on tasks related to security testing, project management, programming, systems architecture, and requirements analysis. Please contact:

Raytheon
870 Winter St.
Waltham, MA 02451
(781) 522-3000
Organization internship weblink: http://jobs.raytheon.com/en/career-paths/campus-recruiting/leadership-development-program

Target
The Target internship program offers interns the opportunity to work in different areas of business related to retail covering divisions of buying and planning, store management, and supply chain management from a technology orientation. You, as an intern, will have the opportunity to work with professionals within various levels of the organization related to the application of technology strategies and planning the various levels of projects and functioning within the corporation. Please contact:

Target
1000 Nicollet Mall
Minneapolis, MN 55403
(612) 304-6073
Organization internship weblink: https://corporate.target.com/careers/college-students

Texas Instruments
The Texas Instruments internship program provides training opportunities for interns interested in technology work related to the production of embedded processors and analog chips and would support work, automotive, and home-based electronic equipment across the nation and the world. You as an intern may work on projects under the supervision of system engineers, software engineers, application engineers, and technology sales engineers, among other professionals, during your career training. Please contact:

Texas Instruments
12500 TI Blvd.
Dallas, TX 75243
(972) 995-3773
Organization internship weblink: http://careers.ti.com/intern

Textron
The Textron internship program provides onsite training and executive supervision opportunities for interns interested in gaining skills related to project management, enterprise business systems, business process management, integration, applications management, and other areas of training. You, as an intern, will engage in ten- to twelve-week internships supervise training across different departments within a computer science and information technology focus, and you might be might be selected for a two-year Leadership Development Program. Please contact:

Textron
40 Westminster St.
Providence, RI 02903
(401) 421-2800
Organization internship weblink: http://www.textron.com/careers/growth-development/LDP-IT.php

Thermo Fisher Scientific
The Thermo Fisher Scientific internship program provides opportunities for students to learn about ways to sell analytical instruments, lab support services, and/or lab equipment to make the world a healthier place. You will be trained under the supervision of experts within the industry related to software development research and development to business analysis. Please contact:

Thermo Fisher Scientific
168 Third Ave.
Waltham, MA 02451
(781) 622-1000
Organization internship weblink: https://www.thermofisher.com/global/en/about/careers/itldp.asp

Time Warner
The Time Warner internship program offers opportunities for interns to gain cutting-edge experience related to technologies in the entertainment and media industries in a nine- to twelve-week training internship. You will be given opportunities to work with professionals within the field across many different divisions within the corporation, covering divisions of HBO, Turner Broadcasting System, Time Warner Inc., and Warner Bros within their information technology departments. Among other training opportunities, you may be given real world experience in digital entertainment technology development. Please contact:

Time Warner
60 Columbus Circle
New York, NY 10023
(212) 484-8000
Organization internship weblink: http://www.timewarner.com/careers/areas-of-operation/internships

Valero Energy
The Valero Energy internship program provides training opportunities for computer science majors who are interested in real-world experience related to the development of polymers, jet fuel, asphalt, and/or other energy related products. You as an intern may have opportunities to work on projects related to production, software development, change management, infrastructure, or enterprise. You will also have opportunities to engage in a mentoring program, network through social and volunteer events, and be part of an intern symposium. Please contact:

Valero Energy
1 Valero Way
San Antonio, TX 78249
(210) 345-2000
Organization internship weblink: http://www.valero.com/Careers/UniversityRecruting/Pages/InformationServicesInterns.aspx

Verizon
The Verizon internship program provides both summer and part-time internship training for those interested in working on technology development for machine-to-machine, cloud storage, and/or mobile products. You, as an intern, will work with architects, engineers, developers, and analysts

through different project development and strategic planning initiatives within the corporation. Please contact:

Verizon
2 Verizon Place
Alpharetta, GA 30004
(678) 339-6300
Organization internship weblink: http://www.verizon.com/jobs/campus_internships.html

Viacom
The Viacom internship program for giving interns exposure to many different areas of the entertainment industry, ranging from programming for Paramount, Nickelodeon, MTV, and other well-known media groups owned by Viacom. You, as an intern, may be assigned to a functional unit or a show, depending upon your background and areas of expertise, as well as career interests. Your internship may involve training on interactive Web, multimedia, information technology–related, and/or media technology. In addition, you may also have opportunities to participate in training workshops for general professional skills and/or entertainment-related skill development. Please contact:

Viacom
1515 Broadway
New York, NY 10036-5794
(212) 258-6000
Organization internship weblink: http://www.mtvncareers.com/internships.html

Visa
The Visa internship program provides global internships for students interested in technology applied to business. You, as an intern, will be trained in the application of technology in business related to cybersecurity Web engineering, systems analysis, and Java programming. Please contact:

Visa
One Market Plaza
San Francisco, CA 94105
(650) 432-3200
Organization internship weblink: http://usa.visa.com/careers/university-recruiting/undergraduates.jsp

Walmart Stores
The Walmart Stores internship program offers training opportunities for students related to information technology, programming, system administration, information technology analysis, software engineering, and/or data science. You, as an intern, can be trained in terms of understanding how information technology relates to all the various aspects of business within retail business industry. Please contact:

Walmart Stores
702 S.W. 8th St.
Bentonville, AR 72716
(479) 273-4000
Organization internship weblink: http://careers.walmart.com/university/

Western Digital
The Western Digital internship program offers opportunities for students to be trained in different areas of technology products and services related to cloud storage, media players, and digital storage. You, as an intern, will work with electrical engineers, computer science professionals and computer engineers in the development and execution of projects for computer applications, software development, and/or computer software validation. Please contact:

> Western Digital
> 5601 Great Oaks Pkwy
> San Jose, CA 95119
> (949) 672-7000
> Organization internship weblink: http://www.wdc.com/en/company/employment/college.aspx

Xerox
The Xerox internship program has opportunities for interns to work on real-world projects with staff and experts within the field related to consumer support and technology as they relate to trends within the business world and the global economy. You, as an intern, can be trained within the information technology group as it relates to understanding better customer service infrastructure and applications of business services to better serve clients and the development of technology solutions for a growing technology base (e.g., applications management and cloud computing). Please contact:

> Xerox
> 45 Glover Ave.
> Norwalk, CT 06856-4505
> (203) 968-3000
> Organization internship weblink: http://www.xerox.com/jobs/internship/enus.html

Hospitality Services

Field Training in Hospitality Services

A&A Marketing Group
The A&A Marketing Group's internship program offers training for interns with a specific focus on sales, fundraising, and business development. You, as an intern, will learn and develop team management, problem solving, sales, leadership, customer service, communication, negotiation, human resources, and/or goal-setting skills. You also can participate in marketing events and help with giving presentations to clients. Please contact:

> A&A Marketing Group
> 7929 Brookriver Dr. Ste. 635
> Dallas, TX 75201
> (469) 300-9894
> Organization internship weblink: http://www.aamarketinggroup.net/index.html

Disney Hospitality
The Disney Hospitality internship program provides interns with a variety of onsite training, encompassing housekeeping, merchandise, recreation, and/or the food and beverage department. You will gain real-world experience within a Fortune 500 company that is a leader within its industry. You, as an intern, will be an active part of professional networking and training events, which will further enhance your professional development within the field. Please contact:

>Disney Hospitality Internship
>1375 Buena Vista Dr.
>Lake Buena Vista, FL 32830
>(407) 824-2222
>Organization internship weblink: https://jobs.disneycareers.com/search-jobs?k=hospitality

Hyatt International
The Hyatt International internship program offers a paid internship program that provides practical experience and hands-on training related to hotel management and service. You will have a variety of experiences that will give you great real-world training in the management of a multinational corporation within the hospitality industry. Please contact:

>Hyatt International
>71 S. Wacker Dr., Fl. 12
>Chicago, IL 60606
>(312) 750-1234
>Organization internship weblink: http://www.hyatt.jobs/university-recruiting/internships/

The World Trade Council
The World Trade Council internship program provides training related to entrepreneurial projects and business management. You, as an intern, will have experiences working with trade shows, art shows, graduations, and other projects related to large group activities. Further, you will be given exposure to various aspects of business management, ranging from managing payroll to hiring and ordering supplies, among other financial responsibilities under this business management experience. Please contact:

>The World Trade Council
>1257 S. Halsted St.
>Chicago, IL 60607
>(312) 566-5400
>Organization internship weblink: http://theworldtradecouncil.org/internships

Communication/Journalism

Field Training Resources in Communication/Journalism

- Society of Professional Journalists – The Society of Professional Journalists is the nation's most broad-based journalism organization, dedicated to encouraging the freedom of the press and the standards of ethical practice in the industry. The society and the Google News Lab have collaborated to provide training of journalists wanting to utilize

Google-related search tools in their news research and/or reporting. Website: https://www.spj.org/

- Donald W. Reynolds National Center for Business Journalism – The Donald W. Reynolds National Center for Business Journalism presents free, full-day workshops specializing in business journalism. Online journalism seminars are also offered by the Reynolds Center and would be beneficial to professionals at various stages of training. Statewide journalism associations, publications, and universities conduct these training workshops. Website: http://www.businessjournalism.org/

- Wharton School of the University of Pennsylvania – The Wharton School of the University of Pennsylvania offers week-long seminars for business journalists. The seminars are taught by the faculty, cost about $2,000, and cover topics related to the global economy, accounting principles, corporate strategy, and financial markets. Website: http://www.wharton.upenn.edu/

- Poynter Institute – The Poynter Institute offers training topics from diverse areas of specialization and would be appropriate for professionals at various levels of training need. Training seminars are presented online and at the St. Petersburg, Florida, campus. The cost of the training seminars varies by the focus of the training. Website: http://www.poynter.org/

- Maynard Institute for Journalism Education – The Maynard Institute for Journalism Education promotes training professionals in news organizations about issues of diversity throughout workplace operations and staffing. The perspective behind the training initiative is for new organizations, and specifically management within the workplace, to engage in practices that better reflect the diversity perspectives of society. Training is provided at different university locations (e.g., Northwestern University). The cost of session participation depends on the content of the training. Website: http://www.mije.org/

Field Training in Communication/Journalism

ABCNews.com
The ABCNews.com internship program offers opportunities for interns to engage in various aspects of news reporting related to generating story ideas and making pitches to section editors about news projects. You as an intern would be trained in how to produce well-written and well-researched stories within a tight deadline under the guidance and supervision of well experienced staff. You will interact with different divisions of the workplace, in addition to gaining experience in various aspects of news and entertainment journalism. Please contact:

ABCNews.com
47 W. 66th St.
New York, NY 10023
(212) 456-2700
Organization internship weblink: https://xjobs.brassring.com/tgwebhost/jobdetails.aspx?partnerid=25348&siteid=5039&jobid=304657

American Society of Magazine Editors Magazine
The American Society of Magazine Editors Magazine internship program provides interns with the opportunity to engage in various aspects of online and print publication projects, ranging

from reporting and editing to fact-checking and/or copyediting activities. You, as an intern, will engage in various aspects of magazine journalism. Please contact:

American Society of Magazine Editors Magazine
757 Third Ave., 11th Fl.
New York, NY 10017
(212) 872-3700
Organization internship weblink: https://asmeinternship.secure-platform.com/a/organizations/main/home

Associated Press
The Associated Press internship program offers paid, twelve-week tailored training experiences for those qualified individuals who have established training in multimedia formats. You, as an intern, will work with Associated Press staff on the production of video, photography, written work, and/or interactive reporting projects under their mentorship and guidance. Please contact:

Associated Press
1 World Financial Center #19
New York, NY 10281
(212) 621-1500
Organization internship weblink: http://www.ap.org/company/careers/news-internship

Bloomberg
The Bloomberg internship program offers training opportunities for interns in financial and business news. You, as an intern, will be trained in various aspects of this specific area of research and reporting on business, economic, and market-related financial news. Please contact:

Bloomberg
731 Lexington Ave.
New York, NY 10022
(212) 318-2000
Organization internship weblink: http://jobs.bloomberg.com/job/New-York-2016-Summer-Print-News-Internship-Job-NY/300195700/

Business Insider
The Business Insider internship program offers several different opportunities for training within the news-related industry, and interns will have the opportunity to work with different departments related to this business-related publication. You will be mentored in various aspects of publication research and production. Please contact:

Business Insider
150 Fifth Ave., 8th Fl.
New York, NY 10011
Organization internship weblink: http://www.businessinsider.com/page/careers

CBS News
The CBS News internship program gives educational training to interns interested in broadcasting, multimedia production, and journalism practices. You, as an intern, would be exposed

to various levels of news research and reporting, as well as the dissemination of information through multimedia forums. Please contact:

CBS News
51 W. 52nd St.
New York, NY 10019-6188
(212) 975-4321
Organization internship weblink: http://www.cbsnews.com/news/cbs-news-internship-program/

Chalkbeat
The Chalkbeat internship program provides interns the opportunity to be reporters covering news issues emanating from local public schools across four bureaus. You as an intern can engage in education-related newspaper reporting on topical issues in school systems. Please contact:

Chalkbeat
1250 Broadway, 30th Fl.
New York, NY 10001
(917) 388-9035
Organization internship weblink: http://jobs.chalkbeat.org/jobs/chalkbeat-summer-education-reporting-internships/

Chicago Tribune
The Chicago Tribune internship program provides the opportunity for interns to engage in twelve-week paid internships. You, as an intern, will be mentored and given opportunities to engage in different training-related newspaper activities across different departments in the newsroom. Depending upon availability and the needs of the workplace, you may be engaging in work related to newspaper reporting and/or research involving copy editing, design, photo/video, business, sports, lifestyle, entertainment, metro, events, and/or social media. Please contact:

Chicago Tribune
435 N. Michigan Ave. Ste. 600
Chicago, IL 60611
(212) 210-2786
Organization internship weblink: http://www.chicagotribune.com/chi-chicago-tribune-internships-20140811-story.html

CNN
The CNN internship program offers interns a wide variety of training experiences throughout many different departments within the organization. You, as an intern, will be exposed to various aspects of news research and reporting that can have an impact upon national and global issues. Please contact:

CNN
One CNN Center
Atlanta, GA 30303
(404) 827-1700
Organization internship weblink: http://jobsatturner.com/careers/internship-jobs/job-list-3

Dow Jones

The Dow Jones internship program offers paid summer internships in all aspects of newspaper reporting and writing. You as an intern will be given the opportunity to have supervised training related to conducting news editing, business reporting, digital media, and data-related journalism. Please contact:

> Dow Jones
> 200 Liberty St.
> New York, NY 10281
> (212) 416-0520
> Organization internship weblink: https://www.newsfund.org/PageText/Prg_HomePages.aspx? Page_ID=Prg_CollegeIntern

Esquire

The Esquire internship program provides opportunities for interns to work with staff and gain reporting and editorial experience in the magazine's offices. You, as an intern, will be immersed in a research-intensive experience, and you will gain real-world experience in how to balance multiple timelines and multiple tasks in the completion of your daily duties under the supervision of staff members. Please contact:

> Esquire
> 300 W. 57th St.
> New York, NY 10019
> (212) 649-4020
> Organization internship weblink: http://ed2010.com/job/spring-2016-print-editorial-intern/

Los Angeles Times

The Los Angeles Times internship program gives opportunities for a ten-week intensive training program across many different divisions within the newspaper, with reporting and other duties ranging from Metro/Local to the Washington, D.C., Bureau. You will have the opportunity to be trained and mentored in different news activities, from research activities about news events to multimedia design of the latimes.com website. Please contact:

> Los Angeles Times
> 202 W. 1st St.
> Los Angeles, CA 90012
> (213) 237-5000
> Organization internship weblink: http://www.latimes.com/about/la-los-angeles-times-internship-program-htmlstory.html

NBCUniversal

The NBCUniversal internship program has a ten-week paid summer program where interns are trained in various aspects of media and entertainment. You, as an intern, will be given broad-based experiences and provided with mentorship for your career development. Please contact:

NBCUniversal
30 Rockefeller Plaza
New York, NY 10112
(212) 664-4444

Organization internship weblink: https://sjobs.brassring.com/TGWEbHost/jobdetails.aspx?partnerid=25354&siteid=5108&jobid=285098

New York Magazine

The New York Magazine internship program offers a three-month Junior Reporting-Writing Internship program. You, as an intern, will be trained in journalism-related activities, getting experience in conducting research and reporting news stories for the Daily Intelligencer, New York Magazine's news website. Please contact:

New York Magazine
75 Varick St.
New York, NY 10013
(212) 508-0700

Organization internship weblink: http://nymag.com/newyork/jobs/#jun-rep

New York Times

The New York Times internship program offers the following opportunities:

1. David E. Rosenbaum Reporting Internship in Washington – This New York Times internship experience trains you in writing about government and policy. As an intern, you will receive in-depth training in how to become a print journalist in Washington, D.C., and other related venues. Reporting internship weblink: http://www.nytco.com/careers/Newsroom-Summer-Internships/#3

2. Interactive News Internship – This New York Times internship provides you with the experience of working at an interactive news desk, giving you wonderful experience in terms of how to be agile and responsive to a dynamic research and reporting environment. Interactive news internship weblink: http://www.nytco.com/careers/Newsroom-Summer-Internships/#4

3. Video and Digital Internship – This New York Times internship experience trains you in the duties of digital production related to producing articles, photos, and multimedia for the website, among other production projects. You, as an intern, will assist editors/producers by conducting and compiling research for breaking news events and/or special sections of the publication.

Video internship weblink: http://www.nytco.com/careers/Newsroom-Summer-Internships/#8
Digital internship weblink: http://www.nytco.com/careers/Newsroom-Summer-Internships/#9
Please contact:

New York Times
620 8th Ave.
New York, NY 10018
(212) 556-1234

NPR
The NPR internship program offers a well-respected training experience that produces many different well-known leaders within the field. You will be provided with a work-based training experience, which will well prepare you for entry into this industry. Please contact:

NPR
635 Massachusetts Ave. NW
Washington, D.C. 20001
(202) 513-2000
Organization internship weblink: http://www.npr.org/about-npr/181881227/want-to-be-an-npr-intern

Politico
The Politico internship program provides opportunities for editorial internships for undergraduates. You, as an intern, will be involved in all aspects of content creation and production, with duties ranging from conducting reporting and researching to copy editing. Please contact:

Politico
1000 Wilson Blvd. #8
Arlington, VA 22209
(703) 647-7999
Organization internship weblink: http://www.politico.com/employment/editorial-internship-edi0008

Popular Science
The Popular Science internship program provides training either part-time or full-time over approximately twelve weeks. You, as an intern, will work on projects for both the print magazine and Popsci.com. Your training activities will include hands-on activities involved in conducting research, assisting in reporting projects, and writing news stories, "front-of-book" segments, sidebars, and/or blog posts. In addition to these activities, you may also be involved in shooting and editing video, working on interactive graphics, assisting with Web production, and doing social media postings, among other activities. Please contact:

Popular Science
2 Park Ave., 9th Fl.
New York, NY 10016
(800) 289-9399
Organization internship weblink: http://www.popsci.com/contact

Reuters Global
The Reuters Global internship program provides formal training to interns before they start working with staff in the workplace. You, as an intern, will receive opportunities to work with a senior editor, and you will be assigned a mentor to help you learn the different knowledge and skills related to conducting work in this globally focused organization and broader industry. Please contact:

Reuters Global
2001 Marcus Ave. #S200
New Hyde Park, NY 11042
(516) 327-2425
Organization internship weblink: http://jobs.thomsonreuters.com/go/Reuters-Global-Journalism-Internship/206847/

Scripps Howard
The Scripps Howard internship program gives interns training opportunities to engage in activities that will hone their reporting, writing, editing, and photography skills. You, as an intern, will meet and be coached by experts within the industry for many different constituents and areas of specialization related to the focus of the publication (e.g., the Washington Post, the State Department, and the Pentagon) in how to better understand the many different steps involved in the process of covering the news. Please contact:

Scripps Howard
312 Walnut St. #280
Cincinnati, OH 45202
(513) 977-3000
Organization internship weblink: http://www.shfwire.com/apply

Student Press Law Center
The Student Press Law Center internship program gets opportunities for interns to engage in research writing and editing a publication work. You, as an intern, will engage in various aspects of publication and production of information related to current law cases and associated controversies ongoing in the legal system. You will also be trained in writing information for the Law Center's website. Please contact:

Student Press Law Center
1608 Rhode Island Ave. N.W. #211
Washington, D.C. 20036
(202) 785-5450
Organization internship weblink: http://www.splc.org/page/internships

Baltimore Sun
The Baltimore Sun internship program provides opportunities for extensive training in the field of journalism and other related fields within the newspaper industry. Interns will have the opportunity for "hands-on" experience in newspaper production and career-related mentoring within various aspects of reporting and/or related areas of training, working with professionals recognized within the field. Please contact:

The Baltimore Sun
501 N. Calvert St.
P.O. Box 1377
Baltimore, MD 21278
(410) 332-6000
Organization internship weblink: http://www.baltimoresun.com/bal-mary-j-corey-internship-summer-2014-ngux-htmlstory.html

Boston Globe
The Boston Globe internship program provides twelve-week internship opportunities for students interested in work-related experience in being a reporter, designer, photographer, and copy editor. You, as an intern, will receive mentoring and feedback related to your writing and workplace performance, as well, as you will have the benefit of a writing coach to assist you in your writing skill development during your training. Please contact:

   The Boston Globe
   1 Seaborn St.
   Boston, MA 02124
   (617) 436-3710
   Organization internship weblink: https://services.bostonglobe.com/aboutus/career/career.aspx?id=7282

Chronicle of Higher Education
The Chronicle of Higher Education internship program provides opportunities for student journalists to be full-time reporters in the Washington, D.C. newsroom. As an intern, you will be trained in newspaper reporting related to the collection of information for the specific topic of this publication. Please contact:

   The Chronicle of Higher Education
   1255 Twenty-Third St. N.W., 7th Fl.
   Washington, D.C. 20037
   (202) 466-1000
   Organization internship weblink: http://chronicle.com/page/Internships/640

Daily Beast
The Daily Beast internship program seeks interns who are self-motivated and dependable to work in their social media team. You, as an intern, would be given opportunities to be trained in how a publication produces work related to pop culture, current events, and linkages to social media. Please contact:

   The Daily Beast
   7 Hanover Square
   New York, NY 10004
   (212) 445-4600
   Organization internship weblink: http://careers.jobscore.com/jobs2/thedailybeast/social-media-intern/bjI9aGoSGr5zbidG1ZS6tF

Denver Post
The Denver Post internship program has summer paid internships for students interested in working within the newspaper industry. You, as an intern, will have the opportunity to work in various departments in the newspaper and interact with professionals within each of these areas of specialization (e.g., features reporting, photography, and graphic design). You will have the opportunity to train in various aspects of subject-specific reporting and/or various aspects of newspaper production. Please contact:

The Denver Post
101 W. Colfax Ave.
Denver, CO 80202-5177
(303) 832-3232
Organization internship weblink: http://www.denverpost.com/internships

The Miami Herald
The Miami Herald internship program offers internships in news, copy editing, photography, and videography design, multimedia, business reporting, and sports reporting. You, as an intern, will engage in a variety of onsite training activities to provide a comprehensive training experience within the newspaper industry. Please contact:

The Miami Herald
1 Herald Plaza
Miami, FL 33132
Phone: (305) 376-2111
Organization internship weblink: http://www.miamiherald.com/customer-service/about-us/article3861569.html

The Seattle Times
The Seattle Times internship program has paid ten-week summer internships for undergraduate journalist students interested in learning all aspects of newspaper production. You, as an intern, will work on varied assignments and attend weekly training sessions under the mentorship and training of a Pulitzer Prize-winning staff. Under the mentorship of a staff member, you will create and complete a skill-development plan. Please contact:

The Seattle Times
1000 Denny Way
Seattle, WA 98109
(206) 464-2111
Organization internship weblink: http://company.seattletimes.com/careers/#internships

The Washington Post
The Washington Post internship program offers paid opportunities for students interested in training to be reporters, news/digital designers, copy editors, multi-platform producers, graphics reporters, photographers, and/or videographers and social media producers. You, as an intern, will get real-world, practical training in how to engage in this competitive industry and to better understand the skill set needed to be a success within the industry. Please contact:

The Washington Post
1150 15th St. N.W.
Washington, D.C. 20071
(202) 334-6000
Organization internship weblink: http://careers.washingtonpost.com/intern/news/introduction

Time Inc.
The Time Inc. internship program places and turns in different departments based upon appropriate knowledge, skills, and abilities to optimize training outcomes and "fit" within the training

site. You, as an intern, will be mentored and supervised by editors, publishers, and other workplace professionals in the industry throughout your training. You also have opportunities to network with publication executives and engage in a Shark Tank-style event. Please contact:

Time Inc.
260 Cherry Hill Rd.
Parsippany, NJ 07054
(973) 939-7201
Organization internship weblink: http://www.timeinc.com/careers/internships/

USA Today
The USA Today internship program offers opportunities for undergraduate journalist to work at a publication organization that will give you real-world skillset training in the operation of a news room. You, as an intern, will have the opportunity to work with professionals for various aspects of newspaper reporting and production staff. Please contact:

USA Today
7950 Jones Branch Dr.
McLean, VA 22108
(703) 854-3400

USA Today College
The USA Today College internship program presents undergraduate student journalists with opportunities to work in a multimedia reporting workplace. You, as an intern, will be given real-world training opportunities to understand what is entailed in this publication related to college-related topics. Please contact:

USA Today
7950 Jones Branch Dr.
McLean, VA 22108
(703) 854-3400
Organization internship weblink: http://college.usatoday.com/correspondent/

U.S. News & World Report
The U.S. News & World Report internship program recruits for various positions based upon need (e.g., an intern in the Opinion section). Internships can be paid and over a twelve-month period. You, as an intern, will be given "hands on" experience in working on various aspects of the publication's output (e.g., creation of op-eds). Please contact:

U.S. News & World Report
4 New York Plaza, Fl. 6
New York, NY 10004
(212) 716-6800
Organization internship weblink: http://usnews.hrmdirect.com/employment/job-opening.php?req=302032&&cust_sort3=17279&&nohd#job

Wall Street Journal
The Wall Street Journal internship program provides opportunities for interns in their different newspaper bureaus across sections of the U.S. You, as an intern, would be given opportunities

to work with reporters and newspaper editors related to many aspects of the production of this newspaper, from newspaper reporting to the production of articles. Please contact:

Wall Street Journal
200 Liberty St.
New York, NY 10281
(212) 416-2000
Organization internship weblink: http://dowjones.jobs/new-york-ny/summer-2016-reporting-internships-in-the-americas/33B85B0361A74DDB9F10DF571CC9B11E/job/

WIRED

The WIRED internship program offers fellowships in editorial work on various sections of the magazine and/or magazine departments, ranging from the front-of-the-book sections and gadgets research to fact-checking. You, as an intern, will get great hands-on experience related to different departments involved in the production of this magazine. Please contact:

WIRED
P.O. Box 37706
Boone, IA 50037-0706
(800) SO-WIRED
Organization internship weblink: http://www.wired.com/about/jobs-magazine-fellowships

Appendix C

Learning Contract Template

Information about Student and Faculty Supervisor

Name of student intern: _____
Name of faculty supervisor: _____
Contact info for faculty supervisor: _____
Proposed term of practicum/internship: Fall _____ Winter _____ Spring _____ Summer _____

Information about Proposed Practicum or Internship Site

Name of site: _____
Address of site: _____
Contact info for site: _____

Description of Proposed Activities Onsite (About 200 Words):
_____
_____
_____
_____
_____
_____
_____
_____
_____
_____
_____
_____
_____

Onsite Training Goals

Site-Related Goal #1: _____
Activities:

    1.
    2.
    3.
    4.
    5.

Site-Related Goal #2: _____
Activities:

1.
2.
3.
4.
5.

Site-Related Goal #3: _____
Activities:

1.
2.
3.
4.
5.

Site-Related Goal #4: _____
Activities:

1.
2.
3.
4.
5.

Site-Related Goal #5: _____
Activities:

1.
2.
3.
4.
5.

Other Site-Related Goals:
_____
_____
_____
_____
_____
_____
_____

Academic Objectives

Academic Objective #1: _____
Activities:

1.
2.
3.
4.
5.

Academic Objective #2: _____
Activities:

1.
2.
3.
4.
5.

Academic Objective #3: _____
Activities:

1.
2.
3.
4.
5.

Academic Objective #4: _____
Activities:

1.
2.
3.
4.
5.

Academic Objective #5: _____

Activities:

1.
2.
3.
4.
5.

Other Academic Objectives:

_____
_____
_____
_____
_____
_____
_____
_____
_____

Signature Approvals for Learning Contract

Student:

_____   _____

Print Name   Signature

____/____/____

Date

Faculty Supervisor:

_____   _____

Print Name   Signature

____/____/____

Date

Site Supervisor:

_____   _____

Print Name   Signature

____/____/____

Date

CPSIA information can be obtained
at www.ICGtesting.com
Printed in the USA
LVHW061814060319
609737LV00018B/57/P